THE CHARISMATIC MOVEMENT:
IS THERE A NEW PENTECOST?

SOCIAL MOVEMENTS
PAST AND PRESENT

Irwin Sanders, Editor

THE CHARISMATIC MOVEMENT:

IS THERE A NEW PENTECOST?

MARGARET POLOMA

TWAYNE PUBLISHERS

THE CHARISMATIC MOVEMENT
Is There a New Pentecost?

SOCIAL MOVEMENTS PAST AND PRESENT

**Library of Congress Cataloging in
Publication Data**

Poloma, Margaret M.
    The charismatic movement.

(Social movements past and present)
Includes index.
1. Pentecostalism—United States
I. Title. II. Series.
BR1644.5.U6P64   1982   306'.6'0973   82-11983
ISBN 0-8057-9701-7

FOR MY MOTHER

CONTENTS

ABOUT THE AUTHOR

Margaret M. Poloma is a professor of sociology at the University of Akron. She is the author of *Contemporary Sociological Theory* (Macmillan) and approximately thirty published articles in the areas of family research and Christian sociology. She served as co-editor of *Sociological Focus* for five years and is currently an associate editor for three other professional journals.

Professor Poloma is on the Steering Committee of the Christian Sociological Society and edits its Newsletter. Raised Roman Catholic and continuing to worship regularly with a Catholic congregation, she has more recently become actively involved with the First Assembly of God (Akron). This dual-religious citizenship has provided an opportunity to observe the charismatic movement from both a mainline church as well as from a Pentecostal denomination.

PREFACE

A Research Chronicle: Being A Sociological Witness To Dialogue

My research on the charismatic movement began over five years before I considered writing a sociological account. In 1974, my newly found religious faith began to merge with my previous training as a social scientist. Since then, the latter has never ceased to challenge the experiences of the former, and the challenge grew as I proceeded to research unfamiliar aspects of the charismatic movement for this book. I have thus attempted to maintain the objectivity desired by all researchers. No doubt it has eluded me at times, just as it has escaped others who have conscientiously sought it. Both my particular orientation toward social science research and my own religious experiences have surely but unintentionally colored my study.

Any analysis bears the subjective imprint of its researcher, whether intended or not. With the advent of "reflexive sociology" (Gouldner 1970), however, it has become more acceptable to lay out the personal assumptions that have the potential to influence the work. I agree with social scientists who recognize that good sociology requires personal involvement, despite the biases that may result. I must admit that my own knowledge of the social world is intertwined with my self-knowledge, with my position in the social world, and with personal efforts to change this world. I also appreciate the difficulties of analyzing one's personal assumptions: the desired reflexivity may be approached but never completely achieved. It is therefore important for me to set forth briefly my personal assumptions about sociology as well as the charismatic movement.

My sociological perspective tends to be eclectic. I consider different theories to be useful in explaining different kinds of phenomena. This multifaceted approach to sociological theory applies to my treatment of various aspects of the charismatic movement. Ideology, organizational structure, and the socialization process—to name only three components of the movement—each required a particular analytical orientation. While the different theoretical perspectives utilized may be obvious, what may be less obvious to the reader is what Friedrichs (1970, p. 290) has termed the paradigm of a "primary level," that is, the image a sociologist has of him or herself. It is from this self-image that other assumptions about the nature of sociology proceed.

Friedrichs (1970) characterizes the sociologist's self-image as being either that of a "prophet" or of a "priest." A religious prophet is someone who is critical of the social world and who heralds a need for conversion to avert an impending catastrophe. Just as biblical prophets were often at odds with their own people as they called for religious renewal, so too have sociological prophets been at odds with the practices of their own discipline. Sociology was born of a secular prophecy. Its putative founder, Auguste Comte, sought to establish sociology as a universal religion that would scientifically discover the secret of perfect social harmony and the perfectibility of man (Friedrichs 1970, pp. 69–70). But just as religious prophecy fails, so too did sociology lose its prophetic thrust. With the attempt to establish sociology as a respected academic discipline came the institution of a sociological priesthood. Priestly sociologists, like their religious counterparts, were more likely to accept and justify the existing social order than prophetic sociologists who criticized the social world and offered plans for its redemption.

As a sociologist I have never been comfortable in either role. The priestly position, reflected by a systematic, "scientifically neutral" view of the social world, leaves me uneasy. Yet I am even more fearful of the prophet who speaks with authority but refuses to allow scientific procedures to serve as a means of enlightenment. Like the Apostle Paul, I need to "test prophecy"—even sociological prophecy—and in doing so, I have found much of it wanting.

Fortunately, neither extreme need be the lot of the sociologist. As Friedrichs (1970, p. 327) has observed, one can be a "witness to dialogue" between priests and prophets. Thus I seek a middle ground, a dialogue between sterile scientific analysis of charismatics undertaken by priestly sociological practitioners and the vital, prophetic nature of the movement itself.

My approach as a "sociological witness" stems from a dialectical world view involving three factors, identified by Wardell and Benson (1979, pp. 232–33) as production, contradiction, and totality. "Production" is "an ongoing process through which people construct the conditions of their existence." At the same time, the process of social life is not static, rather, it is dynamic and open-ended due to "contradiction." As Wardell and Benson (1979, p. 236) note: "The dialectical method implies that any social order, while socially produced, contains the origins of its own replacement, as well as the basis for its own existence. On the one hand, the structure encourages the reproduction of the present social arrangement, while on the other it negates that order and encourages the creation of alternatives." "Totality" is the "whole set of social relationships and practices that characterize a particular historical setting" (Wardell and Benson 1979, p. 240). It includes both the observed and the emerging orders and the contradictions through which these orders are produced.

Throughout this analysis of the charismatic movement I have discussed production as well as contradiction while using totality (the larger social structure within historical context) as the stage upon which the drama unfolds. Such a dialectical paradigm readily incorporates major theoretical frameworks, including structural functionalism, conflict, symbolic interactionism, and exchange, as appropriate for purposes of more detailed analysis of a specific phenomenon. I also utilize data from survey research, participant observation, and historical sources.

Although I am reluctant to label my sociological orientation—labels serve as a kind of useful shorthand but also tend to convey false impressions—I would describe my approach as "existential sociology," which has been defined as "the study of human experience-in-the-world (or existence) in all its forms" (Douglas and Johnson 1977, p. vii). It seeks to understand human experience primarily, but not exclusively, through direct personal experience. Kotarba (1979, p. 351) has observed that such an approach is particularly conducive to analyzing the charismatic movement. Given this approach, I believe that may own involvement in the charismatic movement contributes to my analysis.

The reader should also be aware of my own "search for truth." During my years as a graduate student and my study of the sociology of religion in the late 1960s, I put aside what I believed to be the religion of my childhood and drifted into agnosticism. In part I was convinced by the literature of this period which wrote premature obituaries and performed elaborate postmortem on institutionalized religion. Unlike Peter Berger (1967, 1969), a sociologist whose works I greatly admired, I was unable to follow a model of separating the role of Christian believer from that of sociologist. While Berger appeared comfortable in wearing the hat of a sociologist in 1967 to write what he admits read "like a treatise on atheism" and in assuming the hat of a believer in 1969 for a sequel, I found such hat-switching less satisfactory. I consciously chose the hat of a sociologist and allowed reason to edge out faith as my guiding principle.

It was a religious experience, not reason, which several years later led me on my quest for God. After completing an evaluative research project for a local church, I began to question some of the assumptions I had accepted as fact during my graduate school years and made what the philosopher Kierkegaard would have termed a "leap of faith." I prayed my own version of the prayer of an agnostic: "God, if there is a God, save my soul, if I have a soul." In immediate response to this prayer made in the privacy of my study, I experienced a sense of the Holy and an awareness that I could no longer in all honesty claim to be an agnostic. The quest had begun. Nine months later I awoke in the middle of the night to experience another spiritual breakthrough which brought an acceptance of the risen Christ as my personal Savior. Shortly after that I became involved in a prayer group with charismatic Catholics.

To use Milton Yinger's analogy, I view the stained-glass window from the inside. I am sure that at times my interpretations reflect this vantage point. Reports on the stained-glass window of Pentecostalism from the outside may yield, at times, a somewhat different, but no more or less valid, analysis than those coming from a trained observer on the inside. I have made every attempt to be an honest "witness to dialogue," but I do not believe a value-free, "objective" analysis is possible or necessarily desirable in practice.

The researcher's own direct, personal experience may actually serve to improve the analysis. Experience becomes an original source of data. This is especially important for discovering the hidden aspects of human experience, such as physical sensations and deep emotions, especially "socially dangerous" ones, that are not always discernible from observations of others. One's experience also provides a basis for comparison with the experience of others. The researcher can use his or her own experience and perceptions to judge the credibility of accounts given in settings marked by intense conflict and deceit.

Experience generates points of inquiry. Ongoing personal involvement always turns out to be richer than the rationalized presuppositions brought into a setting. It also facilitates a theoretical understanding of real events. The true participant observer who operates with good faith and realizes, through self-observation and introspection, the complexities he or she faces in making sense of a phenomenon is reluctant to espouse unrealistic and simplistic explanations for other people's behavior (Kotarba 1977, p. 260).

When appropriate, therefore, I have not hesitated to share with the reader personal experiences that may cast light on the charismatic phenomenon under discussion. I did, however, make every attempt to distinguish such experiences from other sources of information.

The empirical data that undergird this work come from both primary and secondary sources. I reviewed hundreds of books and articles published by charismatic publishing houses; familiarized myself with charismatic magazines, including *Catholic Charismatic, Charisma, Logos, New Covenant,* and *New Wine*; and studied newsletters distributed by Episcopal, Lutheran, Presbyterian, Eastern Orthodox, United Church of Christ, and United Methodist charismatic renewal services. I exchanged correspondence with a number of national leaders of the charismatic movement with whom a personal interview was not possible. I also conducted personal interviews, attended conferences, and participated in worship services to corroborate the written materials.

During the course of this research I conducted over forty interviews, each lasting from two to four hours, with knowledgeable persons who could serve as informants on some aspect of the charismatic movement. Most of these interviews were with ministers, while others were with informed members of the laity who were able to direct me to sources of literature, to confirm my interpretations, and to provide leads for additional relevant research avenues.

I attended services at over twenty different charismatic worshipping communities, often conducting informal discussions with one or more persons after the services. I visited a Roman Catholic, an Episcopalian, and an Assemblies of God congregation at least ten times each. The remaining congregations, visited only once or twice, include representatives of the following groups: Roman Catholic (2); Assemblies of God (4); United Christian Assembly (1); Presbyterian (1); Church of God (2); nondenominational charismatic (5); Four Square Gospel (2); and Apostolic (2). In addition, I attended two meetings of the Full Gospel Businessmen's Group International in Akron, Ohio, the location of the largest FGBMGI in the United States. These visits allowed me to evaluate better the observations and research findings reported by others on charismatic worship and teaching.

I also attended six teaching conferences and one week-long camp meeting sponsored by various denominations. These include three local conferences sponsored by St. Luke's Episcopal Church (Bath, Ohio), a Church of God camp meeting held in Canton, Ohio, a United Methodist conference on the gifts of the Holy Spirit, the third annual charismatic conference of the United Church of Christ, and the Northeast Conference on the Holy Spirit, sponsored by the Assemblies of God. Each of these provided innumerable valuable insights on aspects of the charismatic movement.

The chapter on charismatic communities makes use of information gathered during a three-day visit to both Sojourners Community (Washington, D.C.) and New Jerusalem Community (Cincinnati, Ohio). I also visited the Son of God Community (Cleveland, Ohio) and have had considerable contact for over six years with "Mana Community" (Akron, Ohio). These visits provided information on community life as well as on the larger charismatic movement.

The chapter on the media is based in part on over 100 hours of watching charismatic television programs, with most of the viewing time spent on Jim Bakker's *PTL Club* and Pat Robertson's *700 Club*. I also viewed periodically Oral Roberts, Ernest Angley, Richard Hogue, David Lombardi, and Kenneth Copeland. I not only watched David Mainse's *100 Huntley Street* (filmed in Toronto), but I also had the opportunity to visit the studio and to be part of the audience.

The interviews, participation in conferences and worship, observation of communities, and television programs provided the primary data to support, modify, and sometimes question what others have written on aspects of the charismatic movement.

Despite my own involvement, I wish to emphasize that the intent of this book was in no way to prove or disprove the faith of charismatic Christians. Such proof is outside the realm of social science. My object is simply to describe their ideology, their history, and their emerging institutions, and to attempt to explain at least partially its potential impact. As a charismatic Christian, I respond affirmatively to the question-title of this book. The modern world is in the midst of a fresh outpouring of the Holy Spirit, just as the first Christians experienced the Pentecost nearly 2,000 years ago. To those who are more skeptical, Christians and non-Christians alike, I repeat the words of the Pharisee Gamaliel, as reported in the Book of Acts: "For if their purpose or activity is of human origin, it will fail. But if it is from God, you will not be able to stop these men; you will only find yourselves fighting against God" (Acts 5:38–39). The final outcome of this social movement thus awaits the judgment of history.

Margaret M. Poloma
University of Akron

ACKNOWLEDGMENTS

Never before in a research project have I been so indebted to so many individuals and groups for information as in this study of the charismatic movement. I wish to acknowledge some of those to whom I owe a special debt of gratitude.

The idea of tackling the seemingly impossible task of analyzing the charismatic movement owes its origin to George A. Hillery, Jr. It was George who introduced me to the series editor, Irwin Sanders, suggested the topic, and encouraged me to pursue it. Even more than providing the topic and encouragement, George's own research demonstrated the possibility of allowing personal religious beliefs to be a source of much-needed light while still pursuing the objectivity desired in social science.

Other colleagues, both in sociology and in related disciplines, who took the time to correspond, to forward information, to serve as sounding boards, and/or to read sections of the manuscript include Charles Faupel, George Gable, Jeffrey K. Hadden, John Langrod, H. Newton Maloney, William Martin, David O. Moberg, Mary Jo Neitz, James S. Tinney, and Teresa Sullivan. I express my appreciation to each of them for serving in one or more of these roles.

This project would have been an impossible one without the support and assistance offered by various charismatic groups, old and new friends active in the movement, and many ministers. The Service Committee for Orthodox Renewal, Presbyterian Charismatic Communion, Lutheran Renewal International, and Episcopal Renewal Services all freely gave of newsletters and other materials to support the analysis. Brick Bradford of Presbyterian Charismatic Communion patiently corresponded with me, and Charles Irish of Episcopal Renewal Services graciously consented to an interview during which he provided a number of invaluable leads in the initial stages of the project. Jim Dailey of the Rex Humbard Foundation not only supplied information on the Humbard ministry but reviewed the chapter on the electronic church in light of his work experience with Rex Humbard ministries as well as the Christian Broadcasting Network. Sojourners Community (Washington, D.C.), New Jerusalem Community (Cincinnati, Ohio), and the Son of God Community (Cleveland, Ohio) arranged for visits which were spiritually uplifting as well as informative. A special thank you to Jim Wallis and Bob Sabath of Sojourners, Geri Raddell of the Son of God, Bob and Star Mierenfeld and Richard Rohr of New Jerusalem.

Ministers and priests who in spite of heavy schedules made the time to talk with me and whom I would like to gratefully acknowledge include the reverends Donald Bartow, David Burnham, Robert Carlson, E. L. Cushman, Edward E. Decker, Richard Dobbins, Thomas Dunphy, C. Herschell Gammill, Charles Irish, Ron Jackson, Larry Kline, Donald Kline, Earl P. King, E. Eugene Meador, Richard Rohr, Derrill Sharp, Bishop Francis Smith, Lane Sargeant, Robert Trapani, and T. H. Voss. Kenneth Ferraro, Lorrine Holman, Gerald Koser, JoAnn Collier, Bill and Gretchen Cooperider, Joanne Hodoh, Charles K. Moore, Arthur Palacas, Susan Bartone, and Esther Slater also supplied invaluable information for this study and/or read sections of the manuscript. Acknowledgements would be incomplete without noting the service provided by Jane McCandless as my research assistant during a critical stage of the project. The hours of library work as well as those spent with me in the field are much appreciated.

Two minister-friends provided assistance that went far beyond most others involved in the study. Ed Decker and Eugene Meador read drafts of the manuscript and offered suggestions that undoubtedly strengthened it. I benefited from Ed's training in counseling psychology as well as the ministry and his knowledge of Pentecostalism. Eugene was able not only to correct some factual errors but also to raise poignant questions relating to the charismatic movement. Some of his questions I attempted to answer while others, particularly those dealing with the cyclical nature of the routinization of charisma, require further research. I am grateful to both for their insights as well as their prayer support.

The joy of working on this project was further kindled by Irwin Sanders, editor for this series. Irwin provided all the encouragement and help an author-researcher could ask from an editor. His criticism was always constructive, and this work owes much to his careful reading and critique of earlier manuscript drafts.

I also wish to thank my colleague and husband T. Neal Garland who patiently endured TV dinners and endless conversation about my observations. Having a spouse who is trained in social science but does not share my personal enthusiasm about the charismatic movement offered me a source of balance and a different perspective.

It goes without saying that errors are not the responsibility of any of those whose assistance I have acknowledged. For an author, as for a president, the buck stops here.

PART I

A Historical and Theoretical Introduction

CHAPTER 1

The Spirit Falls Afresh: The Rise of the Charismatic Movement in the Twentieth Century

When the day of Pentecost came, they were all together in one place. Suddenly a sound like the blowing of a violent wind came from heaven and filled the whole house where they were sitting. They saw what seemed to be tongues of fire that separated to rest on each of them. All of them were filled with the Holy Spirit and began to speak in other tongues as the Spirit enabled them. (Acts 2:1–4)[1]

The biblical Book of Acts, an eyewitness account of the founding of the early Christian church in the first century, testifies to God's power through His Holy Spirit. Christians through the centuries have accepted this account as historical fact, although modernist or liberal theologians have questioned the validity of interpreting literally large portions of Scripture. At the same time that many theologically liberal Christians are reinterpreting and discrediting miracles reported in the Bible, another group of Christians affirm the accuracy of the Scriptures and further insist that miraculous events reported in the Bible are happening today, in the twentieth century. They represent different religious denominations, diverse social classes, all races and nationalities. These believers are known as Charismatics, Pentecostals, or neo-Pentecostals, and they are having a decisive effect on religion worldwide.

Pentecostal churches, once viewed as "fringe religions," are among the fastest growing denominations in the United States, at a time when most established Protestant churches are experiencing declines in membership. Once viewed as a lower-class phenomenon, Pentecostalism now crosses all income, occupational, and educational lines. Its beliefs have also filtered into the mainstream of Christianity through the neo-Pentecostal groups forming within all major religious denominations.[2]

The beliefs of these charismatic Christians may appear nonrational to those who do not share their faith. In an age of supposed rationalism and religious skepticism, these men and women are believers in the direct intervention of God in daily life and are willing to act on this belief. They assert that through the power of the Holy Spirit within them miracles are being performed before their very eyes: the blind are made to see, the deaf to hear, and the lame to walk. The "gift of healing" is available, they claim, to all Christian believers. Prophecy in its different manifestations is another gift believed to operate in charismatic churches. Glossolalia, or "the gift of tongues," is accepted as a prayer language and also as a means of prophecy.

While the intensity of their belief in such "signs and wonders" may distinguish them from both liberal and fundamentalist believers, charismatics do share basic tenets with other orthodox Christians. Together they believe in the sovereignty of God, who created all things and keeps them in existence. They acknowledge the human race's fall from God's grace through sin and accept humankind's redemption from sin through Jesus Christ. They accept the biblical account of Jesus' life, death, and resurrection and believe that it is through Him that Christians are "born again" into a new spiritual life. Both orthodox and charismatic Christians believe that God kept the promise made by Jesus to send the Holy Spirit to be an Advocate or Helper for those who have accepted Him. The basic theology of the Holy Spirit is shared by both Catholic and Protestant orthodox Christians, but the charismatic emphasis on personal experience of the Holy Spirit and the miracles believed to be brought about by Him today have led some orthodox Christians to condemn the charismatic movement as heresy.

It is sufficient for this discussion to define "charismatics" as Christians who accept the Bible as the inspired word of God, but who also emphasize the power of the Holy Spirit in the lives of those who have accepted Jesus Christ as their Savior. The release of the Holy Spirit's power is ordinarily seen as a type of "second blessing" experienced in an event (or as part of a process) known as the "baptism of the Holy Spirit." Although there is not a unified theology of this Spirit baptism in charismatic circles, especially with regard to glossolalia, the term has come to identify those who are bona fide participants in the life of the Holy Spirit.

A word must be said at the outset about the terms "charismatic," "Pentecostal," and "neo-Pentecostal." These groups of believers share the basic orthodox Christian tenets and an emphasis on the power of the Holy Spirit in their lives, but their histories differ. Pentecostalism, as we shall see, might be termed "classical charismatic" because its churches date back to the first quarter of the twentieth century and mark the beginning of the charismatic movement. The largest Pentecostal denominations include the Assemblies of God, the United Pentecostal Church, International; the Church of God; and the Church of God in Christ. However, the Pentecostal experience did not confine itself to these and other newly established churches. By the 1950s men and women in non-Pentecostal denominations were experiencing the "baptism of the Spirit." Unlike many of their predecessors, however, these neo-Pentecostals did not always join Pentecostal churches. In the 1960s, as both the Catholic and Episcopalian churches experienced a touch of Pentecostalism, the term "charismatic" began to be applied to those who were baptized in the Spirit.[3] The term has caught on and has been used in writings to refer to neo-Pentecostals and sometimes to Pentecostals. Throughout our discussion we will use the term "Pentecostal" to apply to classical charismatics and "neo-Pentecostal" to refer to the movement's growth in non-Pentecostal denominations. "Charismatic" will be used as a more general term to refer to both Pentecostals and neo-Pentecostals.

The Rise of Pentecostalism

Pentecostalism may be seen as a product of nineteenth century American revivals, especially Methodist revivals. A Methodist convert of this period described a revival meeting in much the same fashion as Pentecostal meetings would be described in the next century:

I have been at meetings where the whole congregation would be bathed in tears and sometimes their cries would be so loud that the preacher's voice would not be heard. Some would be seized with trembling and in a few moments drop to the floor as if they were dead, while others were embracing each other with streaming eyes and all were lost in wonder, love and praise. (Damboriena 1969, p. 15)

Such meetings were part of the Second Great Awakening (1820–60) in American religion (Pritchard 1976), but fervor of this type is difficult to maintain. The fires of Methodist revivalism, which stressed holiness and the experience of a "second blessing" (a precursor to the Pentecostal experience of "Spirit baptism"), were seen by some to be dimming even before the Civil War. Dissent arose in Methodist denominations prior to the Civil War from those who felt that "holiness" and "second blessing" were not being taught with enough zeal (Woodbridge et al. 1979, p. 73). It was out of the theology of the founder of Methodism, John Wesley, that the holiness sects developed in the second half of the nineteenth century.

During this era a conservative Christian ideology prevailed. The evangelical Protestants, led by theological conservatives, clearly dominated American religion (Wells and Woodbridge 1975, p. 13). In the years that followed the Civil War, however, the rise of science influenced some theologians to move away from conservative theology. By the turn of the twentieth century, evangelicals were leading attacks on education and institutions of higher learning with a new intensity. The stage was set for the battle between "modernists," or theological liberals, and "fundamentalists," the upholders of theological conservatism.[4]

While fundamentalism did not originate from Wesleyan sources as did the Holiness and later Pentecostal sects,[5] it has been viewed as an influence upon the Pentecostal Revival (Menzies 1975, p. 84). Although not accepted by hard-core fundamentalists to this day, Pentecostal doctrine was more in line with fundamentalism at the turn of the century than with modernism (Marsden 1975, pp. 124–25). The reconciliation of a strain of fundamentalism and Pentecostalism may be seen in the current use of the term "evangelical Christian," which embraces both moderate fundamentalism and Pentecostalism within its fold. Strict fundamentalists still disagree with Pentecostals, mainline churches, and often each other, over literal interpretations of Scripture.

The doctrine that separates most Pentecostals from other evangelical Christians is the statement on Spirit baptism. With the exception of one controversial item, the Statement of Truth drawn up by the Pentecostal Fellowship of North America was based upon the earlier Statement of Faith of the National Association of Evangelicals. The controversial text reads: "We believe that the full gospel includes the Holiness of heart and life, healing for the body and the baptism in the Holy Spirit with the initial evidence of speaking in other tongues as the 'Spirit gives utterance" (Nichol 1966, p. 4). In order better to understand the significance of the Pentecostal doctrine of Spirit baptism and its relationship to glossolalia, it is important to consider the events that led to the establishment of Pentecostal denominations in the United States.

The United States: Birthplace of Modern Pentecostalism. The birthdate of modern Pentecostalism is set by some at 1901 and by others at 1906. Both dates are significant for the movement. In 1901, in Topeka, Kansas, Charles Fox Parham left some forty students of his Bible college to search the Scriptures for evidence of Spirit baptism; while it was from the Azusa Street Mission in Los Angeles in 1906 that the movement spread.[6]

Charles Parham, a Holiness evangelist, started Bethel Bible College in Topeka in 1900. He was convinced that a further outpouring of the Holy Spirit, greater than any that had yet been experienced, was possible. As Parham left these students in 1901 for a three-day speaking engagement, he instructed them to study the Acts of the Apostles in search of biblical evidence of baptism with the Holy Spirit. Upon his return, the students reported that they had found the biblical evidence for Spirit baptism: speaking in other tongues.

The result of this search seemed to be confirmed when, on December 31, 1901, one student began to speak in tongues as Parham laid hands on her as he prayed for the baptism of the Holy Spirit. Soon the majority of the students had similar experiences of speaking in tongues. The significance of this event was not that these students were the first in recent times to claim such an experience, for, as we shall see later in our discussion, glossolalia has a long history. The significance of this event was, rather, "that for the first time the concept of being baptized (or filled) with the Holy Spirit was linked to an outward sign—speaking in tongues" (Synan 1971, p. 95).

During the next four years, Parham preached a series of revivals, spreading the Pentecostal message throughout Kansas and Missouri. In 1905 he moved to Houston, Texas, and opened another Bible school. A black preacher, William J. Seymour, who would soon lead the Azusa Street Revival, was one of Charles Parham's new students.

Seymour had already accepted the Holiness doctrine of a "second blessing." Under Parham he received a "third experience," the baptism of the Holy Spirit evidenced by speaking in tongues. In 1906 Seymour moved to Los Angeles and began a sustained revival.[7] From there Pentecostalism spread both in the United States and in Europe. As church historian Vinson Synan (1971, p. 114) observed:

The Azusa Street revival is commonly regarded as the beginning of the modern Pentecostal [sic] movement. Although many persons had spoken in tongues in the United States in the years preceding 1906, this meeting brought this belief to the attention of the world and served as a catalyst for the formation of scores of Pentecostal denominations.

From Azusa Street the faith spread throughout the country, from the Northwest to New York, through Ohio and Indiana, into the South, and north to Canada (Synan 1971, p. 114). The spread of the movement, however, did not occur without opposition and internal dissent.

Criticism and Controversy.   As might be expected, established sects and denominations were not likely to react favorably to Pentecostalism's new doctrine—or kindly to the very expressive form of worship found among converts of the Azusa Street Mission. Eighteenth-century Methodism has been described as "a reaction against a prevailing creedal rigidity, liturgical strictness, and 'iron-clad institutionalism' that had largely depersonalized religion and had rendered it incapable of serving the needs of the individual" (Synan 1971, p. 22). The Holiness movement reacted against the institutionalized practices that had ossified Methodism by the end of the Civil War. The revival fires of Pentecostalism, however, produced divisive controversies. Even some Holiness groups attempted to suppress or repudiate Pentecostal doctrine.

A common complaint leveled against Pentecostalism was the disorderly nature of its services, in which believers purported to allow the Holy Spirit free reign. At times this zeal for allowing a free movement of the Spirit undoubtedly went to extremes, causing even those churches with some predisposition toward Pentecostalism to frown upon the preoccupation with glossolalia that characterized so many meetings (Nichol 1966, pp. 65–76). They also took issue with the way prophecy was abused in the services where some members "placed greater emphasis upon themselves as prophets and upon their utterances than the leadership of the appointed pastor or the instruction which the scriptures give" (Nichol 1966, p. 76). Historical evidence suggests a breakdown of order at many Pentecostal services akin to the disruptions that led the apostle Paul to write his letter to the first-century church at Corinth. (1

Cor. 12–14 were written by Paul to curb the apparent misuse of the gifts of the Holy Spirit.) In part due to some Pentecostal extremes, in part to the rigidity of some established denominations, and in part to the largely lower socioeconomic status of the early Pentecostals, the Pentecostals found themselves at odds with established denominations. Although they did not originally see themselves as a separate entity, thinking instead of themselves "as a movement within the Christian Church, used of God to revitalize it," before long it was apparent that their doctrine and practices were not readily acceptable by the non-Pentecostal Christian (Nichol 1966, pp. 55–56).

In addition to conflict with non-Pentecostals, Pentecostalism experienced doctrinal problems within. Given the emphasis on personal experience, new revelations and scriptural insights were commonplace. Several of these, of major importance at the time, caused splits within congregations and led to establishment of new denominations. One particularly significant area of dissension was Trinitarian theology. Orthodox Christianity teaches, as does most of Pentecostalism, that there are three *persons* (the Father, the Son, and the Holy Spirit) in *one* God. Some Pentecostals departed from this orthodox Christian belief in two ways: one group of unitarians asserted that there was but one person in God and that person was Jesus; the other asserted that there is but one God and three manifestations (not persons) of this divinity (the Father, the Son, and the Holy Spirit). The latter group of unitarians form one of the largest American Pentecostal denominations, now known as the United Pentecostal Church, International. While the "Jesus only" groups of Pentecostals do represent a major shift from Trinitarian theology, the unitarians who emphasize *three manifestations* rather than *three persons* in a single Godhead appear to be more at odds over semantics than actual belief. It could be asserted that the vast majority of Pentecostals are trinitarians (including the United Pentecostal Church), and that they profess orthodox Christian belief about God.

Such controversy and conflict was in some ways functional for the early Pentecostal groups in that it helped to establish structural boundaries. The different Pentecostal denominations forming these boundaries developed largely as a result of outgroup hostility and in part from theological disputes within the early Pentecostal movement. These structures in turn kept alive the ideology of Pentecostal belief, which, over fifty years later, began to filter into mainline denominations.

Call to Order and Growth. The arising controversies and conflicts clearly pointed to a need for organization. Despite Parham's original anti-organizational bias, Pentecostalism soon discovered the need for becoming an institution. Ostracism by other churches, problems and splits caused by partisanship, invasion by confidence men who posed as Pentecostal preachers, and a need to finance mission work all led to a growing conviction that some type of structure was needed. It became apparent that "lack of discipline for unscrupulous persons, lack of standards, divisiveness, and unhealthy competition proved to be a high price for absolute independence" (Menzies 1971, p. 84). Out of this need, a confederation of local Pentecostal churches known as the Assemblies of God was founded in 1914. It now is the largest predominantly white Pentecostal denomination in the United States, with over one million members.[8]

It is nearly impossible to present an accurate picture of the total number of Pentecostal churches, much less to present an accurate membership figure for members of Pentecostal congregations. Perhaps hundreds of independent Pentecostal churches, some of them still of the storefront variety and supported by lower-class members, dot the nation's cities.[9] Another two dozen groups—many of them rather obscure—have only a regional impact, are ethnically oriented, or remain on the outer fringes of the Pentecostal movement because of a preoccupation with some bizarre practice (such as snake handling). Church historian Nichol (1966) identifies seven Pentecostal organizations that have expanded both nationally and internationally and that presently represent the majority of the Pentecostals in America. Both the predominantly white Assemblies of God and the predominantly black Church of God in Christ have claimed to be the largest Pentecostal denomination in the United States. The Assemblies of God reports over 1,283,000 members, and the Church of God in Christ also claims over one million members.[10]

The other major Pentecostal denominations include the United Pentecostal Church (420,000), the Church of God (Cleveland, Tennessee; 377,800); the Pentecostal Church of God in America, Inc. (110,700); the International Church of the Foursquare Gospel (89,200); and the Pentecostal Holiness Church (86,100). The growth in most of these major Pentecostal denominations has been phenomenal over the past twenty-five years—especially in view of the decline in membership of most mainline churches. For example, both the Assemblies of God and the

Church of God (Cleveland) membership has nearly tripled during that time and the Church of God in Christ and the Pentecostal Holiness Church have more than doubled in size.[11] Such increases in part have contributed to a decrease in much of the mutual hostility and suspicion between Pentecostals and other major orthodox Christian denominations as Pentecostal churches move out of sectlike status to take their place among the established denominations in the United States.

During the early decades of their history, however, Pentecostal churches tended to be misunderstood, ignored, or condemned by other religious groups. Despite their theological kinship with fundamentalism, fundamentalists closed the door to fellowship with Pentecostals. In a 1928 convention for the World Christian Fundamentals Association, a group organized in 1919 as the major voice of the movement, the Pentecostals were soundly condemned (Synan 1971, p. 205). It was not until 1943 that the Pentecostals were accepted into a non-Pentecostal church body, the National Association of Evangelicals. With Pentecostals coming into more frequent contact with non-Pentecostal Christians and with the development of the neo-Pentecostal movement since the 1950s, Pentecostals have enjoyed a more respected position within the orthodox Christian community. The relationship between the Pentecostals and the neo-Pentecostals has been of mutual advantage. While the excesses of earlier Pentecostalism exist to warn the neo-Pentecostals of potential pitfalls, the often highly educated neo-Pentecostals are repudiating once and for all the notion that the charismatic movement attracts only the poor and undereducated.

The Rise of Neo-Pentecostalism

While the rise of classical Pentecostalism can be traced to the influence of the Azusa Street Revival, neo-Pentecostalism appears to have four main sources: (1) the influence of David du Plessis, (2) the Full Gospel Businessmen's Fellowship International, (3) the Van Nuys, California, Awakening, and (4) the Roman Catholic Renewal (Hollenweger 1972, p. 4). Each of these sources can be traced to some Pentecostal influence, but all claim unique religious experiences that served as catalysts for the movement. Each of these sources played a major role in bringing Pentecostalism to mainline churches.

A Man Called Mr. Pentecost.   David du Plessis, a Pentecostal from South Africa, has done more than perhaps any other individual to reach leaders of established denominations with the charismatic message. The son of a white farmer, du Plessis became a leader of Pentecostalism at an early age in his native land. At the age of thirty-one (in 1936) du Plessis was given a prophecy through the evangelist Smith Wiggelsworth which du Plessis (1977, p. 2) reports as follows:

I have been sent by the Lord to tell you what He has shown me this morning. Through the old-line denominations will come a revival that will eclipse anything we have known throughout history. No such things have happened in times past as will happen when this begins. . . . It will eclipse the present-day, twentieth-century Pentecostal revival that already is a marvel to the world, with its strong opposition from the established church. But this same blessing will become acceptable to the churches and they will go on with this message and this experience beyond what the Pentecostals have achieved. You will live to see this work grow to such dimensions that the Pentecostal movement itself will be a light thing in comparison with what God will do through the old churches. There will be tremendous gatherings of people, unlike anything we've seen, and great leaders will change their attitude and accept not only the message but also the blessing.

Wiggelsworth also prophesied that he, du Plessis, was to play a prominent part in this movement.

By 1952 du Plessis had initiated a series of contacts with the World Council of Churches which enabled him to bring the message of Pentecostal doctrine to mainline church leaders (du Plessis 1977). Although he remembered the prophecy given years earlier, he was also apprehensive of these invitations, praying, "Lord, I have preached so much against them, what do I say now? They will not listen to me. Their churches have put our people out of their fellowship." To his amazement, however, du Plessis received a warm welcome. In 1956 he accepted an invitation to speak to ecumenical leaders from all across America—an event du Plessis describes as "one of the greatest experiences of my ministry." His ecumenical work increased during the years that followed, and these activities led to du Plessis's expulsion in 1962 from the Assemblies of God, the denomination he joined and in which he was an ordained minister upon moving to the United States. It was not until 1980 that du Plessis was reinstated as a minister of that Pentecostal denomination—a testimony to both du Plessis's effectiveness as a Pentecostal bridge to mainline churches and to the recognition by the Assemblies of God of their error in opposing his work.

Full Gospel Businessmen's Fellowship International. The history of neo-Pentecostalism has also been shaped by the role of the Full Gospel Businessmen's Fellowship International (FGBMFI). This fellowship was founded by California dairy farmer Demos Shakarian, with support from the Pentecostal evangelist, Oral Roberts. After a slow initial year, the FGBMFI grew rapidly and today has over 2,000 chapters in seventy-one countries, with 150 conventions and workshops held annually (1980, pp. 16–18). Shakarian, who was reared in an Armenian Pentecostal church in California,[12] organized revivals with the cooperation of classical Pentecostal churches throughout the 1930s and 1940s. In 1951 he felt called by God to begin sponsoring breakfasts for businessmen where he could preach the "full gospel" (orthodox Christianity, plus Pentecostal doctrine) and further Christian fellowship.

During the first few years, FGBMFI remained largely confined to cooperation with Pentecostal denominations. Those who experienced a baptism of the Spirit from non-Pentecostal denominations would have been encouraged to join Pentecostal churches. Shakarian (1975, p. 42) believes that the barriers between Pentecostals and mainline denominations began to break down in 1956 in Minneapolis. There, during an annual nationwide FGBMFI convention, five Lutheran ministers were baptized in the Spirit. Shakarian (1975, p. 143) comments:

It was the beginning of a transformation which has since swept Lutheran congregations from coast to coast. Not a rejection of their traditional strengths but the very opposite: an empowering of Lutherans, clergy and laymen alike, to make the statements of their faith a day-by-day reality. Since then we've watched the same power sweep many denominations—Presbyterians, Baptists, Methodists, Roman Catholics, Episcopalians. Always at first a handful of half-hostile people coming to a meeting out of curiosity. Then the wind of the Spirit blowing through whole churches, whole communions.

Shakarian's FGBMFI is important because it marked a successful outreach of Pentecostals to non-Pentecostals that did not result in a new denomination, but rather in a strengthening of existing classical Pentecostal churches and a spreading of the "full gospel" to other institutional denominations. FGBMFI may be viewed as a bridge between classical Pentecostals and the neo-Pentecostal movement among both Protestants and Catholics.

St. Mark's Episcopal Church: Van Nuys, California. Although some members and ministers of mainline denominations were quietly being familiarized with Pentecostal doctrine and exposed to Pentecostal experiences through the efforts of men like du Plessis and Shakarian, it was not until 1960 that neo-Pentecostalism began to achieve recognition. In 1959 Dennis Bennett, the rector of St. Mark's Episcopal Church (Van Nuys, California), began to meet with a few neo-Pentecostals and himself experienced the baptism of the Holy Spirit. During subsequent prayer meetings with others from his congregation approximately seventy persons also received the baptism (Hummel 1978). On April 3, 1960, in order to still some developing rumors, Bennett shared his experience with his entire congregation. This so outraged some members that Bennett eventually resigned from the Van Nuys congregation (Bennett 1970).

About this time, Bennett was invited to serve a small mission church in Seattle. Rather than remain in a church where a small group would continue to oppose him, Bennett chose to accept the offer at St. Luke's. He recognized that this new assignment was to a small, nonprestigious church, quite different from the prosperous Van Nuys congregation.

Despite his attempt to discourage people from joining—and forsaking their own churches, St. Luke's Church flourished. From 1960 to 1970 an estimated 8,000 to 10,000 people were baptized in the Holy Spirit at St. Luke's, but, as Bennett remarks, "we have always insisted they return to their own churches to share what has happened to them." During that same period the church grew from a mission church that "never quite got off the ground," with an annual income of $12,000, to a congregation of 1,000 members, with an annual income of $170,000. As St. Luke's grew and prospered, so did Dennis Bennett's reputation and role as a leader of the neo-Pentecostal movement—a role he continues to play today.

The Roman Catholic Renewal. The neo-Pentecostal movement within the Catholic Church developed during the early post-Vatican II years in the late 1960s. The Second Vatican Council had opened wide the windows of a seemingly changeless institution, allowing diverse experiments with both liturgy and theology. While some of the more modernist-oriented positions are being condemned and silenced currently by the Vatican, neo-Pentecostalism, which is compatible with Catholicism's orthodox Christian framework, has been blessed by Pope Paul VI and the current Pope John Paul II (1981).

The Charismatic movement in the Catholic Church is usually traced back to the famous "Duquesne Weekend." In mid-February, 1967, thirty students and faculty from Duquesne University in Pittsburgh spent a weekend in prayer and meditation on the first four chapters of the biblical Book of Acts. Most knew little about either Pentecostalism or Protestant neo-Pentecostalism, although most had read Pentecostal David Wilkerson's 1963 testimony on the power of the Holy Spirit in his life, *The Cross and the Switchblade*. As they prayed Saturday evening, many were baptized in the Spirit.

There was no urging, there was no direction as to what had to be done. The individuals simply encountered the person of the Holy Spirit as others had several weeks before. Some praised God in new languages, others quietly wept for joy, others prayed and sang. They prayed from ten in the evening until five in the morning. Not everyone was touched immediately, but throughout the evening God dealt with each person there in a wonderful way. (quoted in Hummel 1978, p. 49)

In early March of the same year, one of the participants, Ralph Keifer, visited Notre Dame University and met with a small group at the home of Kevin Ranaghan, a doctoral student, and his wife Dorothy. As he reported to them what had happened at Duquesne, the Ranaghans and about thirty of their friends joined praying that they might be filled with the Holy Spirit. Many of them had experiences which changed their lives (Ranaghan and Ranaghan 1969). The importance of this meeting for the history of the Catholic charismatic renewal is that the Ranaghans have remained as leaders, writers, and teachers, greatly influencing the development of the movement. Within a month, what had begun at Duquesne spread to the University of Notre Dame and to a Catholic parish serving Michigan State University (O'Connor 1971, p. 16). The growth of the Catholic Charismatic Renewal has been phenomenal. Ranaghan (1981) estimates that over six million Roman Catholics in the United States identify themselves as charismatics. Thousands of prayer groups and a number of ministries, including those sponsoring conferences, publications, and ecumenical activities, have developed to further the renewal.

The Catholic Charismatic Renewal has an emphasis somewhat different from classical Pentecostalism. While the Catholic Renewal seems to emphasize houses of prayer, full-fledged religious communities, and prayer groups, Pentecostals appear to be more concerned with the local church and evangelism. The differences of emphasis are due to different ideologies and corresponding religious structures, to be discussed below (Sandidge 1976, p. 16). The Catholic Charismatic Renewal is firmly rooted in the Catholic Church and its history (Ranaghan and Ranaghan 1971), just as neo-Pentecostalism is, to varying degrees, rooted in its own denominationalism. Although they lack a unified theology that may be termed "Protestant," the different denominations have attempted to integrate the Pentecostal experience into their denominational theology. Similarly, classical Pentecostalism, often said to be weak in theology (see Hollenweger 1972; Block-Hoell 1964), has also developed varying traditions and theologies among the various Pentecostal denominations. The charismatic movement can be viewed as a river of the Holy Spirit, into which flow the tributaries of religious denominations. While classical Pentecostalism has served as a major influence, so have the denominational ties of neo-Pentecostals.

Pentecostalism and Neo-Pentecostalism Contrasted

Despite a common emphasis on the power of the Holy Spirit, many differences exist among charismatics. There are denominational differences unrelated to Pentecostal issues, as well as many differences of beliefs on specific charismatic issues. Moreover, older, institutionalized Pentecostal churches often view suspiciously the new enthusiasm of Protestant and Catholic charismatics. (Nearly every Pentecostal minister the writer interviewed expressed a strong support for the neo-Pentecostal movement but also hoped that advice from classical Pentecostal circles would be sought and heeded in order to avoid mistakes made by earlier participants in the movement.)

There are differences in the basic theology of the works of the Holy Spirit between Pentecostals and neo-Pentecostals. Neo-Pentecostals are less likely than classical Pentecostals to hold that Spirit baptism is necessarily accompanied by speaking in tongues. While tongue-speaking is desired and may be more practiced in neo-Pentecostal gatherings than in Pentecostal ones, neo-Pentecostals may view other spiritual gifts such as healing or prophecy as possible evidence of Spirit baptism. This difference is significant, particularly in light of the Statement of Faith of the Pentecostal Fellowship of North America, which doctrinally links glossolalia with Spirit baptism.

Despite efforts of Pentecostals like du Plessis and Shakarian, suspicion and sometimes condemnation may be found in some Pentecostal leaders' and ministers' attitudes toward neo-Pentecostalism. In a recent revival meeting in a classical Pentecostal church, the traveling evangelist stressed the impossibility of the Spirit-filled Christian remaining in "dead" mainline congregations: "He will wither and no longer be open to the movement of the Holy Spirit." Many such individuals doubt that there will be any major renewal or revival among either Protestant or Catholic churches and that Spirit-filled members of both traditions should leave their respective churches for Pentecostal ones. In another large Pentecostal gathering the speaker intimated that the neo-Pentecostal experience may represent a simulation by Satan of the *real* baptism. There is a range of reactions to neo-Pentecostalism, from guarded suspicion to cautious acceptance of this development. Some ministers have faced censure from their own denominational leaders for being influenced by neo-Pentecostalism and for fraternizing with such believers.

Pentecostals and neo-Pentecostals both lament the loss of spiritual vitality in the church and celebrate the baptism in the Holy Spirit as the means to a new life. Both groups expect that extraordinary evidence, such as tongues, prophecy, and healings, will be part of a charismatic community's heritage. They show their commitment to the authority of the Bible, and particularly emphasize the Acts of the Apostles as a prescription for the normative pattern of the Christian church (Logan 1975, pp. 33–34).

Neo-Pentecostals tend to remain active within their own denominations, upholding their different traditions and backgrounds. Theologians and ministers often debate theologies, but the impression of the writer is that there is a grass roots ecumenism in evidence, particularly among neo-Pentecostals. Charismatics speak a common religious language and share special religious bonds, whether they are Pentecostals, Catholics, or Protestants. Nondenominational and interdenominational prayer groups and conferences for charismatics have sprung up throughout the United States. While differences are acknowledged, the emphasis is more on the unity of charismatics in the Holy Spirit than on theological differences. To a great extent there is a desire to share a belief in a "full gospel" of a Spirit-filled life with both noncharismatics and nonevangelical Christians. They seem intent to follow the apostle Paul's advice given

to the early Church at Philippi: "If you have any encouragement from
being united with Christ, if any comfort from his love, if any fellowship
with the Spirit, if any tenderness and compassion, then make my joy
complete by being likeminded, having the same love, being one in spirit
and purpose" (Phil. 2:1–2).

Black Pentecostals: A Movement within a Movement

Classical Pentecostal and neo-Pentecostal believers may be showing
signs of increased cooperation, and charismatic unity is much discussed,
but there is a significant group that remains largely peripheral to the
charismatic movement. This group is comprised of the different black
Pentecostal denominations and sects. Proportionately more blacks in the
United States are Pentecostal than are whites, and black Pentecostal
churches outnumber white ones, both in the number of denominations
and in the size of congregations (Tinney 1980a). The predominantly
black Church of God in Christ is one of the two largest Pentecostal
denominations in the United States, and the Apostolic (non-Trinitarian)
branch of Pentecostalism is largely black.

For the most part, however, blacks are not a visible force in the
charismatic movement. This fact is evidenced in the nonparticipation of
blacks in the 1977 Charismatic Conference in Kansas City, in the near
absence of articles by black Pentecostals in charismatic magazines and
journals,[13] and in the infrequent appearance of black guests on charismatic television shows (with the notable exception of black Christian enter-
tainers). Of the churches and conferences attended by the author, only the
FGBMFI had more than a few black participants, but whites still outnumbered blacks about twenty to one. The charismatic movement described in this book is largely a white movement with a sprinkling of
black, usually solidly middle-class, participation.

Black Pentecostal scholar James S. Tinney (1978) quipped in his
editorial on the Kansas City Conference, "While 40,000 charismatics
gathered in Kansas City, 4 million black Pentecostals stayed home." He
credited their absence in part to the exclusion of non-Trinitarians and to an
"elitist emphasis on tongues." Although the largest black Pentecostal
church, the Church of God in Christ (COGIC) is Trinitarian, the non-
Trinitarian Apostolic churches have many largely black congregations.[14]

While both COGIC and the Apostolic churches have doctrinal statements on the relationship between Spirit baptism and glossolalia, Tinney apparently believes that black churches have placed less emphasis on tongues than have white churches. In this editorial and in other writings, Tinney (1979, 1980a) speaks for at least some educated black Pentecostals who reject what they perceive to be the exclusivity of the movement, its middle-class white bias, and its conservative politics. Tinney (1978) notes in an editorial that "Black Pentecostals have a more holistic view of church history. If anything, our ties and allegiances more strongly lie with non-Pentecostal Black [*sic*] churches than with white Pentecostal 'brethren.'"

Tinney (1980a) has identified other differences between black and white classical Pentecostals, including church government and polity, the role of women, and church involvement in social action. Blacks tend toward episcopal rather than congregational government and usually bar laity from holding church offices. In contrast to the Assemblies of God and some other smaller white Pentecostal denominations, women are denied ordination in the COGIC and in many Apostolic churches. Tinney also asserts that blacks emphasize social action in churches more than do white Pentecostals.

While Tinney identifies a few possible reasons for the absence of blacks in the movement—largely ideological differences—the segregation of American churches, including Pentecostal ones, cannot be overlooked. Different worship styles, music preferences, and leadership styles appear to have developed for blacks and whites (Tinney 1980a). Two religious cultures have developed within Pentecostalism: one black and one white. Black Pentecostalism can be correctly identified as a segment of the larger charismatic movement, but Pentecostalism fails to reflect the integration that was so evident in its earliest years.

It would be difficult to overemphasize the role that blacks played in the earliest years of the movement. While Charles Parham, a white man, is credited with providing a basic Pentecostal doctrine (glossolalia being the evidence of Spirit baptism), it was William Seymour, a black preacher, who led the famed Azusa Street Revival. Furthermore, it was the black leader of the Church of God in Christ, Bishop C. H. Mason, who ordained a number of whites who later joined the Assemblies of God. From its inception until about 1920, the Pentecostal movement was

strikingly interracial. Pentecostal-Holiness church historian Vinson
Synon (1971, p. 165) correctly notes:

In an age of Social Darwinism, Jim Crowism, and general white supre-
macy, the fact that Negroes and whites worshipped together in virtual
equality among the pentecostals was a significant exception to prevailing
racial attitudes. Even more significant is the fact that this interracial
accord took place among the very groups that have traditionally been
most at odds, the poor whites and the poor blacks.

The racism of the larger society prevailed over this short-lived experi-
ment with integration.

Over the years, many poor whites, particularly in urban areas, have
become solidly middle class, as educational and occupational opportunities are made available to them. The image of the socially and
economically deprived Pentecostal believer of the 1920s and 1930s has
changed since World War II. There remains a lower-class white constituency among Pentecostals, but many have entered the "good life" of
suburbia. Fewer blacks, Pentecostal or non-Pentecostal, have had such
opportunities, as segregation and discrimination continue to blight
American society. White Pentecostals and neo-Pentecostals have also
learned to utilize and to establish media contacts for the spread of their
message. Black Pentecostals, presumably because of lack of resources,
have not utilized the media coverage that would give them greater
visibility in the larger movement.

This is not to deny a black Pentecostal movement. Membership figures
according to race are not readily available, but black Pentecostalism
shows signs of the same vital growth that white Pentecostalism has
experienced. Tinney (1980a, p. 16) comments: "Not even Methodists
outnumber Pentecostals in the black community; and if Baptists don't
watch out, they too may become outnumbered." It appears, rather, that
the black Pentecostal movement is a movement within the larger charismatic movement, but one that remains apart from the white components.

As in most contemporary social movements, the charismatic movement is visibly propelled and led by middle-class men and women who,
for the most part, are also white. They have the financial and educational
resources to develop an institutional base for the movement. Some

middle-class blacks undoubtedly do support aspects of the charismatic movement, but others believe that white Pentecostalism and neo-Pentecostalism have very different ideological and social concerns.

Notes

1. Unless noted otherwise, all biblical quotations are from the New International Version (Grand Rapids, Mich.: Zondervan Bible Publishers, 1978).

2. A recent *Christianity Today* Gallup pool reported that 19 percent of those interviewed consider themselves to be "charismatic." The poll does not permit us to know what the respondents meant by this identification, but it does demonstrate that the charismatic movement has had an impact on believers and that a significant percentage of persons associate themselves with it.

3. A minister from a classical Pentecostal church informed the writer that the term "charismatic" came into use in the late 1960s, when the evangelist and healer Oral Roberts brought in a group of ministers with Pentecostal leanings and suggested that the term "Pentecostal" was too controversial for many mainline churches. The ministers agreed that it might be advantageous to use the term "charismatic" (in lieu of Pentecostal), a term that has come into widespread use through the communications media.

4. Pentecostal-holiness historian Synan (1971, pp. 204–5) agrees that Pentecostalists are basically fundamentalists, but notes that the former watched the great fundamentalist controversy over Darwin's evolutionary theory from the outside. Since most of these fundamentalist leaders were strict Calvinists, the Pentecostals, with their equally strict Arminian theology, were unwilling to become too involved in this controversy. Synan observes, "Because they were never an integral part of the fundamentalist controversy, the Pentecostals emerged without the deep anti-intellectual bias that distinguished much of conservative Protestantism after 1925."

5. Leaders of the Church of God may point out that their denomination has Baptist rather than Methodist roots. Despite its denominational background, its theology is Wesleyan. As Church of God historian Conn writes: "The doctrine of sanctification is distinctly Arminian, and Arminianism rather than Calvinism has produced the greatest revival movements in the nation, particularly in the South. Dr. William Warren Sweet has stated that Calvinist doctrine, with its extreme

views of predestination and election, offers salvation to the few, while Arminianism, with its insistence of free will, offers salvation to all. Calvinism is autocratic, while Arminianism is democratic'' (Conn 1977, p. 21).

6. The Church of God (Cleveland, Tenn.) frequently refers to itself as the oldest Pentecostal denomination, dating back to 1884. Approximately 100 of its members were baptized in the Spirit in 1896. This original group, however, was greatly reduced in number (to around twenty members) by 1902 and did not increase again until after the beginning of the Azusa Street Revival. A. J. Tomlinson, the man credited by many historians as founder of the Church of God, was visited by C. B. Cashwell, an Azusa Street convert, who prayed with Tomlinson in 1908 to receive the baptism of the Spirit. Thus the Church of God, which technically was founded before the Azusa Street Revival, did not develop into a significant Pentecostal sect until after this influential event.

7. For an eyewitness account of the Azusa Street revival, see Bartleman (1980).

8. The Church of God held its first general conference in 1906. By 1914, when the Assemblies of God confederation was founded, it had over 3,000 members in approximately seven states. The Church of God in Christ dates to 1897, but its membership and precise historical growth are difficult to ascertain.

In an attempt to simplify the discussion, my account follows those historians who trace the development of Pentecostalism through the Assemblies of God. The Assemblies of God does have historical links to the older, predominantly black Church of God in Christ, and many unitarian Pentecostals were defectors from the Assemblies of God.

9. For a discussion of the varieties of Pentecostalism in America based on regional ties, ethnic identification, or cultic practices, see Nichol (1966, chap. 9) and Faupel (1972).

10. In private correspondence with the author, black Pentecostal James Tinney (1981) of Howard University asserted that the Church of God in Christ (COGIC) "is larger (in the U.S., though not worldwide) in membership than the Assemblies of God," with a membership of over three million in the United States and 500,000 in other countries. This provides an update of the 1980 *Yearbook of American and Canadian Churches* which reported a figure of 450,000 (based on a 1961 response from the church). While Tinney's information was based on figures given in *The Whole Truth* (COGIC's church paper), they may be inflated. Otha Kelly (1976), a COGIC leader, made a statement in his autobiography that is being used to support a more neutral ground that the Assemblies of God and COGIC are approximately equal in size:

By 1970, the church claimed a membership of one million and a worldwide constituency of three million in over 10,000 churches. In a church body that has an oral tradition, exact statistics are difficult to ascertain—yet major scholars agree that this body numbers well over a million in the United States alone.

In contract to COGIC, the Assemblies of God do keep membership records but their figures may be underestimated. Membership is not stressed in many AG congregations, and the reported figures are based only on membership—not on regular attendance and church participation. Many AG congregations have more regular participants than they do actual members.

11. With the exception of the figures for the Church of God in Christ (see n. 10), all church membership figures have been taken from materials presented in the "Statistical and Historical Section" of the annual issues of the *Yearbook of American Churches*. The latest figures used are from the 1980 edition.

12. Most books on the history of Pentecostalism trace its development through Methodism and the Holiness sects to Parham and then Seymour's Azusa Street Revival, from which it began to spread worldwide. Shakarian's own family background demonstrates the existence of Pentecostals in Europe prior to either Parham's or Seymour's experience, specifically to the Russian Pentecostals, some of whom were responsible for Shakarian's grandfather's conversion in 1891 in Armenia. Shortly after the turn of the century, Shakarian's family and others from the Armenian village of Kara Kala immigrated to the west coast of the United States, reportedly as a response to the prophecy calling them to leave their homeland. The remaining inhabitants of Kara Kala were later wiped out by the Turks in 1914 (see Shakarian 1975, chap. 1). Such ethnic Pentecostal churches account for only a small percentage of Pentecostals in the United States. They did, however, have their origins independent of the American Pentecostal revival. As ethnic divisions lessened, many descendents of such churches presumably became involved in the growing American Pentecostal movement.

13. The near invisibility of blacks in charismatic literature was recently acknowledged in an editorial in a leading charismatic magazine. Strang (1981) called for an end to racial barriers and vowed "to cover the Christian community in America whether it's white, black, Hispanic, or any other ethnic group."

14. Included in Richardson's (1980) discussion of black Apostolic Pentecostal denominations are the following: Church of God (Apostolic), Pentecostal Assemblies of the World, Apostolic Overcoming Holy Church of God, Inc., Church of Our Lord Jesus Christ of the Apostolic Faith, Original Glorious Church of God In Christ Apostolic Faith, Inc., Way of the Cross Church of Christ, Highway Christian Church of Christ, Church of the Lord Jesus Christ of the Apostolic Faith, Apostle Church of Christ in God, Shiloh Apostolic Temple, Inc., Pentecostal Churches of Apostolic Faith, Bible Way Church of Our Lord Jesus Christ World Wide, Bible Way Pentecostal Church, True Vine Pentecostal Churches of Jesus, Mount Hebron Apostolic Temple of Our Lord Jesus of the Apostolic Faith, Inc., United Church of Jesus Christ (Apostolic), Apostolic Church of Christ, Inc., Apostolic Assemblies of Christ, Inc., United Churches of Jesus, Apostolic, United Way of the Cross Churches of Christ of the Apostolic Faith, Inc.,

Redeemed Assembly of Jesus Christ, Apostolic. Richardson observes that splits and schisms have characterized the black Apostolic church from 1919 until the present time.

CHAPTER 2

An Unlikely Environment: Theoretical Musings on the Growth of the Charismatic Movement in Secular Society

> The current resurgence of evangelical Protestantism, coming as it does after an era of painful eclipse and emerging under the high noon of secularism, constitutes a remarkable historical development. The development seems particularly notable because the demise of evangelical Protestantism, both in the popular imagination and the academic mind, had appeared so complete. (Wells and Woodbridge 1975, p. 9)

The drama of a small Jewish sect's growth into a major world religion known as Christianity was, perhaps still is, believed by some scholars of religion to be in its final act. The call to repentance from sin and belief in a personal God seemed to many to be hopelessly out of date in an increasingly scientific and technological society. Terms such as "post-Christian era" and the "death of God" became part of American vocabulary and seemed to describe what was occurring in the history of religion as the twentieth century draws to a close. Science, it was frequently argued, has leveled a lethal attack upon Western Christendom. Sociologists Glock and Stark (1965), in their classic study *Religion and Society in Tension,* provided such a thesis and supporting data to demonstrate "that men will tend to be *either* scientific *or* religious, and not both." They concluded that, given the modern scientist's detachment from religion, "we must

suspect that future American society will either become increasingly
irreligious, or that religion will be extensively modified'' (Glock and
Stark 1965, p. 288). How accurate is this prognosis and where does the
growth of the charismatic movement fit into its thesis?

In terms of the analysis offered by many social scientists of religion of
the last few decades, the rise of the charismatic movement is an anomaly.
Contrary to most predictions, the demise of religion has not occurred, and
some groups are increasing in numbers with remarkable vitality. The
Pentecostal churches are one such group. Winds of the charismatic
movement are blowing even among mainline churches plagued by membership declines in the past decades. Are we in the midst of another
religious awakening, as some historians and social commentators have
asserted? Or is the charismatic religious revival an aside on the contemporary stage, having little or no impact on the larger secular order? It is
the thesis of this book that the charismatic movement is a social
movement—and that as a social movement it is having a decisive impact
on both the larger religious order and upon the secular world. The
charismatic movement represents a departure from the secularization of
religion that has fascinated social scientists during the past decades. Its
emphasis on the reality and power of the supernatural might be termed the
resacralization of religion. While only a minority of Christians are involved in it, many of these men and women are committed to the
revitalization of established churches and, in varying ways, to the changing of the social order.

The Secularization Thesis Considered

A trend toward resacralization, even for a significant minority of believers in contemporary Western society, is not a widely held assumption
among social scientists. Ever since its inception as a field of study in the
1850s, sociology has assumed an increased *secularization* of society.
Auguste Comte, the putative founder of sociology, viewed society as
moving through three major stages: the theological, the metaphysical,
and the positivistic (scientific). Dominance of the theological perspective
was a stage long behind modern society. The age of religion and the rule
of the priestly class gave way first to rationalism and then to the development of a positivistic or scientific society. Other social scientists have
developed variations of that view of the Western world as entering a final

positivistic era of industry and science. This theory has rarely been challenged in social science from the time of Comte to the present day.

The modern world, with its emphasis on science, has left little room for values based on faith rather than reason. This secular emphasis on reason has had a decided impact on our society, including its religious institutions. Robert Bellah (1970, p. 74), a contemporary sociologist of religion, argues that "Modernization, whatever else it involves, is always a moral and a religious problem." The moral problem that Bellah refers to can be considered in light of the steadily growing philosophy of individualism which erodes responsibility toward the collectivity. Another sociologist attempting to deal with modern men and women has similarly observed that since the sixteenth century the group, the guild, the tribe, and the city have become less important than the individual (Bell 1976, p. 16). Traditional religion reflected a group consciousness and met individual as well as group needs. An example familiar to most students is the sense of being a collectivity, a people of God, among the ancient tribes of Israel. This sense of peoplehood could be found also in the early Christian churches, but much of Christianity, argue some sociologists, has succumbed to the modern, secular world, with its corresponding emphasis on the individual over the collectivity.

The familiar concepts of modernization and secularization permeate the literature of social science, which often rings optimistically, and sometimes pessimistically, about the future of humankind. Through the development of science and technology, the modern world has presumably executed the old gods and either mourns their passing or seeks new ones. Many theorists have seen an impending spiritual crisis caused by modernization (e.g., Bell 1976; Gouldner 1976)—a crisis in part created by the breakdown of religious ideology. What has not been seriously considered by many of these scholars is a religious revival that reaffirms for many the reality of traditional Christian beliefs. While such a movement may be viewed as inconsequential it is in fact occurring and is touching the lives of millions of Americans.

There are two antithetical movements occurring in modern society, one of secularization and one of sacralization. One of the ways to observe both of these movements is to consider the patterns of church growth and decline. Overall, secularization, as social scientists have so often observed, appears to be the predominant trend. Church membership and participation figures reveal a crisis in the ecclesia. At the same time, however, the sacralization process can be seen in the healthy organizational state of conservative churches.

Recent Church Growth and Decline. The literature in the social science of religion has noted a radical change in American religion during the 1960s. This theme of radical change toward secularization appeared again and again in both theoretical and research articles of that decade. The research of the period saw a decline in religious involvement (Stark and Glock 1968a; Hadden 1971), a "gathering storm" in the churches resulting from conflicts between liberal clergymen and their more conservative laity (Hadden 1970), and the possibility that ethics would mark the end of Christianity as ethical and moral concerns were increasingly separated from religious belief (Stark and Glock 1968b). All in all, the prognosis for organized Christian religions appeared gloomy. Church membership, attendance at services, and donations all appeared on the decline.

Most of these studies, however, focused on the established mainline Christian churches. Several significant findings in articles from the 1970s modified the secularization thesis promulgated in the previous decade. One such work was Dean Kelley's (1972) analysis of the growth of conservative denominations (e.g., Southern Baptists, Wesleyan Church, Lutheran Church–Missouri Synod, Church of the Nazarene) previously ignored by most researchers. In fact, evangelical denominations, including Pentecostal ones, have been steadily growing over the past decades (Hoge and Roozen 1979). Researchers have further concluded that liberal mainline churches (e.g., United Methodist, Lutheran Church in America, United Presbyterian, United Church of Christ) appear to be losing members to both conservative churches and to the group of "unchurched" Americans (Kelley 1978; Bibby 1978); that there is little evidence of successful proselytization of the unchurched by these conservative groups (Bibby 1978); and that a significant percentage of the unchurched are "born again" believers in Christianity.[1]

It would appear, based upon such findings as well as upon a recent *Christianity Today* Gallup poll, that religious belief is alive and well in America. The editors (*Christianity Today* 1979, p. 15) observe that despite the growing secularization in education and the brief flourishing of "the death of God" theology in the 1960s, faith in a personal God continues strong. They note, "The pronouncements of some social analysts and some prominent churchmen as well, that America has become post-Christian and too sophisticated to need God any more turns out to be grossly inaccurate.''[2]

How do such findings modify the thesis of the secularization of modern society? Is secularization a fact or a theoretical fiction created by social scientists?

Reconsidering a Complex Thesis. As we have seen, most social scientists agree that secularization has been on the rise in modern society. They assert that "man has won control over himself" (Wilkinson 1971) and is less susceptible to religious influences. Wilson's (1966, p. 14) definition is accepted by many as a starting point for any analysis: 'secularization' is seen as "the process whereby religious thinking, practice, and institutions lose social significance." This loss has been viewed as being twofold: "On the institutional level there has been *secularization,* or the shrinking of the institutional authority and the role of religion as the mode of community. On the cultural level there has been *profanation,* the attenuation of a theodicy as providing a set of meanings to explain man's relation to the beyond" (Bell 1976, p. 167). This "loss of faith" is presumably the result of dramatic increases in urbanization and education as well as a less dramatic increase in vertical mobility that is part of our modern world (Demerath 1968, p. 390).

Even in the midst of what seems like a general concurrence with the "secularization thesis" among social scientists, some dissenting voices have been raised (e.g., Bellah 1970; Greeley 1972).[3] For such scholars, religion, instead of becoming increasingly peripheral and vestigial, may again be moving to the center of cultural preoccupations. The charismatic movement is evidence that for a significant number of believers religious ideology remains or has become a central concern.

The relationship between modernity and secularization is thus not clear-cut. There is no question that secularization as a process has been rooted in the country's early history, as evidenced by the constitutional separation of church and state. At the same time, America has proved to be fertile soil for the development of a myriad of religious beliefs. In developing a theory of secularization in light of such history, one author observes:

We must therefore be prepared to see the process of secularization in complex patterns: as a cause as well as an effect of religious groups, movements, and institutions; as proceeding according to a variable sequence of events and leading toward no single outcome; and as involving *a number of reversals and simultaneous but contradictory developments at different levels of a single society.* (Fenn 1978, p. 29; my italics)

In accord with this assertion, secularization may be seen as being both on the rise on some, perhaps most levels of the society, while on the wane on others, especially in some church-related institutions that may have been caught briefly in the secularization trend of the 1960s.[4] Even if secularization continues to exert a profound effect on most of Western society, on particular individuals, and on groups, religion may remain a powerful—perhaps the most powerful—determinant of conduct (Wilson 1966, p. 13).

The preceding considerations raise several questions with regard to the charismatic movement. Why did the charismatic movement develop as a countermovement within a presumably secularized world? How is it organized and how is its ideology disseminated? What is its impact on the larger society? Social scientists are necessarily cautious in attempting to answer such questions, and I share this caution. It seems important, nevertheless, to struggle with some of the reasons for the rise of the charismatic movement—reasons which must be kept in mind throughout this analysis of the movement's structure and consequences.

Toward a Theoretical Explanation of the New Religious Awakening

Sociological theory at its best goes beyond description in an attempt to explain the phenomena under observation. Explanation, however, involves many pitfalls. One trap is to reduce all explanation to a single cause, be it psychological, historical, behavioral, or structural. For example, instead of viewing the rise of a social movement as the result of many interrelated causes on different levels of analysis (individual, small group, and societal), some analyses assume oversimplified psychological causes (followers suffer from personal deprivation or have easily suggestible personalities) or sociological causes (religious social movements result from the activities of socially deprived lower social classes). Explanations should, however, take into account a variety of theoretical frameworks in order to produce a more realistic view of the multiple causes involved in the rise of a social movement.

The theoretical premise of this study is that the charismatic movement must be viewed in the historical context of the American society in which it has developed. Further, it must be seen within the socio-cultural milieu of twentieth-century America, within its ideological context and changing social institutions. At the same time, the movement's success is contingent upon the process of effective socialization which occurs, in the case of classical and neo-Pentecostalism, as potential participants experience a phenomenon known as "baptism in/of the Holy Spirit." In short, the history of the United States has shaped the contemporary culture which has given rise to the charismatic movement. The continuance and effectiveness of this movement, however, depends upon the internalization of its values and goals by members of the society. What follows is a consideration of the historical, the socio-cultural, and the social-psychological background necessary for a descriptive analysis of the organization, ideology, and consequences of the charismatic movement.

Revivals and Awakenings in Historical Context. Despite the strength of secular thought in modern society, traditional religious belief provides a viable ideology for many people. It is *not* my thesis that the charismatic movement or conservative Christianity will replace secular humanistic thought in America, but rather that the traditional religious ideology of charismatics is providing a base for an alternative subculture for many and that it is challenging the secular world's influence on mainline churches. Thus while secularization continues in the larger social order, the charismatic believer is determined to wage battle against an increasingly materialistic and rationalistic culture.

Serious students of American religious history are perhaps less surprised by this current religious revival than are some of their social science colleagues who are deficient in historical knowledge. Revivals and awakenings have been a part of our national heritage and have contributed substantially to the American ethos.[5] At least five such periods have been identified (McLoughlin 1978), including the Puritan Awakening in England (1610–40); the First Great Awakening in the United States (1730–60); the Second Great Awakening (1800–1830); the Third Great Awakening (1890–1920); and the current Fourth Great Awakening.

Each of the past awakenings are believed to have had an impact on society. The Puritan Awakening led to the beginning of the constitutional monarchy in England. The First Great Awakening on the shores of the American continent led to the creation of the American republic. The Second Great Awakening facilitated the solidification of the Union and the rise of Jacksonian participatory democracy. Our Third Great Awakening brought about rejection of unregulated capitalistic exploitation and the beginning of the welfare state (McLoughlin 1978, pp. 10–11). Assessments of the goals and effects of the current Awakening are still speculative. According to some (e.g., McLoughlin 1978), America is headed toward a rejection of the unregulated capitalistic exploitation of mankind that has characterized recent history. Others (e.g., Rifkin 1979) are less optimistic about the saving power of the contemporary awakening.

It is my thesis that the charismatic movement is a significant part of the Fourth Great Awakening, which could be an important agent of social change.[6] A key to its effectiveness, however, will be its ability to prevent a routinization of the charisma that permeates the movement, a problem that threatens the movement's existence. The ideology of the charismatic movement exists in a modern and rational world from which it cannot separate itself. Paradoxically, as it seeks to affect the modern, rationalistic world, the charismatic movement endangers itself and may well succumb to that world before modifying it in any significant way.

History readily demonstrates that awakenings have been a regular feature of American civilization, and it would be shortsighted to claim that the present awakening has ended. Some social commentators and historians point to the historical similarities between the present economic and social crisis and past crises that have brought religious awakenings and reforms. It may be that the charismatic movement has at least the potential to challenge present society's values. The extent to which it succeeds remains to be judged.

The Sacred-Secular Social Order.   While some religious historians observe recurrent religious revivals, other social commentators (e.g., Bell 1976; Berger 1977; Goulder 1976) herald a post-Christian era. Most recognize the ideological vacuum created in industrialized, modernized society by a pervasive materialism and rationalism. The product of this milieu has been termed an "unfinished animal" who seeks a lost spiritual dimension of life (Roczak 1975). Such writing is a variant of a perennial theme in social science: the "old gods" are dying or already dead and the "new gods" are yet to be born. This may be true for segments of the social order, but for many the "old gods" and traditional religious belief are alive and well.[7] A religious world view is basic for charismatic Christians. Many view the yielding of traditional religious belief to increasingly secular values as threatening the very foundations of modern society.

Here we may observe two coexisting and conflicting world views (Roof 1978). On the one hand we find the secular, scientific, and humanistic world views which focus on the natural and social order of this world. The traditional world view posits a supernatural order and the mysterious forces of a sovereign Deity at work in everyday human affairs. These two world views coexist as conflicting approaches to reality. Why persons chose one view over the other—the basic question in understanding the rise of religious consciousness (in both old and new forms)—necessarily involves considering the individual in relation to the social order.[8]

Individuals, Their Society, and Religious Experiences. Modern culture has been accused of frustrating at least three basic human needs or desires: community, engagement, and dependence (Slater 1970). Men and women are social beings and thus desire community. They seek meaning to life that is more than an extension of the ego—meaning that enables each to come to grips with personal and interpersonal problems. This desire is fulfilled by engagement. Furthermore, they seek dependence, which allows them to share responsibility for the direction of their lives. The charismatic movement, in promoting traditional religious ideology, claims that it can meet all three of these needs.

The charismatic movement emphasizes, to varying degrees, the fact that early Christians lived in communities that were more extensive than the American nuclear family. The Church is seen as a "family of God." The gifts accompanying the baptism of the Spirit are intended to be used for the church as the "Body of Christ." Healing, prophecy, deliverance, and other gifts are not intended primarily for the person who has the gift, but for others in the church who receive the healing, experience exhortation through prophecy, or who know deliverance from oppression. In other words, charismata are said to operate primarily within the believing community.

The development of this community also implies engagement. Members are expected and encouraged to spread the gospel. The message of Christianity, with special emphasis on a "full gospel," including teaching about the power and gifts of the Holy Spirit, is a cause that transcends the individual. The changed life of the charismatic believer is a recurrent theme in books and articles of personal testimony, television interviews, and local prayer meetings. This changed life should lead to action, especially through evangelistic efforts and/or social action.

Community and engagement are also accompanied in many charismatic circles by *dependence* to counter the ethos of independence in the larger society. Dependence on God, including manifestations believed to be supernatural, and on members of the believing community receive particular emphasis. It is important for most charismatics to belong to a body of similar believers who promote acceptable codes of moral behavior and moral absolutes in a world where everything seems relative. The community of believers is also deemed necessary to sustain the faith essential for the supernatural to occur, again demonstrating the dependence of one believer upon another.

The growth of the charismatic movement may be attributed in part to its ability to satisfy in modern men and women the age-old search for meaning. The movement's emphasis on personal religious experience compels the believer to accept faith. At the same time, this experience, linked to traditional religious doctrine, serves to counter the extreme rationalism that has crept into Christian modernist theology. Charismatics observe the reality of the secular world but also believe in the reality of a sacred world. While accepting modern medicine, charismatics expect "miracles" to supplement what science has to offer. Noting the frustrations of revolutionaries in changing the social world, charismatics teach a provident God who intervenes in that world. Charismatics see themselves in the world but believe that the power of God can work through them for personal direction and for changing the world.

Human beings, as "unfinished animals," appear to need a spiritual component that science and empiricism have (perhaps unwittingly) denied them. For charismatics this spiritual component is provided by the pervasive power of the Holy Spirit. It is the experience of religious reality that makes the spiritual life a matter of practice as well as theory.

Is the Charismatic Movement a Social Movement?

The term "social movement," as used by social scientists, is a rather diffuse category in the study of human behavior. It includes movements of rural and urban discontent as well as imperialism. It may include collective action of a class, an occupational group, a race, or a nation. Some movements are geared toward moral protest and reform, while others are revolutionary. The focal point for some is age (youth or senior citizens); for others it is gender. It goes without saying that the thrust of the charismatic movement is religious and seeks to challenge some contemporary world views that also shape society's structures and norms (Wilkinson 1971).

As a point of departure for this analysis we will employ Lang and Lang's (1961, p. 490) definition. For them a social movement is "a large-scale, widespread, and continuing elementary collective action in pursuit of an objective that affects and shapes the social order in some fundamental aspect." The charismatic movement, as we have already noted, is large-scale and widespread. Our analysis focuses on the United States, but charismatic beliefs and practices are found on every continent, among all nationalities and races, wherever Christianity exists. The movement is continuing, with an unbroken history dating to the beginning of the twentieth century. It has an objective of revitalizing Christianity by reaffirming the belief in the supernatural that has been sapped by rationalism and secularism. It challenges the prevalent American ethos and seeks to reshape American society. While much of the effort toward change is aimed at personal conversion (Gerlach 1974), such changes also bring certain institutional and cultural transformations.

Basic to the understanding of the rise of any social movement is an awareness of its history. The socio-historical foundations of Pentecostalism and neo-Pentecostalism have been briefly dealt with in the previous chapter. What follows in part 2 is an analysis of other components basic to a social movement, namely, its ideology and the dissemination of that ideology, as well as its organization and structure (Heberle 1951).

The role of ideas in a social movement cannot be overlooked. Embodied in an ideology are the goals of the movement as well as the appropriate means by which these goals are to be realized. The ideology of the charismatic movement is made real through personal religious experiences. Such experiences, however, would be isolated occurrences without some degree of organization and structure that promotes the ideology of the movement and facilitates the desired experiences.

The charisma of the movement provides a good illustration of Max Weber's ideal type of charismatic action, but leaders and followers alike partake of that charisma. In fact, the generalization of charisma in the movement involves the very problems described by Weber regarding charismatic action. The charismatic movement's ideology requires a personal (emotional/affective) experience of the power of the Holy Spirit, but efforts to recruit and proselytize require a degree of rational organization. A certain tension thus exists in the charismatic movement between its charism (affective or emotional action) and its rational activities as a social movement. Weber noted this type of dilemma in discussing the ideal type of charismatic leadership:

If the tide which once elevated a charismatically led group out of the routine of everyday life flows back into everyday channels, then charismatic domination, at least in its pure form, is undermined in most cases: it becomes "institutionalised" and changes course, until it either becomes purely mechanical or is imperceptibly superseded by totally different structural principles or becomes mingled and blended with them in a variety of forms. . . . (Weber 1978, p. 236)

In the case of the charismatic movement, adherents believe that they were elevated out of the routine of everyday life and that they experienced the signs and wonders of charismata being demonstrated at conferences, on television, and reported in books. The attempt to package and sell the movement, however, has brought a degree of institutionalization that threatens to mechanize the experience and render it inauthentic. This process was well under way in classical Pentecostalism by mid-century. A reprieve from widespread routinization of this religious charisma has been brought about through a resurgence of Pentecostalism, first in some Protestant denominations, later in the Catholic Church, and most recently among other Protestant denominations.

The charismatic movement involves a dynamic, dialectical relationship between basic components, especially ideas (ideology), experience (including recruitment strategies), and organizations or structures. Another integral part of the movement is its social impact, apparent in two specific areas: its relationship with mainstream churches and its potential impact on politics and social action.

In summary, it is my thesis that secularization and sacralization are coexisting phenomena reflecting different world views. While the rise of the secular has often been noted, the sacralization of large segments of society goes unheeded. The charismatic movement is part of a larger sacralization process (the evangelical Christian movement), in which traditional Christian tenets are accepted as one component of a dualistic reality. More than a personal revival, the charismatic movement attempts to take its place among other major religious awakenings that have had a significant impact on the course of American history.

Notes

1. For a study of the unchurched in American society, see the Princeton Religion Research Center and the Gallup Organization, Inc. *The Unchurched American* (1978). Those who have been alienated from organized religion criticize it for "having lost 'the real spiritual part of religion' and for being 'too concerned with organizational as opposed to theological or spiritual issues.'"

2. The belief in Christianity is also pervasive. This same poll reports that 90 percent of the respondents believe that Jesus was more than simply a great teacher, although they are reluctant to accept Him as fully God and fully man. The editors comment: "We Americans may not know exactly who he is, but we know who he is not: he is not *just* another one of us." Almost half (45 percent) of the general public believes that personal faith in Christ is the only hope for entering heaven, which further attests to the pervasiveness of Christian tenets in American society. Not only is belief in God alive and well, but belief in Jesus Christ continues as the dominant religious tenet in America. *Christianity Today* (1979, p. 16) observes: "It shows how drastically wrong pessimistic forecasts of a decade ago were when we were told that America had outgrown Christianity and was ready to substitute a secular society or a secular church for the fundamental truths of Christianity."

3. In his prognosis for the future of religion, Greeley (1972, p. 251) suggests the possibility of a resurgence of interest in mystical and otherwordly religions toward the end of the present century. Greeley's prognosis may be more accurate than many who have advanced a crude theory of secularization.

4. Wilson (1979, p. 270), the sociologist whose definition of secularization is most often cited, has recently criticized the vagueness of this concept. He observed that secularization as a process is often confused with secularism as a creed. Secularization as a process, as evidenced by the separation of church and state, had its seeds sown early in the history of the United States. Secularism as a creed is more difficult to identify, but as Greeley (1972, p. 132) has observed, it is highly questionable "that nothing of the sacred, or not very much of it, is left in human life." It may be true, Greeley concedes "that men are not motivated by

religion in their daily lives"—but we lack data from other centuries to make an accurate comparison (Greeley 1972, p. 128).

In addition to the difficulties created by confusing secularization as a process and secularism as a creed, those who have studied secularization have used different referents to document the presumed change. For example, Wuthnow (1976) characterizes secularization, "the process whereby religious thinking, practice, and institutions lose their social significance," as a discontinuous pattern "marked by distinctive shifts." Rigney (1978), on the other hand, asserts that while secularization, as measured by new church construction and church attendance, presents an irregular development, there has been a linear decline in church membership, ordination of clergy, and number of religious books published.

5. McLoughlin (1978), in discussing religion and social change in America, attempts to distinguish between "revivals" and "awakenings." Revivalism entails personal conversion, salvation, regeneration, or spiritual rebirth. Awakenings, on the other hand, "are periods of cultural revitalization that begin in a general crisis of beliefs and values and extend over a period of a generation or so" (McLoughlin 1978, p. viii). It is my contention that the personal experience of "revival" in the lives of charismatic Christians has become part of a religious "awakening" with significantly larger scope than a simple changing of individual lives.

6. Gerlach (1974, p. 670) notes that many studies of religious movements focus on traditional religion "as system celebrator, integrator, and maintainer" but view any deviation from the norm as a "sect" or "cult." There is generally a failure to examine religious movements as producers of change. Gerlach, in challenging the prevalent views of many researchers, notes that Pentecostalism is not "a sect activity and an opiate for the deprived but . . . a far-flung movement of change."

7. The vitality of the "old gods" of conservative Christianity was demonstrated in the 1980 presidential election. The validity of the claims of Jerry Falwell's Moral Majority in seating conservative candidates remain to be demonstrated, but the close correlation between those backed by Moral Majority and those elected cannot be disputed. The climate has changed considerably from the late 1960s and 1970s to one that upholds family and country, if not religion, and a certain amount of such sentiment seems necessary for the maintenance of social order.

8. See Glock and Bellah (1976) for examples and discussion of how young people are expressing "a new self-awareness and spiritual sensitivity." The "new religious consciousness" treated by different authors include religions with Asian influence, secular types of religion like transcendental meditation, derivatives of Western tradition as diverse as the Church of Satan and the charismatic movement, as well as other religions and quasi-religions flourishing in the San Francisco Bay area.

PART II

Features of the Charismatic Movement: Ideology, Practice, and Structures

CHAPTER 3

The Search for Meaning: The Charismatic Movement and Ideology

If there is going to be renascence of religion, its bearers will *not* be the people who have been falling all over each other to be "relevant to modern man.". . . . strong eruptions of religious faith have always been marked by the appearance of people with firm, unapologetic, often uncompromising convictions—that is, by types the very opposite from those presently engaged in various "relevance" operations. Put simply: Ages of faith are not marked by "dialogue, but by *proclamation.* (Berger 1977, pp. 191–92)

In the first two chapters we attempted to sketch the social milieu in which the charismatic movement developed. That milieu produced what may be called a "dialogue" between the sacred and secular worlds. Some church theologians not only flirted with secular values, but also questioned traditional religion by seeking to demythologize the Bible and even to proclaim the death of God. While this secularization of religion has captured the imagination of social researchers and provided material for the news media, another movement has been quietly underway—a movement that proclaims an ideology rather than allowing its ideology to be weakened through dialogue between a secular and a religious culture.

A viable ideology is basic to any social movement. This ideology, or generalized belief statement, provides, among other things, a statement of purpose, a doctrine of defense, an indictment of existing social arrangements, and a plan for action (Lang and Lang 1961, p. 537). The ideology of the charismatic movement is no exception. Its stated purpose is a renewal or revival of the Christian faith—a renewal that includes an emphasis on Spirit baptism and use of the accompanying gifts of the Holy Spirit. Its doctrine of defense includes Scriptural references and personal testimonies that serve to justify the need for Pentecostal teachings in the churches. Pentecostals and neo-Pentecostals alike indict the godless materialism of the larger culture and often criticize churches that have grown cold. The ideology has spread through organizations and quasi-organizations committed to making the movement's teachings known to non-Pentecostal Christians and non-Christians alike. The focus of this chapter will be the first two components of a social movement's ideology, namely, its statement of purpose and its doctrine of defense. Before turning to a discussion of specifics of charismatic ideology, it will be helpful to consider the nature of ideology and its relation to religious social movements.

Ideology and Social Movements

The Nature of Ideology.   The word "ideology" has been used in numerous ways since its introduction at the end of the eighteenth century.[1] Originally employed in a positive sense, the word now has both positive and negative connotations. We intend to use the term broadly as "referring to any theoretically articulated propositions about social reality" (Berger, Berger, and Kellner 1973, p. 159). It is an "expression of the world-view of class"—in this case the world view of a religious class of persons (Larrain 1979, p. 13).

In discussing religious ideologies, Schwartz (1970, p. 1) defines them as "ethical doctrines and theological dogmas which not only reflect secular exigencies but also influence ordinary social conduct." As such, religious ideologies do more than proclaim to believers a means of salvation in a later life. They move men and women to action in the social world in which they live. Not only do these ideologies arise in a specific cultural milieu, they also have an impact on it. Schwartz (1970, p. 51) observes: "as an intervening variable, ideology specifies the meaningful connection between religious belief and social action. It mediates between an actor's position in the social structure and his status expectations, on one hand, and his religious outlook, moral code, and secular behavior on the other."

Ideologies may thus be viewed as belief systems which provide a sense of meaning that propels adherents to social action. Religion has been a powerful source of ideology throughout history but has suffered the corrosive effects of secularism. Hardon (1969, p. 34) compares the charismatic with the noncharismatic church response to secularism:

Commentators on the religious movements in the country point out that the Pentecostals offer what other more sedate churches have failed to give their people: a sense of the sacred and a realization of God's saving grace in those who believe. Not unlike the situation that gave rise to modern Pentecostalism, as Christianity becomes overly intellectual and lacking in concern for basic human needs, it creates new forms that promise personal experience to the faithful and the benefit of divine assistance in visible signs.

Gerlach and Hine (1970, pp. 160–78), in their study of a classical Pentecostal group, observe some general characteristics of the Charismatic movement's ideology that distinguish it from the world view of the larger society:

(1) *Dogmatism and certainty.* There is the element of rigid belief that motivates and supports radical attitudinal and behavioral change. It is a belief system marked more often by proclamation than by dialogue. Charismatics tend to be rigidly certain about their fundamentalist view of the Bible as the Word of God and just as certain that manifestations of the power of the Holy Spirit have been promised in that Word.

(2) *Codification of beliefs into a common rhetoric.* Pentecostals and neo-Pentecostals have a common rhetoric or language not fully understood by those unfamiliar to the movement. Terms like "revelation," "baptized by the Spirit," "praying in a heavenly tongue," "being slain in the Spirit," "receiving an anointing from the Spirit" are illustrations of phrases having specific meanings in most Pentecostal circles that even non-Pentecostal evangelical Christians readily misinterpret.

(3) *Paradox of power.* Pentecostals and neo-Pentecostals have an ideology that includes personal power and control over one's own destiny: "in Christ I can do all things." At the same time there is the paradoxical assertion of an omnipotent God that may cause the outsider to regard the charismatics as taking a fatalistic or passive attitude toward the control over events. Both positions—of self activity and control and of passivity and control by God—are present in a delicate balance in the ideology of the movement.

(4) *Split-level nature.* The charismatic movement's ideology contains two levels of belief: the universal and the specific. Universal beliefs include those few concepts (the Bible as the Word of God, the importance of Spirit baptism, the presence of the gifts of the Holy Spirit) on which there is some agreement by virtually all members of the movement. The ideological specifics involve those infinite variations on theological themes that promote both ideological and organizational diversity. The charismatic Episcopalian, for example, places some emphasis on liturgical worship form and sacraments in relation to the workings of the Holy Spirit, while the independent charismatic teacher of Baptist origin does not. Other universal beliefs, including the power of God to intervene in the daily affairs of men and women, as reflected in divine healing, contain ideological components specific to certain subgroups of charismatics.

(5) *Ideal-real gap.* In all ideologies there is an ideal expressed in both the formulated beliefs and the day-to-day lives of adherents. Charismatics are no exception in demonstrating incongruities between belief and action, but the disparities may be less than within many other groups. Some students of Pentecostalism have noted that "even severe critics of the movement consider Pentecostalism as a gap-closer in that it attempts to actualize Biblical ideals of spiritual experience, witnessing, and church participation" (Gerlach and Hine 1970, p. 168).

(6) *Ambiguity.* While often dogmatic and closer to the biblical ideal than many Christian churches, Pentecostal belief is also paradoxically ambiguous. Some aspects of the ideology are clearly stated, but other tenets outside of widely accepted Christian beliefs often remain unclear. Charismatic ideology regarding specific gifts of the Holy Spirit, including healing, prophecy, revelation, and tongues, go beyond the theology of most traditional Christian churches. Much ambiguity on specific points remains, as charismatics of different denominations struggle to develop an ideology that is consistent with both their beliefs and their personal and collective experiences of the power of God.

The Function of Ideology in Social Movements.   Ideology serves four primary and interrelated functions for a social movement: organizational cohesion, a source of constitutive ideas, a means of recruiting members, and an expression of meaning. Ideology enables a movement to organize and often unify members of diverse backgrounds. Charismatics share a commitment to conservative Christian theology that often transcends differences of race, social class, and religious denomination. The charismatic ideology thus serves as a source of cohesion (especially among neo-Pentecostals) and evidence of such cohesion, even under social conditions fostering divisions, in turn reinforce the ideology of the power of the Holy Spirit.[2]

Those engaged in social movements must also know what they are about. Heberle (1951, p. 24) refers to the expression of such awareness as "constitutive ideas" or "those ideas considered most essential to the movement." These ideas include the final goals or ends of the movement, the ways and means by which the goals are to be attained, and the reason for the endeavors of the movement. The ideology of the charismatic movement meets these requisites. It spells out in detail the goal of religious revival and the importance of using the gifts of the Holy Spirit to facilitate this revival.

This knowledge is disseminated not only in churches but also through Christian television and magazines. Personal testimonies abound to support the ideology of the movement. Formal teachings are thus supplemented with account after account of the power of the Holy Spirit to change lives. The more abstract ideology, along with the concrete personal witness of religious charismatic experience serves as a means to recruit other believers.

The ideology of the charismatic promises to provide meaning to life in a seemingly meaningless world. Sociologist Daniel Bell (1976, p. 28) defines our contemporary problem as a "spiritual crisis," in which "the new anchorages have proved illusory and the old ones have become submerged." Bell raises the question: "What holds one to reality, if one's secular system of meanings proves to be an illusion?" His response is "the return in Western society to some conception of religion." The ideology of the charismatic movement has rejuvenated traditional Christian belief for large groups of believers and has replaced the new illusory anchorages with renewed and revived religious systems of meaning.

Gerlach and Hine (1970, p. 61), discussing the ideology of charismatic groups, note:

The ideology is, perhaps, the key to the infrastructure of the movement. In spite of the fact that personal, organizational and ideological differences continually split groups, the conceptual commonality of the Baptism experience and the conceptual authority of a non-human leader provide a basis for continuing interaction between the resulting splinters.

United in a core belief, the Pentecostals can proceed to unite against genuine opposition, or against what they believe to be opposition.

Having introduced the concept of ideology and discussed some of its major functions for a social movement, we will now turn to a presentation of the salient ideological tenets of the charismatic movement that distinguish it from other evangelical and fundamentalist Christian groups.

Common Charismatic Tenets

Baptism of the Holy Spirit. In my account of the rise of the Charismatic movement in the twentieth century, I have traced the theological doctrine of baptism in/of the Holy Spirit to the founder of Methodism. John Wesley's teaching of a "second blessing" was reemphasized in the Holiness movement of the second half of the nineteenth century. It was the Holiness movement that paved the way for Parham and his students' Pentecostal experiences in Kansas City in 1901 and Seymour's Azusa Street revivals of 1906–8. What distinguished Parham's and Seymour's theology of the baptism from earlier Holiness formulations was the insistence that the evidence of the baptism of the Holy Spirit was the gift of tongues or glossolalia. This remains the position of most classical Pentecostals, while neo-Pentecostals are more cautious in asserting that tongues[3] usually, although not necessarily, accompanies baptism of the Spirit. Despite differences in theologies and in definitions of Spirit baptism, charismatics agree that a full Christian life involves "something more" than conversion or being "born again."

Basham (1973a), a spokesperson for the charismatic movement from the Christian Church (formerly the Disciples of Christ), defines Spirit baptism as follows: "The baptism in the Holy Spirit is a second encounter with God (the first is conversion) in which the Christian begins to receive the supernatural power of the Holy Spirit into his life. . . . it is given for the purpose of equipping the Christian with God's power for service." Basham, as a neo-Pentecostal, does not insist that glossolalia is the sign of this baptism as would most classical Pentecostals. While Pentecostals, including both the Church of God and the Assemblies of God, accept the theological doctrine that the Spirit baptism is "evidenced by speaking in tongues," neo-Pentecostals are less willing to make such an absolute statement. Basham (1973b, pp. 78–79), in another work, states a position acceptable to many Charismatic believers in mainline churches:

So we must admit that the baptism of the Holy Spirit can be received without the manifestation of tongues, but we encourage no one to seek the baptism without expecting tongues. Both our understanding of spiritual gifts and our willingness to receive them affect what gifts and manifestations will appear. *Something is missing in your spiritual life if you have received the Holy Spirit yet have not spoken in tongues.* Those Spirit-filled Christians who have not yet spoken in tongues will receive a precious added assurance of God's presence and power when they do.

Despite this theological difference on the doctrine of Spirit baptism between classical Pentecostals and neo-Pentecostals, there are elements common to Baptism experiences described in the sociological literature. Classical Pentecostal Jerry L. Sandidge (1976, p. 13) notes four such elements: (1) there is a genuine spiritual experience, usually distinct from conversion or being "saved" or "born again"; (2) this experience has a definite impact upon a person's life, whether it takes the form of a growing awareness or an instantaneous revelation; (3) charismatics can often pinpoint the date and place that such an encounter with God occurred; (4) there is some activity of the gifts and graces of the Holy Spirit operating in the Christian's life.

Those charismatics who speak theologically of the baptism of the Holy Spirit generally do not view the experience as a matter of salvation. Salvation or being "born again" can be experienced by Pentecostal and non-Pentecostals alike. Spirit baptism, once a normal experience for all Christians, gives a power to Christians to live a life in accord with Christian ideals. Womack (1968, p. 64) describes the history as follows:

In light of the whole history of the church up to the Council of Nicea, it seems clear that what happened to the baptism in the Holy Spirit was a gradual deemphasis over the years. During the first century *all* Christians were baptized in the Holy Spirit and spoke with other tongues; in the second century *most* of the Christians had this experience; by the third century *some* Christians were filled with the Spirit; and in the fourth century the baptism in the Holy Spirit was apparently forgotten.

Thus the central ideological tenet for charismatics is Spirit baptism. Not only is it said to be a definite experience (or series of experiences in a more gradual process), but it is said to bring a new power into a believer's life. This power takes the form of the "gifts of the Holy Spirit," of which glossolalia is but one gift. Given the centrality of tongues to Pentecostal doctrine of Spirit baptism and the importance of this gift in neo-Pentecostal circles as well, I will first consider the phenomenon of glossolalia and then discuss some of the other gifts operating in charismatic communities.

Gifts of the Holy Spirit

Glossolalia or the Gift of Tongues.

While Peter was still speaking these words, the Holy Spirit came upon all who heard the message. The circumcized believers who had come with Peter were astonished that the gift of the Holy Spirit had been poured out even on the Gentiles. For they heard them speaking in tongues (or other languages) and praising God. (Acts 10:44–46)

Of all of the gifts of the Holy Spirit, glossolalia has most fascinated secular researchers and non-Pentecostal theologians and has provided subject matter for charismatic writings. Secular studies include anthropological, linguistic, historical, and psychological research related to glossolalia. Mills's (1973) bibliography lists over 100 books, articles, and theses on the topic. Numerous others have appeared since its compilation. Cardinal Leon Joseph Suenens, the Belgian charismatic Roman Catholic prelate, provides a balanced view of the phenomenon. Tongues is neither miraculous (as many charismatics might claim) nor pathological or diabolical (as many of its critics have proposed) (Suenens 1975, pp. 99–104). Rather, it is a "form of non-discursive prayer—a preconceptual expression of spontaneous prayer." To the uninitiated it appears as babbling in nonsense syllables and to involve altered states of consciousness. To the believer it is a surrendering of mind and heart to a form of prayer believed to be biblically encouraged.

Suenens notes that there are over thirty biblical references to tongues. Bible-believing Christians who are critics of glossolalia (see Rice 1976; MacArthur 1978) dismiss the contemporary phenomenon as a counterfeit of the biblical one, but charismatics disagree.[4] On the basis of linguistic and social science data compared with accounts of tongues in Scripture, it would appear safe to assume that the contemporary experience of tongues is not unlike that found in the early church. As such it appears to be a natural human potential utilized in different times and places by both Christians and non-Christians over the centuries.[5]

Historical Examples of Glossolalia.   Mills (1973, p. 18) notes that the "phenomenon of speaking in tongues does not belong solely to the Judeo-Christian tradition." Numerous other examples of similar phenomena have been found in the religions of the Near East. Bunn (1973, p. 46) further states that glossolalia is actually "a common religious phenomenon." Although it is not usually part of the officially sanctioned religion of the priests, rulers, and educated classes, it is frequently found among the uneducated masses. Among the latter there have always been those who, "when possessed by the spirit of the deity, delivered messages in strange tongues." While Bunn's association of tongues with the uneducated may be historically accurate, such a relationship may be questioned today. Many well-educated professionals not only admit to speaking in tongues but serve as leaders of the charismatic movement. Bunn does, however, document the existence of tongues in other cultures and in other religions.

Those who have traced the history of glossolalia in Christianity begin with its occurrence in the New Testament. Records from the early church suggest that it was practiced extensively until around A.D. 250 (Frodsham 1946; Hunter 1980)—a time during which the early Church Fathers took a stand against the Gnostic and Montanist heresies. Both of these movements included tongue-speaking (Williams and Waldvogel 1975, pp. 64–66), and both were divisive in producing major crises in polity and theology apart from the issue of glossolalia. During the third and fourth centuries tongues became more a matter of historic interest than religious experience, and by the Middle Ages there was little evidence of any form of glossolalia in either Eastern or Western Christianity.

Hinson (1973, p. 73) divides the history of tongue-speaking in the Christian church into four periods: (1) "early showers" (A.D. 100–250); (2) "long drought" (250–1650); (3) "later showers" (1650–1900); and (4) "later rain" (1900 to the present). During the third period tongues was reintroduced around the seventeenth century (probably among the Ranters and the Quakers in Britain and among the Huguenots in France). It was believed to accompany the Wesleyan revivals and the frontier revivals in the United States of the 1800s. Hinson (1973, p. 65) observes that both "the Shakers and the Mormons assigned it an important part of their constitutions." Since 1900 and the development of the charismatic movement tongues has become a phenomenon that has crossed religious, educational, and social class lines, as well as geographic boundaries.

The Multifaceted Nature of Glossolalia. Episcopal priest and Jungian scholar Morton Kelsey (1968) has summarized the most common explanations for glossolalia. It has been regarded as frenzied and ecstatic speech taken over from Eastern cults in the early Christian church and later abandoned; an emotional abnormality that allows a violent release of pent-up emotions in a rush of irrational sounds; a form of diabolical possession; a miracle through which one speaks in one's own language but is heard by others in their own; a pastoral device given by God only to the early church; a rare mystical gift; and an expression of the unconscious psyche that is not necessarily a symptom of psychological abnormality. Some of these explanations, both psychological and theological, refer to phenomena other than speaking in tongues.

Samarin, a linguist who studied tongues, points to the importance of distinguishing "xenoglossia" from "glossolalia." Xenoglossia is "the demonstration of knowledge of a language not learned in the normal way" (Samarin 1973, p. 130). The Pentecost experience recorded in the Acts of the Apostles—where Parthians, Medians, Elamites, Mesopotamians, Cappadocians, Egyptians, and Libyans all heard the Christian believers (who were Galileans) "speaking in their own language"—is an example of xenoglossia. Samarin deliberately omits "emotionalism" as part of his definition and insists that tongues is not gibberish. He nevertheless defines "glossolalia" as "a meaningless (from a linguistic viewpoint) but phenomenologically structured human utterance believed by the speaker to be a real language but bearing no systematic resemblance to any natural language, living or dead" (Samarin 1968). He later characterizes it as "a vocal art believed by the speaker to be a language and showing rudimentary language-like structure but no consistent word-meaning correspondence recognizable by either speaker or hearer" (Samarin 1973, p. 131). When glossolalia is compared with the native language of the speaker "it is seen to be both derivative and innovative" (Samarin 1973, p. 138), involving different sounds, for example, but with the speaker's native accent. Some of Kelsey's classifications can thus be regarded as xenoglossia, while others are apparently forms of glossolalia.

Modern charismatics view xenoglossia as a gift not given to all believers or regularly experienced by a single believer. Claims by many to have had the experience have not been experimentally verified.[6] I have read and heard enough diverse accounts of xenoglossia from credible sources to believe those scientists who at least tentatively accept its occurrence.

Such scientists explain xenoglossia as a parapsychological or psychic phenomenon or, more often, as an example of cryptomnesia (Samarin 1973, p. 132). Cryptomnesia or "hidden memory" is the expression of "conscious thoughts considered to be original but which in reality are only memories." Samarin (1973, p. 132) does not believe xenoglossia stands up to rigorous scientific testing, because most cases are "reported by uncritical people who are predisposed to believe in them." From a scientific point of view, the occurrence of xenoglossia remains to be empirically proved and explained.

Glossolalia, not xenoglossia, has been the subject of the psychological and anthropological research on tongues. Mayer (1973), an anthropologist at Wheaton College (Illinois), sees glossolalia as a learned experience and a natural phenomenon. Kildahl (1972, p. 74), a clinical psychologist studying glossolalia, also believes the phenomenon to be a learned one, but not at all abnormal or pathological. Kildahl found that glossolalia does not occur only among manic, hysterical, or compulsive individuals, as some believe, but rather appears in "a cross section of all the usual personality types" (Kildahl 1972, p. 49).[7]

Glossolalia occurs primarily in private prayer but may occur among believers in group worship in two ways. The first is "praying together in the Spirit" or in "singing in the Spirit," where the glossolalia prays or sings aloud in tongues simultaneously with others. Both are usually pleasing and soothing, even to many noncharismatics who have been present at such worship. Prayer or singing often begins spontaneously, with one or two voices joined by others, and ends just as spontaneously. Glossolalia may also occur when a single person speaks aloud in tongues and someone else interprets the message in English. This "interpretation" is usually not believed to be a verbatim translation of tongues, but rather conveys what is believed to be a message or prophecy from God. At times the interpretation is provided by one, two, or three others who have a sense of the meaning of the Lord's words. This phenomenon is closely related to prophecy, another gift of the Spirit.

Exploring the Gift of Prophecy.   The term "prophecy" has several meanings in charismatic vocabulary. Because those meanings differ from popular usage, the word is easily misunderstood by non-Christians and noncharismatic believers. *Webster's* dictionary defines prophecy as a "prediction of the future," while another definition refers to prophecy as an "act or practice of a prophet." Prophecy may take the form of a divination, a vision, an exhortation to others, a revelatory insight into the past, or an interpretation of glossolalic utterance. Significantly, *Webster's* defines "prophet" as "a person who speaks for God, or a god, as though under divine guidance." It is in this broader sense of God's word being spoken through men and women that the concept is most often used in charismatic teachings.

Prophecy has been a part of the Judeo-Christian religious heritage and of most other major religions of the world. Many Christians tend to think of prophecy as an Old Testament phenomenon, linked with names like Daniel, Ezekiel, and Jeremiah. Prophecy, however, is also a recognized gift in the New Testament, and prophets were important figures in the early Church. Noncharismatic Christians are likely to insist that prophecy, like tongues, was a gift given to the early Christian church but withdrawn at the death of the last apostle. Charismatics are generally evangelical, Bible-believing Christians who do not equate contemporary prophecy with the Scriptures.[8] Many recognize the dangers associated with encouraging prophecy, which allows an individual to speak in the name of God. But, as Yocum observes (1976, p. 62), "To shun prophecy because of its inherent dangers is no solution. . . . In some way, the church must keep the benefits of true prophecy while avoiding the dangers of false prophecy." Yocum urges his readers to be attentive to the advice Paul gives in 1 Thess. 5:20–21: "Do not despise prophesying, but test everything; hold fast that which is good." A major test for prophecy is that it not contradict the Bible. In fact, much prophetic prediction seems to revolve around the Bible, and particularly the book of Revelations.

Using the Bible to Predict.   A theme of biblical prophecy is the imminent return of Jesus to the earth. Modern-day disasters such as famine, earthquakes, and floods have been identified as the apocalyptic events predicted in the Bible.

Much predictive prophecy revolves around the modern state of Israel. Communist powers, it is believed, will continue to swallow up more and more nations of the world. The Soviet Union, with the backing of her allies, will attack Israel, God's chosen nation. Specific interpretations differ but the general agreement of such prophetic writings is that the battle of Armageddon is drawing near and that God will be the final victor. This will not happen, however, before there is much suffering and hardship all over the globe. Some believe that Christians will be taken in rapture (mysteriously removed from the earth to "meet Jesus in the sky") before the onset of this darkness; others believe that Christians will not be spared the tribulation.

This belief is not necessarily unique to charismatic ideology. The popularity of Hal Lindsey's *The Late Great Planet Earth* (1970), which develops such a thesis, demonstrates that it is neither of charismatic origin nor a belief limited to charismatics. Charismatics often differ from their fundamentalist and evangelical contemporaries in claiming additional confirmation of such interpretations. Charismatic writer David Wilkerson (author of *The Cross and the Switchblade,* a book of considerable importance to neo-Pentecostals) received a vision in 1973 "of five tragic calamities coming upon the earth" (Wilkerson 1974, p. 11)—a vision he felt compelled to share and to interpret in light of Scripture in *The Vision* (1974) and *Racing Toward Judgment* (1976).

Prophecy as Exhortation. Charismatics probably see exhortation as the most common form of prophecy. Those who communicate prophecy usually continue with exhortation or "speech which revives, renews, or strengthens people. It builds up their hope and gives them new courage" (Yocum 1976, p. 89). Jeremiah-like prophecies, predicting doom and desolation, are usually followed with exhortations on God's faithfulness to those who believe in Him and do His will.

Exhortative prophecy is frequently given in neo-Pentecostal gatherings and, from the author's observations, less frequently in established Pentecostal churches. Pentecostal congregations appear more likely to experience prophecy in the form of tongues, the interpretation of which takes the form of exhortative prophecy. Some writers have questioned whether tongues was necessary for the prophecy to be given. In any event, prophecy, or "speaking God's word," is most likely to take the form of exhortation in both Pentecostal and neo-Pentecostal gatherings.

In 1977 a nondenominational charismatic conference was held in Kansas City. It was attended and favorably viewed by representatives of principal charismatic groups as well as by classical Pentecostals. Prophecies from the General Sessions of the Conference were published (*New Covenant* 1977, p. 10) along with responses from some representative charismatic leaders. For those readers who have not heard a prophetic utterance, an illustration may prove informative. The first is a promise (predictive prophecy) and a work of encouragement; the second, a call to repentance.

Mark down this day and remember it. . . . Call to mind; declare it publicly. Have no fear, because I am faithful to my word, and I will fulfill it. I am going to restore my people and reunite them. I am going to restore my people the glory that is mine, so that the world will not mock or scorn them, but so that the world might know that I am God and king and that I have come to redeem and save the earth. . . . I am restoring my people, bestowing upon them honor and glory, bringing back to them the glory that is proper to my people, and making them look again like a kingdom, the kingdom of God on this earth.

I am not pleased with the state of my church, the condition of my people. . . . There is suspicion and hostility among you; there is argumentativeness among you. . . . Some of you are still more committed to your friends and your neighbors and your acquaintances than you are to my people, to those who bear my name. . . . It is important that you turn away from all those sins that keep you separated from your brothers and sisters. Now is the time for you to turn away from those things. I will give you the understanding and the strength that you need . . . to be one people.

The reader familiar with the prophetic writings in the Old Testament will readily see the similarity between these contemporary prophecies and those of old. At times they may be delivered in King James English, which has been criticized by charismatic leaders as somewhat inauthentic. The question may arise in the reader's mind: How are these prophecies "tested" as the Apostle Paul insists they be. One of the tests is their compatibility with the Scriptures. Anything that contradicts the Bible would be automatically rejected. Another test is "confirmation": Is the same message repeated by different persons and before different prayer groups? Finally, some prophecies are recognized to be the product of the speaker's own thoughts or wishes, which, while harmless, may not be viewed as genuine by other members of the group. The truth of prophecy is not really subject to objective confirmation. It is the product of a faith and ideology beyond the scope of empirical research.

Prophetic Revelations and Words of Knowledge.   In some instances prophecy apparently pertains to events in the life of a specific individual. At prayer meetings, for example, a revelation such as the following might come to light. "There's a man here who has come for the first time to our prayer meeting. He is having a difficult time being faithful to his wife because he finds a young woman he works with to be very attractive. The

Lord wants this man to try to build a stronger relationship with his wife and to rely on daily prayer to secure the strength he needs to be faithful.'' Such revelations are generally tested to the satisfaction of prayer group participants.

On one occasion a woman had prayed with and counseled a young female friend and then invited her to attend a prayer meeting. This prayer meeting usually consists of 250 to 300 persons, so a newcomer does not stand out in the assembly. The woman was thus surprised when a revelation communicated by someone else in the group clearly applied to her young friend. It referred to a person visiting for the first or second time who was struggling with her personal and professional life. The woman, knowing that she was the only one in the room who knew her friend's needs, went up to the leader of the prayer group. He said that two persons had sent up a similar message to be cleared by him, and, given the independent sources, he believed it to be prophetic. Although he did not know for whom the message was intended, he believed it applied to someone in the room.

Prophecy as a "word of knowledge" or as "revelation" is used in prayer groups of varying sizes, in counseling situations, and in various other charismatic organizations. In discussing the relevance of prophecy for the community, the Apostle Paul writes to the church at Corinth: "While I should like you all to have the gift of tongues, I would much rather you could prophesy, since the man who prophesies is of greater importance than the man with the gift of tongues, unless of course that latter offers an interpretation so that the church may get some benefit" (1 Cor. 14:5). Given the role that prophecy plays in the charismatic community, it is not surprising that it has influenced charismatic activities and organizations, to be discussed below.

Personal and Private Prophecy. Labonte (1974) observes that prophecy may be either personal and private or directed toward a community. The discussion thus far has centered on the public use of the gift. Many charismatics, however, believe God may speak His word to them privately, just as He speaks in the community. It is not unusual to hear a person say "God told me" or "the Lord showed me," although some might not identify such revelations as prophecy.

Most personal testimonies written by charismatic Christians contain personal prophecies. Marshall (1978) describes several such prophecies in her book encouraging Christians to seek experiences of the Holy Spirit.

A believer, for example, might be led to deplane from an aircraft that later crashes, to phone a friend who at that moment is contemplating suicide, or to visit a particular office when seeking employment. Whether or not these revelations are termed "prophecy," the term seems less important than the testimony of the experience.

Critics of personal prophecy will raise questions about cultists who have gone insane and "heard" voices directing them to action. Those who have experienced personal prophecy (and it appears to be a widespread experience) usually recall that the voice they heard was inaudible. It took the form of a gentle yet compelling inner sense, discernible from personal feelings and desires only through extensive prayer. Furthermore, the Word of God in the Bible is the final guide. One could not be told by God to murder, steal, or in anyway violate the Judeo-Christian moral code. In many cases the inner sense is confirmed by other believers, whose "spirit may give witness" in support of the prophecy's message. As with public prophecy, personal prophecy is fraught with dangers, yet these dangers are minimized for those involved in Christian community and the rewards of experiencing direction from God are great for such believers.

Other Gifts of the Holy Spirit.   Many charismatics, although not all, point to the list of gifts in 1 Cor. 12 as being those that will be present in a Christian community. In addition to the speaking and interpretation of tongues and prophecy, these include wisdom, knowledge, faith, healing, miracles, and discernment of spirits. Gelpi (1971) is among those who argue that gifts of the Holy Spirit include all "true acts of piety" and that Paul's list in 1 Cor. was intended to be a sample rather than an exhaustive compilation. Noting this theological difference between many Pentecostals, who are more likely to accept a list of nine gifts, and the neo-Pentecostals, who may add to such a list from other sections of Scripture,[9] I will limit my brief discussion to the nine as listed.

Basham (1973b) groups these nine gifts into three major categories: inspiration, revelation, and power. The first category includes the speaking and interpretation of tongues and prophecy. The gifts of revelation include knowledge, wisdom, and discerning manifestations of good from evil spirits. All three center on knowledge secured by extraordinary means, which might include prophecy or tongues. The gifts of power include faith, healings, and miracles.

The "gift of faith" as a manifestation of power should not be confused with the faith of every believer (Jorstad 1973; Culpepper 1977). Rather it is the faith that Jesus described to his disciples as being capable of casting a mountain into the sea (Matt. 17:20). In other words, it is a faith in the reality of miracles. One such miracle is listed separately as a gift of power—that of healings. Like tongues and prophecy, the power of healing is an ideological tenet central to charismatic thought and action. The nature of this gift and its relation to the health profession will be discussed in chapter 5, which deals with divine healing. Examples of miracles, or occurrences that "seem to contradict the so-called laws of nature" (Culpepper 1977, p. 141), are present in almost every autobiographical charismatic witness. The gift of miracles "goes beyond the miraculous healing of the body to include miracles of every sort." Many claims of miracles are probably exaggerated, but those making the claims believe it is beyond the realm of science to prove or disprove such miracles.

Additional Comments on Ideology

This brief discussion of the baptism and gifts of the Holy Spirit does not exhaust the distinguishing ideological features of the charismatic movement. The ideology discussed in this chapter should be viewed as the basic beliefs of groups that could be identified with the movement. Some groups stress the development of personal and community relationships; others stress evangelism; others emphasize pious behavior and standards; some others, interdenominational cooperation among charismatic believers; still others, deliverance and exorcism from unclean spirits. Most charismatics, however, frown upon the bizarre practices of some cultists among them, such as those who ritually handle snakes.

Practices in worship also vary greatly. Most charismatics believe that God calls worshippers together and that there should be an active participation and a joy in such worship services. The expression of this "praising the Lord" differs greatly. Some stress the emotionalism that provided the nickname "holy rollers" to early Pentecostalists. Others are sedate in their worship. There is much variation in how and when gifts are manifested in a charismatic community. In some churches, for example, the speaking and interpretation of tongues and prophecy are part of nearly every service. In others they are rarely manifested. The more reserved churches (many are classical Pentecostal rather than neo-Pentecostal) are critical of those who "hang from the chandeliers" in worship services.

The degree to which charismatics involve themselves in secular society appears to vary considerably. The author has observed that the "gospel of wealth," which teaches that prosperity is to be expected by Christians as their heritage, is criticized by many classical as well as neo-Pentecostal groups. Similarly, the call to convert the world through evangelism or social action differs from group to group.

All charismatics, however, accept the Bible as the Word of God and believe in the need for conversion and salvation, the desirability of Spirit baptism, and the manifestations of gifts of the Holy Spirit.

In discussing the ideology of any religious or secular social movement, there is a tendency to emphasize the unity of the group under consideration. It would be equally misleading, however, to dwell on the movement's disunity, especially in the case of the charismatics. Despite the suspicions and criticisms that divide Pentecostals and neo-Pentecostals there is much evidence of attempts to resolve differences. Likewise, neo-Pentecostals and Pentecostals seem to be cooperating across denominational lines without giving up what each regards as the essentials of a denominational heritage. What enables such movement toward unity of spirit is not style of worship, standards of morality, or styles of evangelism. The diverse groups of charismatics are united by a belief that signs and wonders are gifts bestowed upon Christian believers.

Most evangelical Christians agree that Jesus walked on water, healed the sick, changed water into wine, ordered the raging sea to be stilled, and withered a fig tree with His curse. Jesus is also reported to have told his followers that they would do greater things than He had done (John 14:12). Charismatics are a growing number of Christians who expect the miraculous to happen in their lives because they profess to be Jesus' followers. While Pentecostalism has frequently been referred to as the "tongues movement," glossolalia has always been viewed as but one of the spiritual gifts. Pentecostals and neo-Pentecostals alike share a receptivity to all of the spiritual gifts reported in the Bible, including prophecy and healing.

The neo-Pentecostal enthusiasm, more restrained but not unlike the first burst of Pentecostal enthusiasm of the turn of the century, is in turn helping to revitalize classical Pentecostalism. Both groups, through a common religious ideology, are making an impact on American religion.

The charismatics are "content to resort to very simple biblical and experiential language" to express orthodox Christian beliefs (Marty 1975, p. 206).

In summary, the charismatics may thus be viewed as orthodox Christians who view their religious experiences as manifestations of their faith. Such experiences probably prove little to the scientific mind bent on empirical proof, but they revitalize men and women who have committed themselves to lives of faith. Even the most skeptical critics have acknowledged their joy in worship and praise and the warmth and love they found at charismatic meetings (for example, see Ward 1975; MacArthur 1978). Without the experiential component, classical Pentecostalism would have become another group of sects and denominations assimilated into an orthodox Protestantism, which shares much of its religious doctrine. Through experiences like glossolalia, Pentecostalism has served as an instrument of renewal among mainstream religious groups and a reaction to the trend toward a rationalized and demythologized Christianity.

Notes

1. For an excellent discussion of the positive, negative, and more neutral uses of the word "ideology," see Jorge Larrain (1979) *The Concept of Ideology*. We attempt to use the term neutrally, in accord with a sociology of knowledge approach that would separate ideology from ideological distortions (negative ideology) or verifiable knowledge (scientific truths). Gouldner (1976) separates religious belief from ideology, but my opinion is that all theology is a form of ideology, as is secular and rational thinking (Gouldner's definition of the concept). Thus ideology is a pervasive element of culture, one that may change in content but is necessary for contemporary as well as traditional cultures.

2. At a recent conference of Episcopalian Charismatics (June 13–15, 1980, in Akron, Ohio) attended by the author, the power of the Holy Spirit to unify diverse social groups was demonstrated repeatedly. Cecil Kerr, a rector from Northern Ireland, shared with the audience his experience of living with Protestants and Catholics a short distance from where violence has repeatedly erupted. Another priest shared with me his experience of seeing charismatics of diverse racial backgrounds worshipping together in apartheid South Africa. A theme of many charismatic groups, especially those committed to Christian living situations, is the power of the Holy Spirit to unify Christian believers despite differing social backgrounds.

Neo-Pentecostal and Pentecostal groups remain wary of each other, but there are signs that both groups desire unity and cooperation. Classical Pentecostal preachers are under heavy criticism for cooperating with neo-Pentecostals, but I have met several who are willing to set aside such criticism and even condemnation to move toward spiritual unity. Divisions of all sorts are apparent to any observer, but charismatics have attempted to overcome past suspicions and mistrust.

3. Since "tongues" is frequently used (and is used here) as a synonym for glossolalia or "the gift of tongues," it is treated as a singular noun.

4. The theological position taken by many Bible-believing critics of tongues is part of dispensational theology. Dispensationalists would emphasize (among other beliefs) that the early church required certain "dispensations" including miracles, prophecy, etc., to be firmly established on earth. Ward (1975, p. 119), in taking that position with regard to charismatics, states:

The temperate tone of modern criticism should not be accepted as a vindication of pentecostalism. In many cases the writer has taken away with one hand everything he has conceded with the other hand. The anti-Pentecostal argument still consists mainly of the following points: (1) the evidential purposes of glossolalia in the Book of Acts are no longer valid; (2) glossolalia was a temporary gift; (3) glossolalia was an inferior gift; (4) glossolalia can be explained as a psychological and human phenomenon.

5. Psychologist H. Newton Malony has undertaken an extensive study of glossolalia at Fuller Theological Seminary, results of which are presented in Maloney and Lovekin (in press). Malony has reviewed existing studies in light of research at Fuller which is available in a mimeographed paper entitled "Debunking Some of the Myths About Glossolalia."

6. An example of xenoglossia was reported in a lecture by Francis MacNutt, former Roman Catholic priest known for his healing ministry. MacNutt described a prayer session conducted at the request of a Sufi Moslem friend. He began to pray in tongues because he did not know specifically what to pray for in English. Much to his surprise, his glossolalic utterances were heard as a prayer of praise in Arabic by his Moslem friend. For a compilation of documented accounts of xenoglossia made by an Assemblies of God minister, see Harris (1973). Harris obtained over seventy-five accounts of such experiences in over sixty languages, largely by writing to district superintendents of the Assemblies of God and to pastors, and then deciding whether sufficient documentation existed to report the incident. Harris (1973, p. 6) notes: "The only alternative to accepting this mass of evidence as valid is to believe those involved are victims of mass deception or parties to a gigantic conspiracy. Either is inconceivable."

7. I do not accept some of Kildahl's conclusions, particularly his finding that the onset of glossolalia requires the presence of an authority figure. I concur with Dennis Bennett (1975, p. 25), who challenges that conclusion.

One is simply overcome with amazement at how they could be put forward as the result of serious research. Anyone in the field knows that many begin to speak in tongues in their private prayers without ever having heard anyone else speak in tongues, and sometimes without even knowing such a thing is possible. Many people begin to speak in tongues in a totally private situation with no one else present, authoritative or otherwise. . . . To say that an authority figure has to be present in order for the person to be able to speak is simply ludicrous. (Bennett 1975, p. 25)

What is needed are more studies on glossolalia (and other spiritual gifts) that move away from aloof descriptions of structure that draw conclusions that are not warranted by the data *and* a move toward studying the meaning attached to the act by participants.

Kildahl could be further criticized for generalizing on the basis of a limited and highly controversial practice of "learning tongues," which involves an atmosphere of heightened suggestibility and the imitation of sounds of one skilled in tongues by an initiate. Although this practice does exist, the author believes that it is atypical.

8. Many neo-Pentecostals, aware that other Christians believe that the gift of prophecy ceased with the early church, are reluctant to use the term or to encourage use of this gift. They are likewise reticent about the practice and interpretation of tongues.

9. Charismatics study the Bible to learn about the gifts, and many may not be concerned about official theological assertions. Shakarian (1975), the wealthy dairyman and founder of Full Gospel Businessmen's Group International, provides a case in point. He prayed, seeking to learn what his special gift was to the church. His answer came in 1 Cor. 12:28, which told him that his gift was to be a "helper."

Others distinguish "spiritual ministries" (which might include Shakarian's "helper" role) from the "spiritual gifts." Donald Gee, a spokesperson for the Assemblies of God, noted: "The suggestive list of nine gifts in 1 Corinthians 12:8–10 (and I now think it is a mistake to always refer to the 'nine gifts' as though the catalogue there is exhaustive) leads on lower down to another list of ministries or offices in the Church of which eight are named . . ." (Gee 1963, pp. 6–8). The gifts are to flow through and assist the ministries of teaching, evangelism, preaching, pastoring, governing, etc.

CHAPTER 4

Religion and Personal Experience: Ideology Made Real

> If men define situations as real, they are real in their consequences. (W. I. Thomas 1928)

People desire to know exactly what is real. That question has intrigued philosophers from ancient days to the present, and their answers to that question have provided different assumptions about how to approach the study of society. Questions about the reality of nonempirical phenomena such as mystical experiences are especially troublesome to sociology and psychology, which are both committed to the empirical study of the world. How can a social scientist approach the reality of a nonempirical event such as the baptism of the Holy Spirit and the accompanying gifts discussed in the previous chapter?

Thinkers steeped in empiricism and accustomed to dealing with observable facts may immediately dismiss such spiritual phenomena as the results of emotionalism and suggestibility. Others may propose that the reality of the Holy Spirit can no more be empirically proved than can God's existence, which most social scientists consider to be outside the realm of scientific verification. The effects of such religious belief can, however, be demonstrated. Social science can objectively study the consequences of a belief system based on unprovable subjective definitions. W. I. Thomas, a sociologist who recognized the interpenetration of subjective experience and objective organization, could thus succinctly note: "If men define situations as real, they are real in their consequences" (W. I. Thomas 1928). If men and women believe in the power of the Holy Spirit and the miracles (signs and wonders) that accompany the proclaiming of the Christian gospel, there will be objective consequences worthy of serious sociological consideration. Experiences and the meanings attached to them are an important key to understanding the growth and consequences of the charismatic movement.

Religions, Values, and Peak Experiences

The late humanistic psychologist Abraham Maslow described a tension that exists between religious ritual and religious experience. No religion can dispense entirely with one or the other. Yet, as Maslow (1970, p. viii) notes:

Most people lose or forget the subjectively religious experience, and redefine Religion as a set of habits, behaviors, dogmas, forms, which at the extreme becomes entirely legalistic and bureaucratic, conventional, empty, and in the truest meaning of the word, antireligious. The mystic experience, the illumination, the great awakening, along with the charismatic seer who started the whole thing, are forgotten, lost or transformed into their opposites. Organized Religion, the churches, finally may become the major enemy of the religious experience and the religious experiencer.

Maslow's brilliant distinction between the experiences of religion and the institutions of Religion is relevant to both sociological and psychological approaches to the study of the development and growth of religious phenomena.

On the one hand, Maslow recognizes the dangers of basing religion solely on the experiences of believers. He observes that without structure, without some institutional basis for worship, "Spontaneity (the impulses from our best self) gets confused with impulsivity and acting out (the impulses from our sick self), and there is no way to tell the difference" (Maslow 1970, p. x). On the other hand, Maslow warns that institutions tend to stifle the experiential component of religious belief. This criticism applies equally to organized religion and to the study of it by social scientists. What is needed, Maslow asserts, is "an experience-based rationality in contrast to the a priori rationality we have come almost to identify with rationality itself" (Maslow 1970, p. vii).

Episcopalian priest-psychologist Morton Kelsey includes in the realm of "experience," extrasensory perceptions (ESP), including clairvoyance, telepathy, precognition, visions, experiences of the departed, psychokinesis, and psychic healing. ESP, or "information that comes to us that bypasses the five senses," should not be dissociated from religious phenomena, according to Kelsey (1972, p. 85). He notes that:

The Bible is a mine of information on ESP or psi phenomena. Nearly every book of the Bible shows the belief that human beings have contact with more than just the physical world and that there are other ways of influencing the world and people besides the physical means. Divination and the works of power are found throughout the Bible. There is even discussion of what kinds of practices are forbidden and why.

Those who attempt to evaluate charismatic experience must, therefore, recognize that "extrasensory perception is a natural part of human knowing which the modern world gradually forgot in its effort to develop as much objective understanding as possible" (Kelsey 1972, p. 21).

The Scientific Study of Religious Experience

Stark (1965, p. 97) observes that since the publication in 1902 of William James's classic study, *The Varieties of Religious Experience,* "virtually nothing of merit has been added to our understanding of religious experience." Although some descriptive work did follow in the 1960s and 1970s, McCready and Greeley (1976, p. 129) could state over a decade after Stark's original observation that "contemporary American social science may name its buildings after William James, but it is not much interested in doing research on the ecstatic experiences about which James's most famous work was concerned."[1] They observe that research on paranormal experiences (which are also an integral part of charismatic ideology) is almost nonexistent. When psychiatry has written about such experiences, its conclusions may be questioned. McCready and Greeley (1976, pp. 129–30) note:

At one time, psychiatrists devoted their free hours to psychoanalyzing the great mystics of the past (who were unfortunately not available for office couches). Despite the physical absence of the objects of interest, psychiatrists like Karl Menninger (in one of his early manifestations) were inclined to write off mystics as self-punitive madmen and madwomen. "Hysteria" was the most frequent diagnosis.

While social science has been more receptive to the legitimacy of psychic phenomena, it still focuses on the relationship between intense religious experiences and socially undesirable (by American value standards) psychological traits (e.g., dogmatism, suggestibility, dependence, etc.).[2] The few researchers in this field seem to be biased against the "healthiness" of psychic phenomena (even though they may view such experiences as being within the range of "normal"). The sympathetic bias of McCready and Greeley or Abraham Maslow is rare. Two alternative conclusions may be derived from the literature on the subject:

1. The ecstatic is an oppressed, unhappy, rigid person who is looking for reassurance and release, which an interlude of self-induced withdrawal provides.
2. The ecstatic is one who has had a "peak experience" that unleashes, however temporarily, the most creative and generous human resources (McCready and Greeley 1976, p. 133).

One such peak experience is that of Spirit baptism and the manifestations of the accompanying gifts. Leaders in the charismatic movement, particularly in neo-Pentecostal circles, frequently assert that personal spiritual renewal must precede institutional church renewal. Some descriptive analysis of such personal religious experiences is an important step toward understanding the growth and impact of the charismatic movement.

Spirit Baptism and Glossolalia

Despite some theological differences noted in the last chapter between Pentecostals and some neo-Pentecostals on the relationship between glossolalia and the baptism of the Spirit, most charismatic believers tend to date their baptism to the first time they spoke in tongues. Autobiographical statements of such experiences abound, and many writers describe them in terms of joy and near ecstasy. Sherrill collected the following accounts of responses to spirit baptism:

I started to praise God in the new language I had been given. There was at the same time a feeling that my spirit had taken wing. I was soaring heavenward on a poem. (Sherrill 1964, p. 113)

For me the gift of tongues turned out to be the gift of praise. As I used the unknown language which God had given me I felt rising in me the love, the awe, the adoration pure and uncontingent, that I had not been able to achieve in thought-out prayer. (Sherrill 1964, p. 82)

The following mass baptism was reported by Gerald Derstine, now a leader of a Christian retreat center in Florida:

One day, without warning, a young man in the class suddenly knelt down and began to cry. . . . This kind of emotion was very unusual in the Mennonite church, and at first we tried to put a stop to it. But before we could, another student was crying. And then another. We tried to pull the weeping students out of the classroom, but as soon as we took one out two or three others began to cry. . . . And then we noticed an amazing thing: strange sounds were coming from the mouths of some of these young people. Were these the "stammering lips" we had read about in the Bible? (Sherrill 1964, p. 109)

Sherrill's investigation of glossolalia and Spirit baptism led him to conclude: "Absolute criteria seem to be about the only things absent from the experience of Baptism in the Holy Spirit" (Sherrill 1964, p. 111). Some have experienced the phenomenon only after much waiting and seeking; others claimed they experienced it without being aware such a phenomenon existed. For some it was an emotionally charged experience; for others, emotions were under control. As Sherrill's wife commented: "If the Spirit is like the wind, blowing where it wants to, fixed rules would be suspicious. It'd be like coming in out of a tornado and switching on an electric fan" (Sherrill 1964, p. 111).

Many people, especially those steeped in an intellectual milieu, regard glossolalia with suspicion. One woman, for example, reported hearing glossolalia at a prayer meeting and reading many accounts of joy and ecstasy experienced by others. She felt no attraction to glossolalia or Spirit baptism but was willing to accept them as religious reality for others. Her own experience of glossolalia began when she was calmly engaged in private prayer. She says that she fully realized that she could start and stop her glossolalia at will, and she remained in an unemotional state of mind. These circumstances, together with her perception of herself as a well-educated person speaking in "nonsense" syllables ("like an idiot"), produced a crisis of faith. She continued praying, both in English and in tongues, and became convinced in her own spirit that God wanted His creatures to come humbly before Him. She felt convinced that if that was the way God wanted her to pray, she must surrender. Contrary to Kildahl's (1975) assertion that the presence of an authority figure brings on glossolalia, her speaking in tongues was prompted only by an inner sense that what she was doing was prayer and was a gift from God. Glossolalia was for her the result of a nonecstatic, deliberate surrender to a faculty that she found she possessed and that assumed greater meaning only as she used it over the years. Judging from this and other accounts, many are impressed by the simplicity of the tongues experience rather than by its ecstatic nature as reported in so much religious and nonreligious literature on the topic.[3]

The meaning attached to glossolalia is very important. Those who pray in tongues believe in faith that these utterances represent a "heavenly language" that enables them to pray when they do not have the words or do not know how. At times glossolalia may be accompanied by intense religious feelings; at other times it represents the Spirit of God who "intercedes with us with groans that words cannot express" and who "intercedes for the saints in accordance with God's will" (Rom. 8:26–27).[4]

The believers who are baptized in the Spirit see glossolalia not only as a form of prayer that praises God but also as a source of deep enrichment of the Christian life. Williams (1978, p. 16) explains that speaking in tongues is an audible reminder of the activity of the Holy Spirit, the practice of which gives the person a growing sense of awe that God is present through the Holy Spirit. This new language, which the person knows he or she did not just conjure up, is a reminder of God's power and presence. Singing in tongues, another phenomenon, adds a new dimension to corporate worship. Furthermore, speaking in tongues often proves to be the doorway into a deeper experience of other gifts of the Spirit in that it represents a total yielding to God and to his power.

Other Experiences of Spirit Baptism.   Most Pentecostals emphasize that glossolalia is the definitive evidence of Spirit baptism, while neo-Pentecostals are more likely to assert that glossolalia is only one indication. Those who accept classical Pentecostal teachings will recount their first experience with glossolalia when asked about Spirit baptism, but neo-Pentecostal testimonies (even from those who pray in tongues) may or may not include such a reference.

On the basis of over fifty written accounts of believers involved in the neo-Pentecostal movement (for these testimonies see Ovries 1980; Manney and Bourassa 1976), I have concluded that the most dramatic experience involves the development of a personal relationship with Jesus. This intuited awareness of God's love represents a shift from knowledge and belief to the experience of a new intimate relationship with God. Neo-Pentecostal witnesses are likely to emphasize how this relationship continues to grow and develop. The experience (whether tongues accompanies it or not) is seen as only the beginning of a changed life. Glossolalia continues to be important to neo-Pentecostals, and it is sought as a desired gift of the Holy Spirit. The focus of much teaching and reported experience, however, is the importance of coming into an intimate and personal relationship with Jesus, which will probably bring the gift of tongues. Thus conversion and Spirit baptism are often regarded as a single experience among neo-Pentecostals.

The peak experience of the Holy Spirit reported in the fifty-two testimonies reviewed usually occurred under one of four circumstances: (1) as a small group of believers gathered around a person desiring the baptism, laid hands on the individual, and prayed for him or her (the experience may have occurred immediately or some short time later); (2) as the individual was privately praying, after being exposed to the concept of a baptism of the Spirit, through literature, witness of friends, etc.; (3) during prayer with the person's spouse and/or one or two others; (4) during a large prayer gathering, without the knowledge or prompting of any others immediately around the person.

The peak experiences themselves are unique and varied. For example, a seventy-one-year-old married man described his baptism as follows:

I was finally prayed with to be baptized in the Holy Spirit, but I was honestly disappointed. I had come to expect a lot, but I didn't feel anything. I know that for some people it had been a tremendous experience, but it seemed as though nothing had happened to me. A week later, in the middle of the night, I woke up crying like a baby and couldn't stop. It just poured out of me. I was really alarmed. I woke up Ernestine and said to her, "what's wrong, I've never done this before in my life! Something's wrong, I can't stop crying!" She said, "The Holy Spirit is touching you. I'm sure of it." And she prayed for me, and I prayed. On that night, I felt a release of all this tension, of deep hurts from the past. . . . Now I realized that I had a hostility in me, all this sin in me, and that I was being set free. God just took it all away. It was extraordinary and beautiful. (Ovies 1980, p. 67)

A forty-two-year-old maintenance man also reported that nothing seemed to happen when he and others first prayed for his Spirit baptism:

Nothing happened that I could tell; there were no bells, no lights or anything, but they told me that the Lord was going to give me more peace in my life. And that's exactly what happened. In just the next few months, I got a lot closer to God, and I began to really experience a change. For the first time in my life I felt at peace. The most wonderful inner peace started coming into me. I couldn't explain it or describe it, but it was the first time in my life that I began to feel secure. (Ovies 1980, pp. 73–74)

A Presbyterian minister described a dream that he had of being baptized in the Spirit and how this dream released him of his prejudice against "Pentecostals, charismatics, and certain gifts of the Spirit." He said that his actual baptism occurred when

Three days later while I was having my morning devotions in my study, I sensed the presence of God and the joy that filled my heart in the dream. I bowed my head and prayed, "Lord, is this the time when I will be able to praise you with my conscious mind even as I did with my subconscious mind?" He said, "When you are ready, speak." I folded my hands and bowed my head and began very softly to praise God in an unknown language. (Manney and Bourassa 1976, pp. 95–96)

Those who wrote up their experiences for the two books reviewed, as well as many others whose accounts were found, emphasized their perception of a changed life after this peak experience. One missionary, who did not give the details of his experience, provides a typical account of the change:

The temptation to describe those days is overwhelming, but I am going to resist it, as it would only be a repetition of what has already become familiar in the happy witness of so many pentecostals: being baptized in the Spirit, the gift of tongues, the rediscovery of prayer, the Scriptures coming alive, the love and peace and joy, the new life in the Spirit that makes the Acts of the Apostles read like autobiography. (Manney and Bourassa 1976, p. 115)

Spirit Baptism and Other Spiritual Gifts

Gifts of Inspiration.   The previous discussion of ideology suggests that spiritual gifts may be divided into three types: inspiration, revelation, and power (Basham 1973). Glossolalia is illustrative of inspiration, both in terms of providing personal edification and, when used with interpretation, of being a source of prophecy. The other two gifts of inspiration are prophecy with and without tongues.[5]

Before delivering a prophecy, a person often has a sense that God wishes to speak through him or her. The initial reaction may be one of doubt, particularly for middle-class neo-Pentecostals, who appear more likely than classical Pentecostals to prophesy frequently at prayer gatherings. This doubt may be allayed by another worshipper who speaks words similar to those of the intuited prophecy. Having acknowledged that God may wish on occasion to use him/her to speak his word, the person would likely be moved to deliver a message believed to be prophetic. Frequently the person speaks the prophecy without knowing ahead of time exactly what he or she will say. Encouragement (or discouragement) from others in the gathering, either during or after the service, will serve to reinforce future prophetic behavior or to extinguish it.

Allowing others to speak in the name of God has many hazards.[6] The classical Pentecostals learned this from early experiences (e.g., a "prophet" contradicting or interrupting the preacher or two "prophets" delivering conflicting messages), and prophecy appears to be much more regulated in their gatherings than in many neo-Pentecostal ones. While anyone in a Pentecostal congregation may speak out in tongues, it is usually the preacher who "interprets" and thus speaks the prophetic word. With the notable exception of neo-Pentecostal pastors, prophetic utterances appear to occur much less frequently in Pentecostal gatherings than among neo-Pentecostals, who may wait for a "word from God" as a regular part of their prayer gatherings.

Prophecy as a gift refers less to foretelling the future than speaking words of exhortation and encouragement. Its use serves to heighten a believer's awareness of God's personal presence among those gathered. Not everyone at any particular gathering necessarily believes that all statements made in a prophetic form come directly from God, but prophecies always speak to some individuals in the congregation, while others may not find the words particularly applicable. There are also those who seem to have a prophetic ministry—when they deliver a prophecy, it has stronger impact than those given by others in the gathering. Many who gather for such prayer meetings are already used to spending time daily in personal prayer and have learned the secret of dialogue with God. One not only speaks to God but learns to listen to God speaking to him/her. Collective "listening" to God's word thus has a deep meaning and serves to reinforce personal prayer experience.

Gifts of Revelation. There is an overlap among these categories of gifts. Prophecy may include both a revelation and an exhortation, and revelations may or may not be delivered through prophecy. Often revelations may be simple statements beginning with "I feel" or "I sense in my spirit." The importance of revelation is that it provides knowledge secured from other than normal means. It may include foretelling; it may be a knowledge about a specific event in someone else's past; it may be a sense that the spiritual power being manifested is not from God; or it may be an ability to suggest a line of action or to give an appropriate message to a person in need. Knowledge, wisdom, and the gift of discerning spirits are grouped together as gifts of revelation (Basham 1973).[7]

Such gifts are very real for those involved in the charismatic movement. The person having the gift often has a presentiment like those that precede prophecy, and it is only in acting on it that the gift will be developed further. A story recently reported by a young woman student may serve as an illustration of revelation.

Sue (not the student's real name) belongs to a neo-Pentecostal church where the gifts are regularly manifested. One Sunday the minister invited anyone "who wanted to be used by the Lord" to gather the following Saturday for prayer at 6:00 A.M. Sue reported that about seventy persons gathered at the church that morning. They began with prayer, simply praising God, and expected that he would speak to them. Before long a woman stated that she sensed that someone who was "hooked on drugs" needed counseling. It was a young man whose mother was on the verge of a mental breakdown because of his addiction. The woman had no idea who the person was. The group continued to pray for clarification. The name "Joe" (not his name) came to one woman. When that name was mentioned, a young businessman remembered the situation of one of his partners, whose son Joe was just released from prison and had a drug problem. His mother was particularly distraught over her son's condition. He asked for prayer before he went off to minister to the young man.

As they continued praying, a man sensed that a young Christian who was "not now walking with the Lord" was in danger of being delivered into the hands of the enemy. With continued prayer the name of "Jane" came to another woman. A man present felt that the name referred to his daughter, whose whereabouts in the city were unknown to him and his wife. They then prayed to be told who should minister to her. At this point Sue said she was weeping, for she had such a heavy heart for this young girl without even knowing what her specific problem was. Another woman said that Sue should go to minister to her. A call to telephone information provided the young woman's address, and Sue was off to visit Jane, whom she had never met. When Jane answered the door, Sue said, "The Lord sent me. May I come in?" After Sue told of their morning prayer service at the church and the sense the community was receiving, Jane broke into tears; she told Sue that she was planning to make a pornographic movie in another city. Both Sue and Jane were convinced that God had indeed spoken to his people.

Illustrations of this sort appear regularly in charismatic witnesses and writings. Harper (1973), for example, in writing about the fellowship at the Church of the Redeemer in Houston, Texas, narrates a striking account. Dr. Bob Eckert, a member of the church, had an idea that he could not get out of his mind—God wanted him to go to Mexico. Dr. Eckert had a very busy medical practice at the time and had no idea where he was to go in Mexico, where he would get the money to go, or what he would do when he got there. He shared his presentiment with another brother in the church, who felt he was called to travel with Dr. Eckert. They began to pray together and, after consulting a map, decided on the place (a remote village) to which they were being called. Once they arrived in the village they sought out the local Roman Catholic priest and explained in the little Spanish they knew that "God had sent them." The priest broke down and wept, saying, "I have been praying for years for God to send a doctor to treat my poor people." Harper (1973, p. 116) comments, "A priest praying in Mexico, a doctor listening in to God in Texas, and the result, a perfect solution." The two men were able to set up a medical clinic, staffed at first by Americans, but now completely run by Mexicans.

These examples of the operation of the gifts of knowledge and wisdom demonstrate certain principles believed important for the manifestation of these gifts. The accounts show that no person could have known in advance, through normal means, the facts later revealed. No person in the group knew of Jane's problem: the word was only that she "would be delivered into the hands of the evil one." Only one man knew Joe's difficulties, but he saw that the word applied to Joe only after the name "Joe" was mentioned. Bob Eckert was not aware of the needs of the Mexican village—only that God had told him to go there. Middle-class charismatics, who are most likely to publish such accounts, emphasize that such knowledge is given to the church, the body of believers, for ministry. Thus the knowledge was revealed in a group prayer session and/or with community support. This knowledge is then said to call a believer to Christian service. Implementing the word frequently requires the gift of wisdom. Sue reported that she knew the words to speak to Jane without ever having met her before or having been aware of her specific problem until she went to visit her. Bob Eckert and his companion were given the wisdom necessary to set up the medical clinic. The gifts are thus interrelated and affect other members of the community. Social support thus becomes a prime factor in interpreting such occurrences as the work of the Holy Spirit.

Gifts of Power. To one degree or another, those involved in the charismatic movement expect God to manifest his power in their lives. Basham (1973) lists the gifts of faith, healing, and miracles as three manifestations of this power. Again, there is overlap among these three gifts. Those who have a healing ministry and those who work miracles also exercise the power of faith. To some extent charismatics expect these gifts to be at work in their communities.

Many charismatics are familiar with accounts of dramatic healings or dramatic miracles, many of which are published by charismatic publishing houses and retold on charismatic television programs. Such accounts boost their expectations for less dramatic miracles and healings that might occur in their own lives.[8]

At a recent healing service, the minister told the following anecdote. A man was working on his barn roof and started to fall. He began crying, "Oh God, save me!" When his fall was halted in the middle of the roof, he said, "Oh God, never mind; I'm caught on a nail." The charismatic believes that the nail is as much of a miracle as a net appearing from nowhere to catch the falling man. Again, there are no coincidences for the true believer. Every nail is an act of God.

Healing might be viewed simply as a specific miracle. Other miracles can range from dramatic changes in weather to the recovery of lost articles or the repair of broken objects. A few years ago a group of young students returning from a large charismatic conference in South Bend, Indiana, excitedly recounted how it had rained during most of the conference. On Saturday evening, while gathered for prayer at the outdoor stadium, they prayed in unison for the rain to cease and the stars to come out. Reportedly, that is exactly what happened. Such stories may embarrass more rationally oriented charismatics who accept tongues and may believe in prophecy but are reluctant to believe that God fills empty gasoline tanks in response to prayer—yet these stories are believed by others. Believers are encouraged to expect miracles, for only then can they happen.[9]

Nonbelievers frequently attempt to provide alternative explanations for these and other stories. It is relatively simple to dismiss what charismatics believe to be gifts of the Holy Spirit as coincidences or as results of overly active imaginations. The nonbeliever can always point to prayer that has seemingly failed: Why is there hunger in the world? Why do volcanoes erupt? Why does drought still plague the earth? Why doesn't charismatic prayer and belief change all this if it really works? It is easier to demand empirical proof (with statistically significant results) than to follow the reasoning of charismatics who experience "unanswered" prayers. I will now consider the ways charismatics minimize the cognitive dissonance of such negative experiences.

Charismatic Experience and Cognitive Dissonance

What does happen in the believer's mind when God appears silent, when the sick man dies, or the mountain remains unmoved by prayer? Part of the answer may be found in Festinger, Riecken, and Schacter's (1956) classic study *When Prophecy Fails*. Festinger and his colleagues studied a flying saucer cult that had predicted the end of the world for the mid-1950s. They were relatively certain that this prophecy would be disconfirmed, but wanted to learn how such disconfirmation would be handled by the group's members. The alternatives discussed by Festinger et al. can be applied to charismatic believers, just as they applied to the small cult that prematurely predicted the destruction of the world.

One way to minimize the dissonance is for the believer to abandon the belief when it appears to be refuted. A couple filled with a faith in God's power to heal experience the death of a sick child. A prophecy assures the growth of a particular charismatic fellowship, but six months later it disbands. Faith-filled believers pray for sunshine—and it rains. Some, perhaps many, who come to the edge of the charismatic movement may experience such failures (i.e., specific prayer requests that are not answered or revelatory prophecies that fail to be actualized) and turn away from the movement. Their commitment is minimal, so it is easy for them to abandon the belief they never fully embraced. Yet Festinger et al. (1956, p. 216) found an "increase of proselyting following unequal disconfirmation of a belief" alongside cases of clear disconfirmation, as when the world did not end when the cultists' prophecy told them it would. This same phenomenon may be seen among charismatic believers and is a key to the movement's present success.

Festinger et al. found that social support was the key variable in determining whether the individual abandoned his or her faith in the cult after the disconfirmation of the prophecy or went on to make an even greater commitment through increasing proselytizing activities. Members of one group involved in the cult received more social support from each other than those of the other group, who were more isolated. The group receiving social support developed a rationale to explain why the world had not been destroyed. It believed that its own faithfulness enabled God to spare the world. Thus they could reinforce one another's beliefs and actually increase proselyting activities. Prior commitment was a necessary bolster for their faith after the disconfirmation, but commitment alone was not sufficient.

For charismatics, as for anyone involved in a social movement, support from like-minded believers is necessary to sustain belief. Most established Pentecostal denominations and many neo-Pentecostals emphasize as part of their teachings that men and women cannot know the mind of God. Thus, faith-filled prayer always brings an answer—God cannot fail people—but the answer may not be in accord with the desires of those who pray. Other charismatics, most notably some television ministers, are likely to blame the failings of the person whose prayer was not answered: the individual lacked faith or did not tithe, for example. In either event, the committed charismatic will selectively focus on the answered prayers and miracles witnessed, rather than on incidents that would tend to disconfirm beliefs.

Those who experience the "hand of God" will inevitably have prayer failures as well as successes. No doubt selective perception enables a person to focus on the successful prayer requests or prophecies, but he or she may also attempt to analyze the "failures." These failures may be redefined as successes because of a faith in God "who always answers prayers"—not because of any statistically verifiable empirical proof. At times extraordinary measures may be employed to help redefine the situation.

An example involves a prophecy a woman received and believed regarding a specific event that was to happen in 1979. Given the time limit and the specific nature of the prophecy, it was susceptible to disconfirmation. The prophecy did not come to pass as she had expected. Mindful of the nature of prayer as dialogue with God, the woman turned to God on the last day of 1979, saying "Lord, I've got to know why this prayer wasn't answered the way I thought you promised it would be through the prophecy." As has happened on other occasions, the woman had the sense that if she opened the Bible at random, she would receive her answer. She immediately opened to Prov. 30, and her eyes fell on verses 5 and 6: "The word of the Lord is flawless. He is a shield to those who trust him. Do not add to what he has to say or he will rebuke you and prove you a liar."

For the woman this random consultation was no coincidence. She interpreted the passage to mean that the prophecy was more limited than she had originally envisioned—she had unintentionally added to God's word. Occurrences such as these are defined as "successes," reinforcing a belief that even "failures" teach something. While not all charismatics accept such rationalizations (nor would they all agree on the appropriateness of playing "Bible roulette"), this illustration serves to demonstrate how "failures" can be reinterpreted by a believer. Since this type of belief is held by "significant others" in the charismatic movement, charismatics obtain the needed social support through experiences of prayer "failures" as well as "successes."

Do the Spiritual Gifts Bear Fruit?

In the absence of well-designed and executed empirical studies, perhaps the best discussion of the consequences of the spiritual gifts for believers is an evaluation by a well-known critic of the charismatic movement of what non-Charismatics can learn from charismatics. After spending sixteen chapters of his book attempting to refute charismatic claims from a theological perspective, MacArthur (1978, pp. 200–202) concludes that noncharismatics have a tremendously important lesson to learn from charismatics, who have stepped into the religious void of many mainline churches. Noncharismatic churches have failed to provide exemplary leadership for people. "In Charismatic churches, however, one almost always finds a strong leader or leaders" (MacArthur 1978, p. 201). In contrast to the lack of open warmth and love in many churches, charismatics work to establish warm and loving fellowships. MacArthur (1978, p. 202) notes that "The church was never meant to be a mental mausoleum." Charismatics go beyond theology and allow their experiences to touch them. Through their belief in divine providence, charismatics have helped noncharismatic churches to "recognize that the church needs more than seminary graduates, beautifully written Sunday school curriculum, and an organizational chart that would rival General Motors. Charismatics have helped pull the church up short to realize that God's

Spirit will build the church, not human ingenuity'' (MacArthur 1978, p. 202). Charismatics have demonstrated the need that people have to participate actively in worship and have shown other Christians the need for greater commitment. Thus even some unsympathetic critics of charismatic theology have come to recognize its religious impact.

Charismatic teachings often warn against overemphasizing religious experience and are critical of those who skip from group to group in search of new religious experiences or new ''highs.'' The emphasis, most will say, must remain on the Giver and not his gifts. If the experience is from God, it is meant to bear fruit—it is meant to be a source of loving service to others. The psychologist-priest John Powell (1974, pp. 54–55) has argued that a genuine religious experience must be lasting, have a real effect on the believer, and be directed toward the spiritual enrichment of others. Taken as a whole, the charismatic movement seems to meet these criteria.

Notes

1. While some research (see, for example, Hood 1980; Hay 1979; Hay and Morisy 1978; Gibbons and DeJarnette 1972; Thorner 1965) has been conducted in response to Stark's challenge, little has been done to analyze the substantive content of such experience (Hay 1979).

2. See Moberg (1979) for a collection of articles that explores psychic phenomena in terms of "spiritual well-being." This edited volume contains conceptual studies of spiritual well-being, theoretical considerations, and reports on both qualitative and quantitative studies bearing upon the topic. A total of twenty-two articles, plus an excellent introduction and conclusion by the editor, makes Moberg's work a significant contribution to the literature.

3. Richardson (1973), after examining psychological interpretations of glossolalia, criticized both the methodologies and the unwarranted conclusions of much previous research and called for further research on the topic. He recommends a longitudinal study of glossolalia that follows the different stages and changes that may be observed until the glossolalist becomes a frequent user of tongues and further study of the meaning attached to glossolalia by the user and the ways in which and the conditions under which it is employed.

Hine (1969) is an important exception to much existing literature which I feel is at best incomplete, and at worst a serious distortion. In her functional interpretation of glossolalia, Hine is able to link it with conversion, changed behavior, and an act of commitment. She further notes:

Through a functional approach to the phenomenon, we have come to assess glossolalia as a nonpathological linguistic behavior which functions in the context of the Pentecostal movement as one component of the generation of commitment. As such, it operates in social change, facilitating the spread of the Pentecostal movement affecting nearly every denomination within organized Christianity, and in personal change, providing powerful motivation for attitudinal and behavioral changes in the direction of group ideals. (Hine 1969, p. 225)

4. Hutch (1980) takes the position that glossolalia is a personal ritual that represents a "deliberate act, purposely undertaken for the religious benefit just as one would enter into any other sort of ritual process." His stance, which criticizes those who have used the aberrant behavior approach (e.g., Kildahl 1972) or the

extraordinary behavior approach (e.g., Goodman 1972), closely agrees with my own experience and observations of glossolalia.

5. I have been unable to find research on prophecy as used within the charismatic movement; but through religious readings on the topic, interviewing informants, and my own experiences and observations, I will attempt to describe its basic workings.

6. Prophecy, which occurs freely at relatively new gatherings, soon encounters restrictions. Even among neo-Pentecostals I have noted increasing structural regulations, especially at larger gatherings. The prayer meeting I attended regularly over a period of the last five years may be used as an illustration. The gathering used to have an informal control of prophetic utterances. If someone gave what leaders considered a meaningless prophecy (one that may have been harmless and in accord with Scripture, but did not seem to have any particular relevance to the way the meeting was progressing) or one through which a single person knowingly or unknowingly tried to manipulate the gathering, the speaker was interviewed privately. (There was always caution about "wandering prophets" who moved about from prayer meeting to prayer meeting with a "word from the Lord.") The would-be manipulator probably would choose not to return while the author of meaningless prophecies would refrain from giving them. As the group grew in size, more regulations were introduced. At present, prophecies must be shared with a representative in the prayer gathering who, in turn, clears them with the leader. The leader then selects the prophecies that may be given to the entire gathering.

7. As with prophecy, I was unable to locate studies dealing with these phenomena and will rely on religious writings and personal accounts and observations to illustrate them.

8. A classical Pentecostal minister told me how he reevaluated the issue of miracles after hearing witnesses given at an upper-middle-class Episcopalian church's prayer meeting. He said he heard reports of miracles there that might have been shared at a camp meeting of lower-class Pentecostal believers twenty-five years ago! As some Pentecostals become more educated, they discourage witness of miracles. The minister was impressed that the faith of the educated and the wealthy was so similar to the simple beliefs of the uneducated.

9. At a recent Pentecostal service I attended the minister addressed this issue as would many other charismatic teachers of both classical and neo-Pentecostal churches. He noted, "We all know someone who has been healed as a result of prayer while someone else was not, but we cannot let this be an excuse to abandon the Lord." Those committed to belief in the operation of the spiritual gifts do not allow seeming "failures" to dampen their convictions.

CHAPTER 5

Faith and Healing: The Charismatic Movement and the Health Profession

"Which is easier to say, 'Your sins are forgiven,' or to say 'Get up and walk'? But that you may know that the Son of Man has authority on earth to forgive sins. . . ." He said to the paralyzed man, "I tell you, get up, take your mat and go home." Immediately he stood up in front of them, took what he had been lying on and went home praising God. Everyone was amazed and gave praise to God. (Luke 5:22–26)

Both spiritual and physical healings were an integral part of the ministry of Jesus of Nazareth and the early Christian church. Nearly one-fifth of the Gospels is devoted to accounts of miraculous healing of physical maladies that, as the passage cited above suggests, were often spiritual as well.[1] Over forty different instances of such healings were recorded in the Bible, but such accounts were meant to be illustrative rather than exhaustive (see John 21:25). The apostles were thus accustomed to Jesus' wonder-working power—a power that he promised would be theirs as well. "And these signs will accompany those that believe: In my name they will drive out demons, they will speak in new tongues . . . they will place their hands on sick people, and they will get well" (Mark 18:16). In the Acts of the Apostles, a book which narrates the history of the early church, the blind did receive sight, the lame did walk, and demons were exorcized. Ten general references to "signs and miracles" or healing all diseases may also be found in this account (Kelsey 1973, pp. 117–22), giving the impression that faith healings were a normal occurrence in the apostles' ministry.

It was only with the increased institutionalization of the church and the development of an Aristotelian-based theology which dichotomized body and soul that miraculous healings became a rarity or a phenomenon not to be expected at all.[2] Just as glossolalia died out by the third century, the expectation and practice of faith healing also declined. The normative view of theologians and intellectuals was that medicine and physicians were to be called upon to "heal the body" while Christianity had as its purpose to "heal the soul." Body and soul were thus separated, and illness came to be viewed commonly as a chastisement from God to be borne rather than relieved through spiritual efforts.

While Christian theologies that developed over the centuries either belittled or opposed belief in miraculous healings, the practice continued in folk religion. It found an outlet in Roman Catholicism through the use of relics and shrines that provided a medium through which cures and tales of cures could be perpetuated. After the Reformation, a less mystical and more rational Protestantism was also less inclined to allow any vehicles for spreading such "superstition," which was tolerated and regulated, if not encouraged, in Catholicism. In modern times, regardless of the denomination, the idea of healing was restricted to special instances, more often regarded as superstition, and further from the center of official Christianity (Kelsey 1973, p. 231). Modern healing sects (perhaps the most noted being Mary Baker Eddy's Christian Science) were opposed as being heretical.

Not until the twentieth century, with the emergence of the charismatic movement, was the belief in healing restored in some Christian groups to a position similar to that of the early church.[3] Particularly among Pentecostals, healing came to be expected as a normal religious occurrence. The early Pentecostals did not specifically seek healings, but many experienced them as they were baptized in the Holy Spirit. While Pentecostals are not the only Christians presently espousing belief in faith healing, they are the ones who rekindled in Christianity an expectation of regular healings in Jesus' name. It is within their fold that twentieth-century healers, including Oral Roberts and the late Katherine Kuhlman, began their ministries. Roberts, Kuhlman, and others practicing divine healing, in turn, were often bridges to a non-Pentecostal audience who sought healings at their hands.

This chapter will deal with four main considerations regarding the spiritual gift of healing: (1) the nature of faith healing; (2) its relation to modern medicine; (3) charismatic ideologies on sickness and healing; and (4) the attempt to institutionalize the gift of healing.

Claiming the Promise: The Sick are Made Well

Most practicing charismatics are familiar with testimonies of physical healings, many have prayed for the healings of others, and many have experienced healings themselves. The claimed healings may range from the relief of a headache to the cure of a terminal illness. Such accounts are reinforced through charismatic publications and television.[4] Faith healing even made the front pages of the daily newspapers when the 1980 Miss America, Cheryl Prewitt, reported that her left leg, suffering impaired growth as a result of an automobile accident, was lengthened through the prayers of a minister at a revival meeting six years earlier. Both Pentecostal and neo-Pentecostal congregations regularly pray for physical healings—and many report that they regularly receive them.

Prayer situations for healing include private prayer, congregational prayer, special healing services or revival meetings, and the electronic church. People who have reported incidents of healing usually do not attempt to provide medical diagnosis or theological explanation. Belief in such healings becomes reinforced through personal experience and through giving and hearing testimonies.

Healing Through Private Prayer. Practicing charismatics may regularly pray for healings for themselves and for others—and believe that they regularly receive results. Witnesses commonly shared include relief of minor headaches, disappearance of lumps or abnormal growths, healing of eye infections, and easing of arthritic pain. It is less important to determine whether these were in fact "healings," than to note that those who give such witness believe that prayer resulted in healing.

Accounts of healings are found in charismatic books and magazine articles and in church and television testimonials. Nearly every issue of the weekly *Pentecostal Evangel,* the official publication of the Assemblies of God, contains such reports. They are endorsed by a local pastor and usually allow some time to elapse between the perceived healing and its report by the magazine. The account selected to illustrate how private prayer may be used in seeking healing involves a young boy who was healed of a brain tumor ten years ago.

In 1971 Kenneth Castleberry, then four years old, was found to have a brain tumor. The whole family gathered around him, anointed him with oil, and prayed for his healing. The physicians called for surgery to remove the tumor, but they found that the tumor had grown so rapidly and was so situated in the brain that they were unable to remove it. The tumor was malignant, and the doctors informed the family that the only thing they were able to do for Kenneth was to drain the fluid to keep the tumor from spreading so fast. A minister who was in the hospital visiting another patient came into the room to pray for Kenneth. The minister reported to the mother, "Your son will live longer than you and me both. God has healed him." The next day, after a peaceful sleep, four-year-old Kenneth said to his mother, "Mommy, do you know what just happened to me? . . . Jesus just opened my head, and I felt Him take my tumor away." The mother reported that the doctors sent the boy home, giving them no hope for the child's survival. Tests performed three years ago show that the tumor has completely disappeared (Castleberry 1981, p. 15).

Healing Through Congregational Prayer. Many Pentecostal and neo-Pentecostal churches have a time to pray for healing as part of regular church services. While it is usually the minister or elder who lays on hands and/or anoints the person with oil, the congregation joins the prayer for healing. From time to time, members give witness of perceived healings ranging from headaches and the common cold to muscle strains and sprains and occasionally of something much more serious.

One recent event which reinforced the belief in the power of congregational prayer at a Pentecostal church involved an elderly lady suffering from a heart problem. She had already been hospitalized for several weeks, but remained so weak that the doctors reportedly could not risk anesthetizing her to insert a pacemaker. One evening during service the congregation united in special prayer for her. That same evening her condition began to improve, and a pacemaker was installed the following Tuesday. Over the weeks she continued to amaze doctors with a slow but unexpected recovery—a recovery that the congregation asserted was a result of the power of God being released through their prayers.

Claims of healing of physical illnesses, emotional difficulties, and forms of addiction are heard within congregations that practice praying for the sick. At times the reported healings occur gradually; sometimes they are instantaneous. Whether the healing is physical or emotional, of a life-threatening condition or a less serious malady, instantaneous or gradual, through modern medicine or without it, God is openly proclaimed as its source.

Special Healing Services. In charismatic circles some men and women are believed to have a special gift of healing, enabling them to conduct healing services with dramatic results. Oral Roberts first displayed this gift for a television audience in the 1950s, and Katherine Kuhlman exhibited a similar gift in the late 1960s and early 1970s. (Oral Roberts has changed his image from a faith healer to a television evangelist to correspond with his change in religious affiliation from Holiness-Pentecostal to United Methodist in the late 1960s. He no longer performs healing services on television.) Perhaps the best known of the television healers is Ernest Angley, an evangelist who is slowly gaining a national audience.

Ernest Angley and his late wife Esther Lee ("Angel") came to Akron, Ohio, in 1954 with nothing more than a tent and their evangelistic fervor. Three years later they opened the $1.5 million, 3,000-seat Grace Cathedral with the support of some 3,000 church members. While refusing to identify with any established denomination, Angley and his wife were both trained at the Church of God's Lee College (Cleveland, Tennessee). After about a dozen years of itinerant tent preaching, the Angleys settled in Akron and watched their ministry thrive.

After Angel's death in 1970, Angley began a television ministry in 1972. He recently leased a building for a television studio in Akron to further expand this part of the ministry. While precise figures were unavailable, Angley's ministry has attracted worldwide attention; on a trip to China he conducted a healing service for deaf children. (Reportedly Angley has been asked to return to share his "technique" for such healing with specialists in China.)

Angley's messages are basically biblical with a delivery style that reflects the Baptist tradition of his youth. Unlike many charismatics who emphasize love as a sermon theme, Angley is more likely to preach an old hellfire and brimstone message of repentance and salvation. His free use of charismatic language ("I saw in a vision" or "God told me"), together with his flamboyant mannerisms, "down-home" countrylike speech, and the ever-present carnation worn on his suit lapel, make him a target for professional comedians. Despite this stereotyped image, which may be an embarrassment to more reserved charismatics, Angley's message and claims are mostly in accord with other "full-gospel" adherents. (Angley is frequently the object of a press that does not understand him or his healing ministry. Although he is at times ridiculed, he has remained above any moral or ethical charges. He appears to be regarded as an oddity, but not a person seeking personal gain.)

The Friday-evening healing service at Grace Cathedral conducted by Angley begins promptly at 7:00 P.M. with congregational singing and ministry by the choir. After approximately a half hour, Angley appears on the platform to spur the 3,000 persons gathered to open praise of God. Following this time of informal worship, Angley then delivers his sermon based on a biblical theme. By 8:30 or 9:00 P.M., nearly two hours after the commencement of the service, Angley begins to get a word of knowledge (through what he calls his X-ray vision in which he claims to see a person's ailments in his mind) regarding specific healings. It starts gradually—"There's a woman on the far right—yes, with the red hat—who is being healed of diabetes. Stand and claim your miracle." The woman stands, and the congregation praises God. Angley continues pointing throughout the audience, claiming specific people are being healed of cancer, arthritis, back ailments, and stomach problems.

Angley then calls certain groups (depending on how "the Holy Ghost leads") to come forward—it may be people afflicted with cancer or hearing problems. After asking if the person is born-again and if he/she smokes, Angley prays and usually the person is "slain in the Spirit."[5] For the next couple of hours, he will pray individually for hundreds of persons in need of healing. Many appear to be touched, although a few will openly demonstrate signs of disbelief. Some may return repeatedly, or even go through the healing line a second time in one evening, seeking healing or even the spiritual sensation of "falling under the power of the Holy Spirit."

Angley's healing services are taken to other cities during the week. In addition to the Friday-evening services at Akron's Grace Cathedral, services are held in different cities during a typical week. An hour-long program is telecast on stations throughout the country, including Angley's preaching and a portion of the healing service.

Unlike Angley, many healers travel a circuit without the benefit of television. Their styles differ in conducting services, but they all instill in their audiences the belief in divine healing. A healing service in an Episcopal church during which a student-friend claimed a healing may be used as one illustration of a service quite different in tone and congregational composition, but not dissimilar in basic belief, from that of Angley's at Grace Cathedral.

The service began with song, prayer, and praise similar to any prayer meeting in this church. The worship was part of an Episcopal communion service that is very similar to a Roman Catholic mass. The visiting priest began to share some thoughts on healing and on the Scriptures, emphasizing God's power to heal. He also noted that there would be times during which he would leave the platform to lay hands on specific persons and to pray "as the Spirit leads." During one of these unobtrusive moves through the congregation (during which the congregation was to continue praying and singing in unison), the priest stopped by my student-friend, who was standing directly behind me. Jennie (not her real name) had been suffering from degenerative arthritis for some fifteen years, but at that time had no immediately obvious symptoms of that disease. As the service progressed following the reception of communion, the priest invited those who wished to come up for prayer to do so. Jennie went up to the alter asking him to pray that her knees might be healed (her kneecaps had been surgically removed several years before, and she was unable to kneel or bend without intense pain). The priest, seemingly ignoring that request, responded with, "I see something wrong with your left shoulder. God wants to heal that." Jennie had had surgery on her shoulder, that produced no immediately visible impairment. As the priest laid hands on her, Jennie "fell under the power of the Spirit," arising to find she had total use of her shoulder. The priest then asked her what was wrong with her knees. Jennie told him that she believed God was doing much inner healing in her life, healing her "from the inside out," but that she would like to be able to kneel and bend. The priest confirmed her self-diagnosis and added, "God wants to do something for your knees tonight." Again he laid hands on her and prayed; again she was slain in the Spirit, getting up to find she could kneel and bend her knees without pain. That event occurred about a year ago at the time of this writing, and Jennie can still use her shoulder, bend her knees, and kneel; moreover, she believes that even more healing will follow.

Published reports of healing services range from attempting to discredit both healer and those believing in healing to uncritically accepting the claimed healings. My experience at a number of such meetings suggests that some are indeed healed, and many, probably most, are not.

It is apparent that despite a common belief in divine healing, the mode of expression differs for the upper-middle-class Episcopalian when compared to the largely working-class congregation of an Ernest Angley. One of the main differences in theology may be observed in the handling of "dissonance" or persons who are not healed—an issue to which I will return later in this chapter.

Healing and the Electronic Church. Prayers for healing, for both the studio and home audience, are frequently part of television services. Much as both Ernest Angley and the Episcopalian priest reportedly receive words of knowledge, knowing who needs special prayer and who God wishes to touch during the service, television ministers report "sensing" God removing cancers, curing arthritis, and healing diabetes. People who believe they have been cured call the station to claim that they have been touched through the prayers of the television church. Even the laying on of hands takes place during the broadcast, as the host asks the person needing healing to place his/her hand up against the hand appearing on the television screen (a technique used regularly by Ernest Angley).[6]

Television allows viewers, particularly those in noncharismatic churches, to accept healing as a normal, everyday experience. Healing services are thus made available to members of mainline churches who may not be exposed to such practices, as well as to those who may elect not to be a member of any congregation. The witnesses provided and the television cast's belief in the power of miracles through television may serve the same function that congregational prayer and healing services do for others, namely, a reinforcement of the conviction that healing is available to believers, which creates a mental framework allowing the viewer to receive such a healing in the future.

Healing: Its Relation to Modern Medicine

Unlike many early Pentecostals, contemporary charismatics teach that physicians and medicine are means through which God may bring healing (Hollenweger 1972). Gone are the old tensions between Pentecostals and modern medicine, as charismatics are represented in the medical professions as in other occupations. FGBMFI (1976) has been one vehicle for bringing charismatic physicians into contact with one another and further dispelling the old tension between faith healing and medicine.

Pentecostals have come to recognize the value of medicine, and some in the medical profession, particularly those who are advocates of holistic medicine, are coming to accept the power of prayer to facilitate healing. They echo Plato's concern: "This is the great error of our day in the treatment of the human body that physicians separate the soul from the body." Those who advocate holistic health (see Otto and Knight 1979) view the process of healing as having several dimensions: mental/emotional, physical, social, and spiritual. Holistic-healing advocates argue that modern medicine's concentration on the physical has omitted dimensions that are vital to maintaining health.

While the mental/emotional and social dimensions of healing are slowly finding their way into medical education, the spiritual dimension is seldom treated (Kelsey 1979, p. 213). In this regard, primitive cultures have demonstrated more awareness of the integration of the spiritual and the physical than has contemporary medicine. Primitive religions employing the shaman acknowledge the presence of evil and destructive forces that must be dispelled with spiritual healing. For them the religious task and the healing task are essentially the same. This is in decided contrast to contemporary Western medicine, which, with the exception of the holistic movement, has become almost entirely materialistic and rational.

Two specific topics frequently discussed in holistic medicine that may have direct bearing upon the practice of spiritual healing are touch therapy and the "laying on of hands," and the role of the mind in the healing process.

Healing Touch and the "Laying on of Hands". The practice of placing hands on the head or shoulder of the person to be healed is a common practice of charismatics when praying for healing. Those who engage in the "laying on of hands" are aware of the biblical references to the practice, but most are also aware that biblical healings may or may not have been accompanied by that outward sign. Few would insist on touching the person in need of healing, but most would be open to the use of touch.

Within the medical profession, particularly among nurses, attention has been given to this ancient healing practice of "laying on of hands." While skeptics both inside and outside the profession regard "touch therapy" as another variety of "tender loving care," proponents insist that it is a skill that requires more than simple TLC. The research of biochemist Bernard Grad and the experiments of Dolores Krieger in nursing lend some support to the physiological basis of touch therapy.

Wardwell (1972) suggests that the laying on of hands effects a patient's healing through a type of placebo effect. Just as sugar-coated tablets relieve symptoms for some patients who believe the tablets are medicinal, so too the laying on of hands may affect the mind rather than produce a physiological response. Several experiments were conducted by Bernard Grad (1979) with mice and barley seed to dispute the placebo explanation. In all of the experiments involving a healer's laying on of hands there were reported differences in the experimental group as compared with the control group. Dolores Krieger (Flynn 1980, pp. 65,-66) has attempted to explain such phenomena, reportedly occurring in humans as well as animals and plants, through the Eastern religious concept of prana, or energy. The practice of touching may actually transmit energy from one person to another. Based on pioneering research begun as early as 1969, Krieger has come to advocate "therapeutic touch," described as "an act of healing or helping that is akin to the ancient practice of laying-on hands," to be used as an adjunct to orthodox nursing practices (Krieger 1973, 1975; Krieger et al. 1979). Others appear to be following Krieger's innovative efforts in utilizing and promoting touch therapy in medicine as one method that takes into account the principles of holistic medicine (Miller 1979; Weiss 1979; Ujhely 1979; Boguslawski 1979; Goodykoontz 1979; Sandroff 1980).

Further research may determine that touch therapy is efficacious in healing, merely another form of communication, or a practice with physiological underpinnings, but these findings will not greatly alter the charismatic's use of the "laying on of hands." The fact that some members of the nursing profession are learning therapeutic touch techniques and asserting that it effects healings in patients simply reinforces the charismatic's belief that the material and the spiritual are inseparable. It remains to be seen whether therapeutic touch, as taught in nursing seminars around the country, has succeeded in duplicating the religious practice of laying on of hands. The possible relationship between the practice as used in nursing and in healing services merits further study and investigation.

The Mind and the Emotions in Holistic Health.   A relationship between stress and disease is widely acknowledged (Pelletier 1977; Selye

1978). Stress diseases include hypertension, heart failure, cancer, and ulcers (Lamott 1975), as well as diabetes, asthma, stomach problems, and arthritis (Kelsey 1973). The rise of psychosomatic medicine has led to a distinction between functional (mental/emotional) and organic diseases, but there is little agreement concerning the diagnosis, much less the etiology, of diseases in the respective categories. It is, however, acknowledged that the nervous system provides a bridge between the mind and physical symptoms in the body, which often makes medicine alone ineffective in dealing with apparently physical problems.

For many charismatics the culprit in such illness is sin, either personal or social. Sin is not defined as an infraction of a set of codified rules but rather as an estrangement or separation of persons from their God. This may result from unconfessed and unrepented personal sin (including the frequently stereotyped "sins" or infractions of rules), but is perhaps more likely to be brought about through a social situation (social sin) affecting the patient. It may be the result of lack of parental love, hostile work situations, or the injustice of a neighbor. While psychotherapy recognizes the potential of repressed anger, hurt, and anxieties to cause physical problems, charismatics believe they have an answer that goes beyond simply bringing the unconscious to the surface to be dealt with intellectually. Two practices, developed to deal with mental and emotional healing, often bring physical healings as well: inner healing and deliverance.

The Practice of Inner Healing. The best-known advocate of inner healing is former President Jimmy Carter's sister, Ruth Carter Stapleton (*Newsweek* 1980; Woodward 1978). Stapleton found that her inability to forgive the emotional hurts she experienced at the hands of her parents and her husband caused a deterioration in her personal life. Only through months of using a meditative technique by which she allowed Jesus to be present in her mind as she relived hurtful situations, was Stapleton able to forgive and to receive an inner healing. Learning from her own inner healing, Stapleton began to pray with others and lecture and write about the process. She has recently established Holavita, a thirty-acre ranch outside Dallas, where she conducts religious retreats for inner healing.

Stapleton (1976, 1977) has presented numerous cases to illustrate the experience of inner healing. The following story of Mrs. X represents but one of them, demonstrating what Stapleton (1976, pp. 41–57) refers to as a "healing of memories." Mrs. X had nightmares, often causing her to scream in her sleep, for nearly thirty-six years. She connected her fears to a burgler breaking into their house when she was four and his being discovered hiding under her bed. Since that time she had been afraid to be alone in a room at night. Stapleton urged Mrs. X to recreate the childhood scene in her imagination. She instructed her to see Jesus coming into the room, taking hold of her hand. Mrs. X responded, "I do feel his love. I feel his warmth." The process of imagining continued with Mrs. X and Stapleton in dialogue, until Mrs. X exclaimed:

Jesus told me to go wake my mother and tell her to set the table with the best crystal and china and to fix a feast because we had an honored guest. So I saw myself get up and wake mother up, and I saw the whole table loaded with all of the wonderful food. Then Jesus walked in. Do you know where he placed that burgler? At the head of the table, as the honored guest. He loves him as much as, if not more than, any of us. (Stapleton 1976, p. 52)

Mrs. X was able to forgive the burgler, which freed her from both the fears and the nightmares.

Not all charismatics are equally open to Stapleton and others who emphasize techniques for inner healing. Most support seems to come from neo-Pentecostal Catholic and Episcopalian priests who, because their denominations practice sacramental confession, have seen how people may be oppressed by emotional hurts and strains. Scanlan (1974), a Catholic priest, has written specifically about the Catholic practice of confession and its relation to inner healing, but he also emphasizes that "all are called to be ministers of reconciliation." Just as any believer may pray for another's physical healing, so too may believers pray for healing of the emotions, the psyche, or the spirit, as needed.

Those who advocate inner healing tend to consider it more important than physical healing, the accomplishment of which may come automatically with inner healing. There exist abundant examples of healings such as the restoration of sight to a person who forgives a parent or the healing of arthritis that follows a marital reconciliation. Reconciliation with others and liberation from anger, hostility, and fear often appear to be the first step to physical recovery.

Deliverance from Evil Spirits.   Another response of charismatics to what the medical profession would term psychosomatic illness is the practice of deliverance. Charismatics believe that evil spirits are a real force in the world but are not as strong as the positive power of the Holy

Spirit. Most leaders caution against excessive preoccupation with Satan, asserting that for believers, the power of Christ far exceeds the ability of the Evil One. At the same time, however, they would not deny the workings of the devil, as depicted in William Peter Blatty's best-seller, *The Exorcist.* Deliverance and/or exorcism are practices through which Satan may be dealt with on some occasions.

Satan is believed to have the power to bind a person both spiritually and physically. Charismatics do not believe that a Spirit-filled believer can be *possessed* by Satan (a condition requiring the much rarer practice of exorcism), but believers are commonly oppressed and in need of deliverance. The devil may have gotten a foothold, believers assert, through preconversion activities of the believer, such as use of drugs or involvement in the occult. The cause is less important to the believer than the fact that the power of Satan appears to be at the root of the person's problem. Given the excessive powers historically attributed to the devil, charismatics are usually cautioned by leaders not to call hastily for deliverance prayer services.

Unlike healing, a practice to be shared by all believers to some degree, those who write on deliverance (and particularly exorcism) suggest caution before embarking on that ministry. Persons involved in the work of deliverance should have the special gift of being able to discern spirits (for example, not all illness requires deliverance from Satan) and to determine whether the prayer should be one for inner and/or physical healing or deliverance. Deliverance is likely to be left in the hands of those displaying a special gift with pastoral sanction (Scanlan and Cirner 1980; Basham 1972).

Don Basham, a neo-Pentecostal who was reluctant to believe in the reality of satanic forces, describes his story of developing a deliverance ministry in *Deliver Us From Evil* (1972). The following account shared by evangelist Maxwell Whyte (and similar to others that Basham himself later witnessed) moved Basham closer toward accepting the validity of a deliverance ministry. The man involved in the deliverance suffered from chronic asthma, was a heavy smoker, and for years had been a semi-invalid. Prayers for healing did not seem to change the situation. One day another minister suggested to Whyte that the man's problem might be caused by a demon:

We took the man into the church basement having read that demons sometimes came out crying with a loud voice, but of course we knew no one who had ever heard one come out! We had been taught to use the blood of Jesus in the presence of the destroyer, so we started to sing some choruses about the Blood. Then we attacked! "In the name of Jesus come out!" . . . This was kept up, and as we pressed the battle hard the demons of asthma and smoking started to cough out, to vomit out. After one hour and twenty minutes we had seen a huge pile of handkerchiefs soaked with sputum, but he was healed! He stood up and breathed down to the bottom of his lungs and exclaimed, "Praise God, I am healed! I can breathe for the first time in my life!" . . . The brother is still healed today, and no longer needs to smoke for Jesus set him free. (Basham 1972, p. 108)

Charismatic Beliefs Regarding Spiritual Healing: Minimizing Dissonance

Charismatics believe that illness is not caused by God, that God wishes to heal men and women just as Jesus was able to heal, and that Spirit-filled Christians have an ability to tap the healing power of God. Most would agree with these basic points, but there are conflicting opinions as to why some persons are not healed. The explanations range from the failings of the afflicted person to a simple assertion that Christians are "wounded healers" who for some reason are not always able to tap the healing power of God. Both of these positions merit some consideration.

Blaming the Victim.   Because God wants men and women to live in health, some believe that sickness must be due to a lack of faith, particularly in failing to proclaim the healing. Summarized in clichés like "confess it and possess it," or "name it and claim it," the profession of health is considered more important than physical symptoms of illness. Refusal to proclaim the healing blocks God's power to heal. One charismatic teacher states unequivocally:

I am fully convinced—I would die saying it is so—that it is the plan of Our Father God, in His great love and in His great mercy, that no believer should ever be sick; that every believer should live his full lifespan down here on this earth; and that every believer should finally just fall asleep in Jesus. (Hagin 1979, p.21)

To receive a healing, one only needs to believe that the healing has been received. What happens if the symptoms remain in spite of prayers for a cure? Some hold that a believer should never say "I know I will receive a healing," but rather, "I *am* healed"—regardless of physical symptoms (Hagin 1979, p. 50).

Such assertions, when carried to the extreme, can have pathetic results. At a healing service where failures to heal are blamed on the afflicted, a young deaf boy was led to the altar by his mother. After being prayed over, the healer asked him through his mother whether he could hear. He nodded negatively. The scene was repeated about four times during the duration of the service, after which time the healer said, "Mother, take him home and work on him; his lack of faith is blocking the Spirit."

Noncharismatic Christians are often severely critical of the practice of blaming the victim. Critics will ask, "What do I tell the sick person who watches such scenes on television and listens to such teachings? Added to the illness is a tremendous guilt." Frequently such comments come from ministers who may have seen the negative effects of the teaching but are not experienced with the positive results of divine healing.

What is less frequently known is that even the person espousing a blame-the-victim ideology may have suffered the loss of a loved one who was not healed. Ernest Angley (1974, p. 19) writes—four years after his own wife died of cancer—that it was not God's will that a person die of a horrible disease: "God promised them healing, if they would have accepted and clung to the golden promises of God, they could have been delivered. God has obligated (sic) Himself to deliver His people and healing is the children's bread." He appears to minimize the dissonance between his theology and his wife's death by (1) noting God told him to surrender his wife, Angel, a week before she died; (2) stressing that Angel wanted to be with the Lord, knowing her work on earth was finished; and (3) claiming a heavenly vision after Angel's death in which God said, "It was my divine will to have taken Angel. By taking her when I did, she will bring more people into my kingdom than if I had left her with you" (Angley n.d.). While Angley claims that "I believe with all my heart that by prayer I could have kept her here" (Angley 1977, p. 131), to have done so would have been a rebellion against God's plan (Angley 1977, pp. 75, 131).

Rather than allow his wife's death to stifle his healing ministry, Angley used it as a benchmark for the third and final phase of his life. The first phase was his early life and salvation as a young man; the second phase was his ministry with his wife, coming to Akron and establishing Grace Cathedral; the third phase is an increase in evangelistic efforts and the beginning of the television industry. As Angley (1977, p. 155) recounts:

I could have allowed Angel's death to destroy this work; however, I realized He took her, not because He did not love me, but because He loved us both so much and He was able to have His way. I looked at the ministers who had not given all to the Lord and still had their wives; but the Lord reminded me that He could have taken them, too; but what blessing would it have been? Souls would not have been brought into the kingdom because of it. 'But I took Angel and will bring many into the kingdom,' saith the Lord.

Wounded Healers in a Wounded World. The position of those who firmly believe in healing but are unwilling to blame the victim's lack of faith includes a candid recognition that many, but not all, are healed. In the words of one healer who himself had been cured of cancer: "I wish all were healed that we pray for. I am sure that more will be when we fully yield to the Holy Spirit to allow God's love to flow more freely among us. As long as many are being healed and God's Word seems to endorse praying for the sick, we shall continue by God's help to minister to the needs of those who come" (Sumrall 1973, p. 107). In other words, those who are ministers of healing are themselves wounded and are imperfect ages of healing. Rather than simply transferring blame from the afflicted to themselves, however, they own that they cannot explain why some are not healed (MacNutt 1977; Dorpat 1980). The famous healer, Kathryn Kuhlman, told a newspaper reporter, "You asked me why everyone is not healed. I don't know. If you think you have questions, I have more" (Jorstad 1973, p. 104).

Numerous books and articles have been written to teach and encourage healing through prayer (e.g., Sanford 1947; Cliffe 1951; Neal 1958; MacNutt 1974). In addition to testimony, such works provide basic guidelines to facilitate prayer.[7] Most would assert—and limited research supports this belief—that the prayer for healing always produces *some* results. A study of Roman Catholic prayer meetings in Portland, Oregon, for example, found that of the 123 persons questioned, 91 percent believed they had experienced a physical healing in response to prayer, while 99 percent reported an inner or spiritual healing. These statistics do not prove that in a single prayer meeting 91 percent of those seeking help were healed, but it does suggest that believers claim success.[8] Even when physical healing does not occur, prayer apparently produces inner or emotional strength.

Bartow (1981, p. 38–42), a charismatic Presbyterian minister, provides an excellent but brief summary of a position in healing that would be in accord with most of the writings reviewed by the author.

Fourteen Tenets

by Pastor Don Bartow

There are basic tenets of the healing ministry which serve as a foundation of our efforts.

The following fourteen will give you a better understanding of the approach and aims of spiritual healing.

I ALL OF GOD

We believe that all healing is of God.

II DESIRES WHOLENESS

We believe that God desires for us wholeness and health. Jesus spent much of His time here on earth healing the sick and He came to always do the Father's will.

III MANY AGENCIES

We believe that God uses many agencies for healing. These include medicine, surgery, psychiatry, physician, prayer, confession, etc.

IV HUMAN CHANNELS

We believe that God works almost invariably through human channels to do His healing. We are to be willing channels to do His Will.

V NOT MAGIC

We believe that Spiritual Healing is not magic, hocus-pocus or sleight-of-hand. It is simply taking God at His word. In faith, believing, you make intercession for healing and thank Him for what is already taking place.

VI WITHIN THE CHURCH

We believe that God's healing power operates within the Church which is the Body of Christ here on earth, but it is not limited to His Church.

VII RIGHTEOUSNESS-SINS

We believe that physical health does not necessarily indicate righteousness nor does illness necessarily indicate specific sins in a person's life.

VIII PROMOTE HEALTH

We believe that Christian witness and fellowship promote health and in many ways prevent illness by providing purposeful living and wholesome companionship. This results in proper stewardship of strength and health.

IX CHRIST'S MINISTRY

We believe that healing was an important part of Christ's ministry here on earth and is intended to be part of His disciples' work in every generation.

X NO FAILURES

We believe that there are no failures in Spiritual Healing. No one can be brought into the presence of the healing Christ without being changed spiritually, emotionally, or physically. In some cases they are changed in all three areas.

XI CHRIST LIVES

We believe that Jesus Christ lives today in His risen power. He is the same today as yesterday and will be the same forever and ever.

XII SALVATION

We believe that the word *salvation* means not only deliverance from sin and death, but also deliverance from physical and mental evils.

XIII REVIVAL

We believe that the revival of Spiritual Healing in the Church today may be the means of the greatest advance in Christianity in this century.

XIV BELIEVE

We believe that what we believe is vital for both our present and our future.

In conclusion I present the question to you. *What do you believe?*

Another variant of the theme that acknowledges divine healing but also recognizes that not all of the sick are healed may be terms "charismatic-dispensationalism." Dispensationalism teaches that divine healing existed in biblical times, but is no longer a gift to be experienced today. Charismatic dispensationalists would assert that God can and does miraculously heal in this age as he did in biblical times. However, healing involving the direct intervention of God is an irregular occurrence depending on His sovereign will and cannot be understood by the finite mind. Thus healings are to be prayed for and expected—and at times they will occur. While those who "blame the victim" and even many "wounded healers" may pray with charismatic dispensationalists "Thy will be done," the former groups assume it is always God's will to heal while the latter are less likely to presume to know God's will in specific cases and despite prayer, to expect healing to be a regular course of events.

Spiritual Healing and Social Organization

Pentecostals, joined by thousands of neo-Pentecostals, are no longer on the fringes of the larger social world. The conflicts between conventional medicine and faith healing, as well as the barriers between secular and religious faith, have given rise to attempts to merge the best of both worlds. The result may be quasi-secular organizations that make some use of spiritual healing. Three such organizations are Oral Roberts' City of Faith, David Wilkerson's Teen Challenge Program, and Richard Dobbins's Emerge Ministries.

"Science and Prayer: Keys to the City of Faith"[9]. The name of Oral Roberts has been linked with spiritual healing for over three decades. Roberts began with a traveling tent ministry, then brought his church to television and radio, and now operates a university and a medical school, with a hospital under construction. In 1978 Oral Roberts became the first man in this century to found his own medical school and has recently opened his own health care center (Wenmeyer 1981; *Newsweek* 1981). Despite some opposition from Tulsa's medical community (Tulsa already has five private hospitals with a 70 percent occupancy rate and does not want additional competition), the charismatic community has responded to the project. Oral Roberts the tent healer has become a university president, but he has not renounced his belief in divine healing.

Both the medical school and the health care center seek to integrate spiritual with modern medicine. According to Dr. Carl Hamilton, who oversees the development of the City of Faith, this medical complex represents "the culmination of President Roberts's call into the healing ministry. The union of prayer and medicine is the climax, the logical apex, of what he has spent his entire life doing." The City of Faith is to differ from traditional hospitals in its application of prayer and medical science for holistic health care. The medical school faculty and hospital staff members are selected on the basis of academic credentials and their ability to share in the mission and ministry of the City of Faith.

Roberts represents an interesting example of the institutionalization of personal charisma. The gift of healing he demonstrated for believers since the mid-1940s led to his vision of a medical institution which heals the sick through science and prayer. Reportedly, when Roberts is asked who will succeed him, his response is the "City of Faith."

Teen Challenge: A Pentecostal Venture into Treating Drug Addiction. Teen Challenge began with the work of Assemblies of God minister David Wilkerson and his ministry with drug addicts in Brooklyn over twenty years ago (Wilkerson 1963). It has grown into an international program (see Gruner 1979a for a cross-cultural study), with centers in 136 cities. Eighty-three Teen Challenge Ministries are found in sixty-four American cities in thirty different states. Teen Challenge seeks to help addicts, not through social service techniques, but through Christian conversion. In principle, Wilkerson is not opposed to social services, psychiatry, or modern medicine, but Teen Challenge operates exclusively with a nonprofessional Pentecostal staff.

Wilkerson (1963) espouses the Pentecostal position that drug addiction, like other social aberrations including alcoholism, prostitution, and homosexuality, is a spiritual rather than psychological or social problem. As such, it requires spiritual solutions involving repentance and conversion to Christ. The three-phase program includes "Induction" (conversion, instilling discipline, building character), "Training" (developing intellectual and emotional maturity in part through work training), and "Reentry" (moving back into a normal church and community life) (Gruner 1979, pp. 191–211). The program centers on the belief that a spiritual rebirth or conversion is essential for a total cure from the addiction and the eventual reentry into a normal life.

Most of the outside studies of Teen Challenge have noted that, while having a "respectable rate of success" (Langrod, Joseph, and Colgan 1972), the success of the program is contingent on its being voluntary (Desmond and Maddox 1980). Its voluntary nature undoubtedly accounts for the low recidivism rates (24 percent) among Teen Challenge rehabilitants (Hess 1975). While such religious programs are helpful to some drug users, they are not voluntarily embraced by the majority. Of those who enter the program, only a minority complete it. A seven-year longitudinal study of New York City's Teen Challenge found that only 18 percent of the admissions completed the program (Langrod, Alksne, and Gomez, 1981)—although this is still a favorable rate when compared with secular programs. Those teens, however, who report a religious conversion (in contrast to those who simply "follow the rules" in order to remain in the program) are rehabilitated through Teen Challenge. The religious experience seemingly central to achieving abstinence in Teen Challenge cannot be programmed, although a climate favorable to its experience may be created. Attempting to package this program for general consumption would inevitably mean a loss of the charisma that is presently an integral part of Teen Challenge.

Emerge Ministries and Counseling Center[10]. Emerge Ministries in Akron, Ohio, is one of a growing number of attempts to combine professional counseling with prayer in dealing with the treatment of emotional problems. Unlike Teen Challenge which does not employ professionals in the treatment of their patients, believing Jesus alone will ultimately cure the addiction, Emerge holds that while God is the ultimate healer of emotions, He can use some professional assistance. Just as prayer for healing of the body and modern medicine are complementary, healing of the emotions and contemporary psychology can be wedded. A case presented in lecture by the founder Richard Dobbins may illustrate the process.

A Christian, Spirit-filled man came to Dobbins seeking help. Despite his conversion and charismatic experiences, he still physically abused his wife. Through counseling, Dobbins and the patient came to the recognition that the man had deep resentments toward his mother. She had retaliated against her husband's infidelity by having an affair of her own, ultimately causing a divorce when this man was a teenager. While he could forgive his father's action, he still held his mother responsible for all the heartache caused him by the divorce. This hostility was being transferred to his wife. Early in counseling the man ceased abusing his wife and came to deal intellectually with his problem, but he saw that deep resentment and hurt were still a part of his life. Dobbins urged him to "pray through the situation." This practice involves praying about a situation until the burden lifts and then using time after prayer to seek new meaning in the situation through meditation. With regular prayer the man could finally announce to Dobbins, "I am healed; I have forgiven my mother."

Dobbins, himself an Assemblies of God minister and a Ph.D. in counseling psychology, began Emerge through the church he pastored for twenty-five years. In the mid-1970s, Dobbins left his congregation to another minister in order to devote full time to Emerge. His vision for Emerge is of "a learning resource center for Christian growth and development" through training, treatment, and research. The teaching is accomplished through workshops and institutes, a radio program, cassette teaching tapes, and pastoral psychology and counseling training offered in conjunction with Ashland Theological Seminary. Treatment includes counseling assistance by a staff of professional counselors, with psychiatric consultation, testing, and evaluation available. Emerge also sponsors ongoing research projects conducted in conjunction with af-filiate churches, which contribute to Emerge financially and are also willing to provide research subjects on topics related to Christianity and mental health. For example, a recent study considered the needs of church members over sixty years of age, and another project will examine the needs of single people in the church. The research contributes to both the teaching and the treatment functions of the ministry.

Can Charisma Be Successfully Institutionalized?

Attempts to apply spiritual healing within an organizational framework support Weber's observations that charisma is always in danger of losing its essence through routinization. Institutions that promote spiritual heal-ing exist within a secular, rationalistic culture that resists their approach. To the degree that such institutions depend on the larger culture, they run the risk of losing their charismatic basis.

Emerge Ministries is perhaps most prone to losing its charismatic foundations, if in fact this has not already occurred. Teen Challenge, which remains free of professional and secular constraints and operates as a religious organization, is least susceptible to the process. The City of Faith only recently opened its doors (*Newsweek* 1981), so its direction is still uncertain. A spiritual event, such as a divine message or vision communicated to Roberts, might spark enthusiasm for the project, but such events are unlikely to be part of its daily operation. In general, past experiences show that the initial charismatic impulse that moves people to action gives way to religious organization and then to secular routiniza-tion. St. Vincent de Paul, for example, cared for the sick and the poor, but his mission led to religious organizations, including hospitals bearing his name, that cannot sustain his charisma. Many institutions bearing de Paul's name today may be religious in outward appearance but intrinsi-cally no different from other secular hospitals or childrens' homes. Teen Challenge has resisted those critics who recommend a professional staff and appears to remain successful in maintaining its religious ideology and practice. Were it to be dependent on federal funds or on accrediting agencies, its ability to maintain this position would be greatly decreased. The City of Faith, still a vision rather than a complete accomplishment, promises to emphasize the spiritual and to provide a revolutionary ap-proach to medical care. There is little reason to suppose that it will not go the same route as other Christian hospitals that have experienced the effects of secularization.

The difficulties in sustaining charisma became clear to the author in the course of her research on Emerge Ministries. Richard Dobbins is a highly gifted and charismatic man who has an ability to learn from his life experiences. At the time of his ordination and early ministry, Assemblies of God was hostile to secular education and psychology, but it afforded Dobbins an opportunity to develop a deeply spiritual perspective. Without greatly diminishing his own spiritual outlook on life, Dobbins has been able to integrate psychological counseling and evangelistic spirituality. There is, however, no known procedure by which Dobbins (or anyone else) can impart his charisma to the staff he hires. Even more problematic than a transfer of personal charisma is the development of a bureaucratic organization at odds with the nurture and practice of spiritual gifts. The latest counseling techniques, case history files, and a staff lacking Dobbins's charismatic power are likely to replace faith healing, revelation, and perhaps even prayer in the treatment of patients.

While such religious organizations do an admirable job of meeting human needs (as do their secular counterparts), the realities of unpaid bills and accrediting agencies' secular standards make bureaucratic organization inevitable—and the maintenance of charismatic gifts an impossibility.

Notes

1. Kelsey (1973, p. 54) reports that out of the 3,779 verses in the four Gospels, 727 "relate specifically to the healing of physical and mental illness and the resurrection of the dead." Thirty-one additional general references are made to miracles that include healing.

2. Protestants inherited this position from Catholics and the Reformation did little to alter it. Even many fundamentalist Christians who claim the Bible as the Word of God are unwilling to accept the principle of contemporary healing. They reiterate the position of the Protestant reformer John Calvin who stated: "The gift of healing disappeared with the other miraculous powers which the Lord was pleased to give for a time, that it might render the new preaching of the gospel for ever wonderful. Therefore, even were we to grant that anointing was a sacrament of those powers which were then ministered by the hands of the apostles, it pertains not to us, to whom no such powers have been committed" (cited in Kelsey 1973, p. 23). This position has come to be known in contemporary evangelical circles as "dispensationalism," a theology used to refute charismatic healings and other gifts of miracles accepted by charismatic Christians.

3. This twentieth-century shift in theology may be seen in the history of the Catholic sacrament of the sick (formerly, extreme unction). Originally developed as a rite to pray for healing, by the seventh century the sacrament became a preparation for death. Only with Vatican II and changes in the rite which occurred since 1970 has the sacrament of the sick been restored as a rite of healing.

4. For examples of testimonials of healing by spiritual healers, see Kuhlman (1962) and Angley (1975); by a medical doctor, see Casdorph (1976); by a family experiencing the cure of the husband's terminal cancer, see Lawson (1977). Testimonials are also regularly found in religious magazines, particularly in *Guideposts* and *Voice*.

5. The terms "falling under the power of the Spirit," "resting in the Spirit," and being "slain in the Spirit" are interchangeable in the literature. As MacNutt (1977, p. 18) defines it: "it is the power of the Spirit so filling a person with a heightened inner awareness that the body's energy fades away until it cannot stand." For other discussions see Coughlin (1977); Kelsey (1978); Maloney (1977); Montague (1977); and Pelletier (1977).

6. Even those who engage in the healing ministry are critical of many techniques used on the broadcast media. One Presbyterian minister, who regularly holds healing services and has attempted to share with others the importance of such services in mainline denominations, reported to the author that, "Only television ministers claim healings 100 percent of the time. The rest of us must minister to those who are not healed, assuring them of God's love and our inability to comprehend his ways. Television ministers need not deal with such 'failures.'"

7. This is in decided contrast, however, to Pattison's (1974) limited psychoanalytic study of forty-three individuals claiming to have been healed. He concludes, "only a very few members of the fundamentalist subculture actually engage in these rituals," and notes that those who received healings saw not the healing but the conversion experience as a life-changing event. While most charismatics would concur that physical healing is not as important as religious conversion, there is reason to question Pattison's assertion that few seek healings.

8. In this study McCartney reported a great variety of physical symptoms and conditions claimed to have been healed. He categorizes them as follows: musculoskeletal problems, 25 percent; neurological, 15 percent; respiratory, 10 percent; cardiovascular, 7 percent; gastrointestinal, 6 percent; endocrine, 5 percent; gynecological, 4 percent; dermatological, 3 percent; and miscellaneous unclassifiable complaints, 5 percent.

9. The section title is taken from Miller's (1979) article on the City of Faith.

10. Information and observations about Emerge Ministries came from the author's interviews with the founder, Richard Dobbins, and the vice-president, Edward Decker, as well as from public addresses by both men in Akron, Ohio, conversations with participants in the program, and the author's own experience of seeking counseling at the Center.

CHAPTER 6

Unless the Lord Builds a House: Structural and Organizational Features

> Religious experience is almost impossible without some
> form of group support. . . . Religious institutions are
> social settings for the encouragement of spiritual life.
> When they seem no longer capable of fulfilling their
> function for significant numbers of people then
> revolutionary or reformist action to improve the
> situation also takes group form. (Bellah 1970)

The phenomenal growth of the charismatic movement from its earliest Azusa Street days in the first decade of this century has been heavily dependent upon religious experience—or, in the terminology of the believer, upon the movement of the Holy Spirit in a person's heart. Yet such experiences can only be sustained with the support and encouragement of other believers. Charismatic ideology teaches that the experience of the gifts of the Holy Spirit (with the possible exception of glossolalia, which is a personal prayer gift) should serve to build the church on earth, rather than simply to satisfy personal needs.

Although many early Pentecostals would have preferred that this church not take on organizational form, excesses and abuses in the manifestation of the gifts, the vulnerability of believers to charlatans, and the need to be recognized by outsiders as a legitimate religion made organizing imperative. Like scores of religious groups before them, Pentecostals needed to create an institutional base for their faith without losing the emphasis on experiencing God that was fundamental to that faith.[1] This is the dilemma that faces fourth generation Pentecostals and first generation neo-Pentecostals alike.

There is a dialectical relationship between religious structure and religious experience. Throughout history we may observe structural reforms that failed to meet the needs of significant numbers of people. In the history of Pentecostalism John Wesley's Methodism provides one ready example. Intended originally to renew the Church of England, this "religion of the heart" began to lose its purity for many believers as it grew into a separate denomination. Those disaffected believers started the Holiness movement. Their quest for a direct experience of God anticipated the Pentecostal movement.[2] Thus new groups meet the needs of those disenchanted with existing religious structures and in time develop structures of their own.

Cameron (1966) observes that a group of people becomes a social movement when its members consciously recognize their dissatisfaction, believe in their ability to reshape their lives, and live under conditions "in which the banding together to change something is both possible and plausibly effective." Charismatic leaders believe there is a "spiritual hunger" even among many churchgoing Americans. They feel they have found in the Bible the nourishment that mainline churches have not been able to provide. Given the religious freedom in America, they have been able to join together effectively into a number of organized and quasi-organized groups to spread their message.

Classical Pentecostal Structures

Synan (1974) has divided the classical Pentecostal denominations into three major categories. The first and the oldest consists of the fifteen denominations that represent the "holiness-pentecostal" tradition.[3] Two of the largest Pentecostal denominations, the Church of God (Cleveland, Tennessee) and the black Church of God in Christ are representative of this tradition. The second group of denominations is often referred to as "baptistic-pentecostal bodies" (not to be confused with the Baptist denomination). Typical of the group is the largest of its nine denominations, the Assemblies of God. Synan (1974, pp. 9–10) observes that the Assemblies of God were organized in 1914 "to serve pentecostals who did not share a Wesleyan understanding of a crisis experience of sanctification." They share with "holiness-pentecostals" the doctrine that conversion is followed by the baptism in the Holy Spirit "with evidence of speaking in tongues," but the "baptistic-pentecostals" are more likely to see sanctification as a gradual process rather than as a "definite work of grace" subsequent to conversion. The third group, the five "unitarian-pentecostal" denominations, developed as a result of a doctrinal division in the Assemblies of God. Rather than adhering to a trinitarian theology that states there are three persons (Father, Son, and Holy Spirit) in one God, the "unitarian-pentecostals" emphasize the oneness of God, with the Father, Son, and Holy Spirit being different manifestations of God. The United Pentecostal Church, International, is the largest single denomination in this category.

Synan's typology is accurate from a theological perspective, but from a sociological perspective most "baptistic-pentecostal" and "unitarian-pentecostal" bodies may be collapsed into a single category. Churches of both groups tend to have a congregational form of government, with the denomination representing a relatively loose federation of churches and ministries. The "holiness-pentecostals," on the other hand, have a highly centralized government. In discussing the structure of classical Pentecostalism, therefore, we will use the Church of God as an example of the "holiness-pentecostal" groups that maintain a centralized government, as opposed to the congregationally governed "baptistic-pentecostals" and "unitarian-pentecostals," exemplified here by the Assemblies of God.[4]

Congregational Government: The Assemblies of God. According to William Menzies's (1971) history of the Assemblies of God, many members of existing churches at the beginning of this century were expelled because of their Pentecostal experiences. At the same time, the disrepute of Pentecostal churches made it necessary for their clergy to function as ministers in a recognized denomination. The need for organization became all the more pressing as personality conflicts at churches and camp meetings created divisive competition. These factors, along with the abuses of traveling confidence men and the doctrinal problems created by the "revelations" of would-be prophets, led to a call for a General Council in 1913. Some of those who urged organization insisted on adherence to Scripture for guiding principles; others feared any organization above the local level.

Charles Parham, the Holiness evangelist considered to be a father of the Pentecostal movement, was among those who feared a central organization. "Let us cease wasting time at this juncture in systematizing or organizing the work of God," he argued, "Let each minister go forward doing his work, and leaving local assemblies under local elders . . ." (Menzies, 1971, p. 94). A healthy fear of what religious organization had done to a free movement of the Holy Spirit in other churches, coupled with a social need for structure, eventually led to the formation of the Assemblies of God.

The participants in the First General Council held in 1914 agreed not to organize a new sect or denomination but to hold an annual convention "to advise scriptural methods of unity and to attend to business for God." Menzies (1971, p. 103) observes that they thought they were creating an annual convention supervised by a small advisory committee. What in fact developed was a foundation upon which the largest Pentecostal denomination was built.

Fear of over organizing was also reflected in a fear of "creedalism" and a consequent reluctance to deal with doctrinal matters. Nevertheless, by the time of the Third General Council in October, 1915, doctrine had to be considered. What came to be referred to as the "New Issue," a position which moved away from traditional Christian trinitarian doctrine to a unitarian belief about the Godhead, led to a formulation of fundamental beliefs. The "New Issue" cost the Assemblies of God about one quarter of its membership at this time and led to the establishment of the unitarian United Pentecostal Church. The resolution, however, also provided the Assemblies of God with a "Statement of Fundamental Truths" and a base upon which to build a more complex organizational structure later.

From 1916 to 1941 the Assemblies of God enjoyed a period of growth and relative tranquillity. Isolated from evangelical Christians because of doctrinal positions on the baptism of the Holy Spirit and its relation to glossolalia and from other Pentecostal groups due to sectarian conflicts, the Assemblies of God quietly developed at the grass roots level without the opportunity for significant cooperation with other denominations. By the early 1940s it was apparent to some that Pentecostalism was here to stay. The Assemblies of God, along with other Pentecostal groups, were invited to join the National Association of Evangelicals (NAE) in 1942. Through cooperation with other Pentecostal bodies that were also members of NAE, the Pentecostal Fellowship of North America (PFNA) was formed in 1948. As part of a confederation of relatively autonomous local assemblies, the Assemblies of God were now recognized by NAE as a force in Christendom and, as the largest Pentecostal denomination, were also important to the success of PFNA.

Cooperation with other evangelical and Pentecostal Christians (which continues today) was only one of the organizational efforts by the Assemblies of God. They also developed Bible schools, Christian day schools, and the liberal arts Evangel College. Extensive missionary outreach, operation of a publishing house, retreat camps, and other such services soon required an expanded structure (Menzies 1971).

At the same time, however, the Assemblies of God continue to guard jealously the sovereignty of the local churches. As recently as the Thirty-Eighth General Council, held in 1979, discussions of church sovereignty resulted in the clarification and strengthening of local autonomy (Minutes 1979, p. 21). Although subordinate to the General Council in matters of doctrine and conduct, local assemblies reaffirmed their right to self-government.

The officers of the General Council are chosen by two thirds of the voting constituency, which includes ordained ministers and delegates. The elected officers are the general superintendent (elected for a four-year term), the assistant general superintendent, the general secretary, and the general treasurer (all elected for two-year terms). Two presbyteries, each with specific functions, serve to govern the Assemblies of God between the biannual council sessions. The General Presbytery has the responsibility of serving ''as the official policy making body when the General Council is not in session,'' while the Executive Presbytery, headed by the general superintendent plus twelve other members, serves to implement the policies put forth by the General Council and/or the General Presbytery. The Constitution and accompanying by-laws of the Assemblies of God thus guarantee local representation and self-determination in government.

The financing of headquarters can be used by an organization as an excuse to solidify a central government by requiring extensive financial commitments from member churches. But financing of the Assemblies of God headquarters appears to be in line with the commitment to local control. Each ordained minister is expected to contribute at least five dollars per month and assemblies at least twenty-four dollars per year, but both are strongly encouraged to give more when possible (Minutes 1979, p. 149). All churches are also expected to take offerings at regular intervals for the support of the missions, Christian education, radio and television, and other such ministries. Reliance on voluntary cooperation rather than strongly mandated financial support of central offices again allows local congregations much control.

In terms of both structure and finances, the Assemblies of God provide an example of effective congregational control and appear resolved to maintain their practices. As noted in the committee report on church sovereignty at the 1979 General Council: "Basic to the committee's considerations was the awareness of God's evident blessing upon our Fellowship since its inception. The committee believes that, to a considerable degree, the historical concept of local church sovereignty has contributed positively to the growth and development of the Fellowship" (Minutes 1979, p. 20).

Centralized Government: The Church of God. Like the Assemblies of God, the Holiness-Pentecostal Church of God (Cleveland, Tennessee) dates back to the early days of Pentecostal growth at the beginning of the century. It too has shared in a steady increase in membership both here and abroad, developing an organizational structure to meet the needs of both members and churches. Like the Assemblies of God it operates a publishing house and a liberal arts college (Lee College in Cleveland, Tennessee), as well as other educational and mission efforts that help to promote its growth. The two churches share most points of doctrine but differ in their history and subsequent organizational development.

The Church of God, founded in 1886 as an outgrowth of the Holiness revival, is the oldest Pentecostal denomination. First known as the Christian Union and then as the Holiness Church, its congregation peaked at about 130 members during its early years (after a Pentecostal-type revival) but declined to about twenty members in 1902. In 1907 it adopted the name Church of God, and membership climbed to nearly two thousand by 1911. The growth of the Church of God has been continuous (although it is about one third the size of the Assemblies of God), with 392,551 members reported during 1978.

Despite its growth since the onset of the Pentecostal movement, the Church of God has experienced schisms and dissent. A. J. Tomlinson, often considered the founder of the church, joined the Holiness Church in

1903 and was baptized in the Spirit in 1908, while praying with Azusa-Street convert C. B. Cashwell. Tomlinson was selected for the newly created office of general overseer in 1909, and the church prospered under his leadership. Tomlinson's impeachment in the 1920s for misappropriation of church funds caused a split in the church (although no actual membership decline was reported during this time, but only a slower growth rate). Tomlinson continued to lead a faction of the church, known as the Church of God, until 1943. (Tomlinson's Church of God continues to exist and reported a membership of 75,890 in 1978.)

Unlike the Assemblies of God, which have steadfastly avoided centralization, the Church of God sought a strong central government almost immediately. Due to excesses in the early Christian Union Church that led to "false teaching and fanaticism," early growth in pre-Tomlinson days first peaked and then waned. Conn (1977, p. 39) observes that during these days "there had been no distinguishable organization or government; even the manner of selecting a minister and admitting new members was informal to the point of being casual." After reorganization in 1902, with provisions for more organization and the eventual inauguration of Tomlinson as a strong general overseer, the stage was set for the development of a strong centralized church.

Tomlinson's impeachment brought about efforts to curb individual power but not the authority of the institution. The power of individual leaders was restricted by the 1926 church constitution, which limits elected church officials to two two-year terms of office. The overseers, both on national and local levels, are elected by the Ordained Ministers Council, as are most other key officers. The national governing body is the Supreme Council, comprised of the General Executive Committee (the general and assistant general overseers and three others) and the Council of Twelve (also elected). The elected boards (missions, education, publications, etc.) function under the Supreme Council, as do the elected state overseers and other regional officers.

From its earliest days the Church of God has been committed to a strong central government. Finances have been one of the means of retaining control. Tomlinson's 1920 plan to control funds and pay ministers through the central office was later abandoned, but the practice of tithing 10 percent of total church income to central headquarters and another 10 percent to regional headquarters has been an effective way to limit the strength of local churches. While this 20 percent tithe is gradually being reduced, the firm financial base of the central organization has enabled it to remain strong.

A recent attempt to further increase the strength of the central administration of the Church of God (Cleveland) has met with defeat. A proposal that Overseers be given the right to transfer local pastors was defeated at the 1980 General Assembly Meeting in Dallas, and some congregations are questioning the centralized church's ownership of local property. Judging from reports of the 1980 conference, including election results, increasing centralization has been at least temporarily halted.

Centralization versus Confederation.   If measured in terms of growth and outreach of services, both the Assemblies of God and the Church of God (Cleveland, Tennessee) represent strong and viable organizations. While the Assemblies of God remains committed to a loose congregationally based federation, the Church of God still favors a strong central government. Both systems work—and both have strengths as well as weaknesses.

The Church of God is in a better position to control its pastors and its member churches because of its central organization. As one disenchanted minister quipped to the author: "My church is rapidly becoming the Pentecostal version of the Roman Catholic Church, with the General Overseer functioning as pope!" Despite such disenchantment, its form of government has allowed the Church of God to deal effectively with aberrant ministers. However, the exercise of centralized authority tends to produce increasing resistance from local churches and pastors.[5] The Church of God may now be at the point of risking alienation of some ministers and congregations in order to further consolidate its power.

The ability to control the activities of pastors and churches through a highly centralized organization has had an impact on the relationship between the Church of God and the neo-Pentecostal movement. While the clergy from both the Church of God and the Assemblies of God has shared with other Pentecostals a certain skepticism about the authenticity of the neo-Pentecostal experience, individual members of the clergy of the Assemblies of God have been more free to bridge the distance between the two components of the movement.[6] Thomas Zimmerman, the highest ranking officer of the Assemblies of God, is often invited to speak at both charismatic and evangelical gatherings. Many persons from the Assemblies of God are now involved in the Full Gospel Businessmen's Group International, an important vehicle for spreading the Pentecostal gospel to non-Pentecostals. Local autonomy makes it possible for Roy Harthern, the former pastor of an Assemblies of God church in Orlando, Florida, to initiate the publication of *Charisma,* a nondenominational magazine "about Spirit-led living." On the other hand, representatives from the Church of God are less likely to venture outside their own denomination. It would appear that until the centralized church takes a stand on behalf of the neo-Pentecostals (which does not appear likely), those ministers from the Church of God who travel the ecumenical road do so at their own risk.

Neo-Pentecostalism in the Mainline Churches

The original Pentecostal vision of renewing the mainline churches has been passed on to the neo-Pentecostals, many of whom remain in traditional denominations to work for the spread of the charismatic movement. The Episcopal and Roman Catholic churches have proved particularly receptive to the movement by establishing organizational structures that allow for its growth. Paradoxically, neo-Pentecostal leaders within these denominations have encouraged strong denominational ties, as opposed to piecemeal integration of theologies and traditions. At the same time, however, they have promoted a spirit of unity and cooperation among different denominations. By examining the development of the charismatic movement in the Roman Catholic and Episcopal churches, we can better understand how other denominations are implementing similar structures to further the movement. It remains to be seen whether the movement realizes the Pentecostal objective of renewing established churches or withers away in other denominations, as many Pentecostals now predict.

The Roman Catholic Church and the Charismatic Renewal.   There is no doubt that the charismatic movement is firmly established within the Roman Catholic Church. Ralph Martin, an international leader of the Catholic charismatic movement, reported findings of a Gallup survey indicating that 10 percent of American Catholics had some contact with the charismatic renewal and 8 percent had attended a prayer meeting within the last month. "That would mean 5 million American Catholics have had some contact with the charismatic renewal and 4 million actually attending a meeting within the month they were surveyed" (Martin 1980, p. 18). The success of the movement within the Catholic

Church may be attributed to its centralized structure and to the approval that the renewal has been given by the church's hierarchy.

The Catholic Church, perhaps more than any other denomination, represents a highly bureaucratic and centralized structure. Only within the past fifteen years has the laity been encouraged to participate more actively in church affairs, but its power is minimal. The episcopacy establishes parishes, assigns pastors and priests, issues teachings, and ultimately has the authority in the church. As in the Church of God, centralization in the Catholic Church has both strengths and weaknesses. Centralization has actually been a blessing for the promotion of the charismatic movement. Regardless of how individual priests or parishioners feel about the charismatic movement, both the papacy and the American bishops have endorsed it. Those who oppose the movement thus may refuse to participate, but cannot actively work against the movement without challenging the church hierarchy.

The Catholic charismatic movement originated at Duquesne University in Pittsburgh and spread to Notre Dame University and Michigan State University in 1967. Under Dorothy and Kevin Ranaghan at Notre Dame and Ralph Martin and Steve Clark at the University of Michigan (Martin and Clark moved to Ann Arbor from East Lansing in late 1967), the Catholic charismatic movement found major leadership and direction. By 1969 it had become so prominent within the Catholic Church that the Committee on Doctrine of the National Committee of Catholic Bishops issued a statement, on November 14, 1969, urging openness to the development of the movement:

It is the conclusion of the Committee on Doctrine that the movement should at this point not be inhibited but allowed to develop. . . . It must be admitted that theologically the movement has legitimate reasons for existence. It has a strong biblical basis. It would be difficult to inhibit the work of the Spirit which manifested itself so abundantly in the early Church. (cited in Scanlan 1979, pp. 135–36)

By May, 1975, when the International Catholic Charismatic Congress was held in Rome, Pope Paul VI added his endorsement to that of the American bishops. Archbishop Jean Jadot (1978, p. 16), then the Vatican's apostolic delegate in the United States, observed, part of the reason the Catholic Church had relatively little difficulty in accepting the charismatic renewal is due to "her long experience with renewal movements.'' Jadot here refers to the many religious movements that are part of Catholic Church history, including the Monastic movement of the fourth century, the thirteenth-century Franciscan movement, and recent renewal endeavors such as the Cursillo and Marriage Encounter movements of the twentieth century. Such renewals, however, have been confined to subinstitutions (usually convents and monasteries) within the church. They do not become new sects, as has happened often within Protestant denominations. As long as their theology is compatible with that of the Catholic Church, and as long as they submit to the church's governing hierarchy, they are allowed to develop sectlike status *within* the Catholic Church. There is some evidence that the charismatic movement is following this pattern.

The acceptance of the charismatic movement can be credited in part to the strategy of its leaders. Rather than setting themselves above or apart from the church or challenging its clerical and hierarchical organization, they have reaffirmed their loyalty to the Catholic Church. Furthermore, they have done so during a rather turbulent time in the church's history. During the early 1960s, after Vatican II, many theologians, priests, and members of the laity used their newly found freedom to attack church policies, doctrine, and structure. Charismatic leaders have, for the most part, upheld traditional teachings and given support to the institutional church. As Father Michael Scanlan (1979, p. ix) recently noted (echoing the highest ranking charismatic Catholic leader, Belgium's Cardinal Suenens):

It is crucial to understand that the charismatic renewal is designed to disappear into a renewed church. It is also crucial to understand that the charismatic renewal does not purport to offer the church anything new; it contends only that God is calling attention to what was the center of the life of the Church for centuries but which has been overlooked or greatly undervalued in the modern church.

Ford (1976) distinguishes between two types or forms of Catholic neo-Pentecostal organization. The "paraecclesial structure" represented by the convenant communities (discussed in chapter 7) provides most of the formal direction for the movement. For example, the Word of God Community in Ann Arbor, Michigan, publishes a magazine *(New Co-venant),* operates a publishing company (Servant Books), and issues cassettes, tapes, and records to help spread its teachings and information on the movement. Working closely with the Word of God, the People of Praise Community of South Bend, Indiana, has helped to develop the Catholic Charismatic Renewal Service Committee (located in South Bend) and has promoted national charismatic conferences. Father Scanlan, a Franciscan priest and member of the Servants of God's Love Community in Steubenville, Ohio, has provided leadership for Catholic priests through an annual conference for priests attended by thousands over the years. As president of the College of Steubenville, Scanlan has also led a charismatic renewal at the college, which has consequently become the Catholic counterpart of the Assemblies of God's Evangel College or the Church of God's Lee College. The highly structured covenant communities are afforded both the manpower and the financial resources to initiate programs and services that will enable the spread of the charismatic gospel.[7]

The less structured and more flexible form of organization "is integrated into Catholic parish and theology" and is a less viable force in the renewal. Although it speaks through the magazine *Catholic Charismatic,* published by Paulist Press, it consists mainly of informal renewal groups within larger Catholic parishes rather than covenant communities. The 1979–80 *Directory of Catholic Charismatic Prayer Groups* lists nearly 3,000 prayer groups in the United States. Many of these are small, parish-based groups rather than covenant communities, with an average of fifteen to thirty persons attending. Once-large prayer groups often decrease in size, but there is a corresponding growth of smaller prayer groups. Ranaghan (1980, p. 18) observes that of the 2,800 American prayer groups listed in the 1979–80 *Prayer Group Directory,* nearly one half are new listings.

Based on the rise and fall of prayer groups and the sale of charismatic literature, Ranaghan raises the question "Has the Charismatic Renewal Peaked?" It appears that many Catholics may be going through the revolving door of experiencing the charismatic movement in prayer groups, but then later drop out. While thousands of Catholics continue to be baptized in the Spirit each year, "the number of known prayer groups and the size of known prayer groups shows little growth." The drop-off of old members seems to cancel out any increase derived from new members. Ranaghan (1980, p. 18) concludes, "If one looks at the Catholic charismatic renewal as a prayer meeting movement, then the charismatic renewal has not peaked, although it has come to a plateau."

The charismatic movement is not likely to survive solely through parish-based prayer groups because of the Catholic Church's policy of assigning and rotating priests in geographically determined parishes.[8] A priest who is a charismatic Catholic must also serve parishioners who are not inclined to the movement, and he may be replaced by a priest who is less sympathetic to the movement and less inclined to offer leadership. At the same time, strong lay leadership is viewed with suspicion by clergy and laity alike. Furthermore, because parish membership is determined by geographic boundaries, the charismatic Catholic may not have access to a viable prayer group without informally leaving his or her assigned parish.

It appears that covenant communities are a much more likely base for the continuance of the movement within the Catholic Church. Its membership is transparochial and voluntary, so it attracts those who desire involvement in the charismatic experience. There is some evidence, moreover, that as time goes on, these communities may become a new religious order within the Catholic Church. Orders such as the Dominicans, the Franciscans, and the Jesuits, to name a few, originally expressed desire for church renewal, and their members joined together for support in their work. In time, each became a sectlike religious group within the larger church. The covenant communities may well become a structured institution within the church. This does not appear to be their desire or present goal, but it is a path that has been traveled before.

Charismatic Renewal Within the Episcopal Church. Although Pentecostal influences began to reach mainline denominations during the 1950s, the movement did not attract nationwide attention until an Episcopal priest, Father Dennis Bennett, shared his charismatic experiences with his congregation. In 1960 both *Newsweek* (July 4) and *Time* (August 15) carried accounts of how Father Bennett had told his congregation about the Pentecostal renewal occurring at St. Mark's Episcopal Church in Van Nuys, California. As a result of the ensuing controversy over the renewal, Bennett accepted a supportive invitation from the bishop of Seattle and moved to a new assignment there.[9] With the support of his new bishop, Dennis Bennett became an important voice for the charismatic movement in the mainline denominations.

The Episcopal Church, like the Roman Catholic Church, illustrates the potential role of central authority in helping the spread of the charismatic movement. Once it had secured the support of the governing bishop, the movement was in a position to grow and develop with minimal opposition. Those bishops who allowed the renewal to occur in their Episcopal dioceses in effect provided a showcase for what Pentecostalism could do for a dying church. A recent report on Bennett's Seattle church explains: "Bennett found in his new congregation a willingness to accept the reality of the Baptism in the Holy Spirit. As a result, St. Luke's grew from a sanctified Sunday morning echo chamber (population: about 3) to a Seattle revival center where thousands upon thousands have found new life in the Holy Spirit" (Roberts 1980, pp. 23–24).

The Episcopal Church, like its Roman Catholic counterpart, had hit upon troubled times in the 1960s. Membership and contributions were declining, as they were in other mainstream churches. Given the troubled times, many Episcopal bishops were willing to take a wait and see attitude regarding the effectiveness of the charismatic movement.

The Episcopal Church, despite its strong episcopacy and doctrinal affinities with Roman Catholicism, differs from the Catholic Church in allowing the parish, rather than the covenant community, to be the source of leadership for the movement. Unless the church is a "mission," as was St. Luke's in Seattle, parishes are in a position to hire their own rectors, who, once called, are almost never removed from their positions. This frees the rector from having to curry the support of factions of his congregation, as may occur in churches with strong congregational government, and allows him to exert decisive leadership. Roman Catholic priests enjoy this same freedom, but they are transferred regularly by the bishop of the diocese. The pastor thus has the opportunity to lead a congregation from the beginnings of a charismatic experience to the maturity of integrating that experience into the parish structure.

The rector's freedom, however, is limited by a second structural feature of Episcopal government. Unlike most Catholics, Episcopalians may choose the parish they wish to join, rather than being assigned to one based on locale. Withdrawing from one church and joining another takes away financial support that can and does serve as a form of congregational check on the rector. It also allows members who may desire to worship in a charismatic congregation to join a renewed Episcopal parish. Both of these factors have served to assist the Episcopal Church in parish renewal.

In the Episcopalian parish, the rector appears to be the key figure in promoting the renewal.[10] In the Catholic Church, lay leadership has usually initiated the movement, but renewal in the Episcopal Church has tended to start with the clergy. The difference in leadership may be also observed at conferences within the two denominations: in Catholic-sponsored conferences clergy and laity share the speaker's platform; in Episcopal-sponsored conferences the clergy are often the only speakers. The importance of the rector has been shown in a recent church-sponsored survey. Asked why they became members of the church, Episcopalians most often cited the clergy (Schwab 1980).

The Episcopal Renewal Ministries (formerly, Episcopal Charismatic Fellowship) is the primary organization through which information on the renewal is disseminated to Episcopalians, and every effort is made to reach the clergy. A mailing of its monthly newsletter, *Acts 29,* reaches about 20,000 persons, including every priest and every bishop within the Episcopal Church. Ministries also makes tapes and teachings available for distribution and sponsors conferences and workshops throughout the country to promote neo-Pentecostalism.

The Charismatic Movement Within Other Denominations. It would appear that the charismatic movement, although best organized among the Catholics and Episcopalians, has a strong structural base among most other mainline Christian denominations as well. The most common structure is some form of service committee similar to the Catholic Charismatic Service Committee or the Episcopal Renewal Ministries. Lutherans, Presbyterians, and Orthodox Christians all have committees which publish newsletters or journals to disseminate renewal information. The threefold function of the Lutheran Charismatic Renewal Service (Christenson 1976, pp. 138–39) may hold for other such committees as well: to provide help and resources (conferences, tapes, literature) for those involved in the movement; secondly; to serve as a point-of-contact between church officials and the renewal; and to relate to those individuals who are outside the denominational structure and to represent their concerns to the church.

The move to establish service committees and to develop organizations that are denominationally oriented appears to flow from regional and national conferences. For example, the United Church of Christ, which has not yet formed an official service committee, held its third annual charismatic conference in 1980. Such quasi-organization is encouraged and assisted by more established groups of other denominations. Speakers from charismatic groups often attend conferences sponsored by other

denominations, and charismatic newsletters and magazines help to promote conferences regardless of the sponsoring denomination. Those who
have developed effective denominational organizations may encourage
others to form similar groups. Larry Christensen, a renewal leader among
American Lutherans, writes of how the Catholic leaders of the Word of
God Community urged him to help Lutheran charismatics get a clearer
grasp of their own identity to avoid defections to the classical Pentecostals or the Catholics. If that were to occur, one leader admonished, "the
distinctive contribution of the Lutherans would be lost." Christensen
expressed surprise at first that such advice would be coming from a
Catholic charismatic leader but then reflected:

I came to see, however, the wisdom of their words. This approach to
cooperation and unity among Christians was not "non-denominational,"
which so readily glosses over differences and reduces everything to the
lowest common denominator. Unity in this way tends to be shallow and
one-dimensional. Their approach was truly ecumenical, which sees each
tradition as having something special to contribute. (Christensen 1976, p.
10)

Some Reflections on the Interplay of Ideology and Structure

The Pentecostal movement stemmed from a Wesleyan theology open to
gradual sanctification and/or "works of grace" beyond salvation. The
strict deterministic stance of Calvinism was less amenable to doctrines of
"second blessings" or "Spirit baptism." No ideology long remains in a
pure form (if, indeed, it ever existed as such), and religious ideology is no
exception. Despite this fact and despite the zigzagging of certain ideological tenets across antithetical camps, dominant strains can be identified.

Dispensationalism and Pentecostalism are two ideological strains
stemming out of Wesleyan and Calvinist positions that are still important
to evangelical Christians (Woodbridge et al. 1979, p. 70). Dispensationalism arose from the predominantly reformed part of the evangelical mainstream while Pentecostalism came from the Methodist component. The belief that God once granted "dispensations" (allowing manifestations of the gifts of the Spirit, including "miracles" and
"tongues," as reported in the Bible) that have since been withdrawn is
opposed by the Pentecostal doctrine that gifts of the Holy Spirit are for all
time and for all believers. Denominations steeped in Calvinism seem

more likely to take a dispensationalist stand and to condemn the charismatic movement. This seems especially true of many Baptists, who, unlike some Calvinist-oriented believers who had begun to "demythologize" the miracles of the Bible, have remained evangelical and fundamentalist in ideology.

Those with a Wesleyan base, however, have less theological difficulties with the movement. This is why someone like Oral Roberts, the famous former Pentecostal healer, could join the Methodist Church in 1968 without abandoning his Pentecostal beliefs.[11] Moreover, large segments of other denominations, while Calvinist in origin, tended toward modernism in the fundamentalist-modernist controversy of the early twentieth century. With the liberal strain still existing in these denominations, the neo-Pentecostal movement enabled some to return to the more fundamentalist position on the Bible abandoned earlier.

Thus two groups of churches may be found among mainstream denominations that support (or at least do not oppose) the charismatic movement: those whose ideology has never been at odds with the basic Pentecostal belief that the Holy Spirit desires to work in "extraordinary ways," just as he did in the early church and those churches fragmented by the functionalist-modernist controversy that have tended toward liberalism. The churches that have remained solidly fundamentalist and dispensationalist in ideology have been less receptive to neo-Pentecostalism, just as they continue to oppose classical Pentecostalism. It is from this group that many of the independent neo-Pentecostal ministries have developed.

Independent Charismatic Ministries

Although we have been focusing on church structure and the rise of the charismatic movement, independent ministries have played a crucial role in the movement's rapid growth. Some of these are television ministries that deliberately avoid denominational ties. Others represent local independent churches that prefer not to align with any established denomination. Still other ministries are service oriented, such as former Mennonite Gerald Derstine's Christian Retreat Center[12] or Ruth Carter Stapleton's Holavita (Whole Life) Retreat. Leaders of these ministries seem to come from Protestant denominations that have refused to allow any charismatic ministries (such as healing or deliverance) to develop within its walls and from Pentecostal denominations in which leaders in the mold of Oral

Roberts have developed but attract more neo-Pentecostals than classical Pentecostal followers. Given the still strong insistence among some Pentecostals that neo-Pentecostals leave their mainline denominations for Pentecostal ones, some such leaders have found it more comfortable to establish their own nondenominational churches and ministries.

One of the most important independent ministries to spread the Pentecostal gospel is the Full Gospel Businessmen's Fellowship International, founded by Demos Shakarian nearly thirty years ago. It has furthered neo-Pentecostalism and also served as a bridge to classical Pentecostalism. Numerous independent ministers have gained prominence by speaking at FGBMFI national conferences or on the circuit of monthly speaker-meetings held by some 2,000 local chapters of the organization. Independent ministries have not only helped to spread the charismatic gospel but, as in the case of FGBMFI, have also played an important role in initiating the neo-Pentecostal stream of the movement.

Social Structure and the Charismatic Movement: Tentative Hypotheses

Some degree of structure or organization is basic to the spread of any social movement. Within the charismatic movement, both formal and informal organizations have developed to further its goals.

Without neo-Pentecostalism, classical Pentecostalism would be another religious denomination but not a viable social movement. By the end of World War II, the largest Pentecostal groups were well on their way to becoming established Protestant evangelical denominations (Wilson 1970, pp. 234–35). As classical Pentecostals experienced a routinization of their charisma and became established denominations, the revival fires of the early decades of this century that sparked the pentecostal development cooled. In part this was due to more rational and educated second and third generations of believers, who, in their attempt to make Pentecostalism acceptable, also extinguished the revival. One Pentecostal minister who is familiar with the development of neo-Pentecostalism reluctantly observed: "There are churches in my own denomination that are Pentecostal in name only. In these buildings Pentecost has been relegated to the realm of doctrine without any correspondent expectation of experience."

The fresh experiences of largely middle-class neo-Pentecostals, disseminated through religious and secular communications media, should help to revive classical Pentecostal beliefs. A greater awareness of Pentecostal experiences not unlike those reported by earlier generations may well be rekindling the dying Pentecostal fires.

The extent to which classical Pentecostalism is open to exchange with neo-Pentecostals appears to be contingent on both church structure and ideology. It appears that a highly centralized Pentecostal organization is more likely to oppose neo-Pentecostalism than a decentralized organization in which leaders are freer to participate in this new burst of Pentecostal enthusiasm.

It appears, then, that there is an inverse relationship between the degree of centralization and the role existing ideology plays in accepting or rejecting a charismatic revival; furthermore, there is an inverse relationship between the degree of centralization and the power of the denomination to promote acceptance (or rejection) of a charismatic revival. Individuals and independent ministries have attempted to circumvent both ideological and organizational obstacles to charismatic revival through the establishment of nondenominational organizations.

Neo-Pentecostalism, in both its denominational and independent ministerial forms, has been a force in rekindling the Pentecostal fires and allowing this early twentieth-century revival to continue as a viable force in the 1980s. In turn, the older classical Pentecostals, particularly those drawn into independent ministries within the last twenty-five years, have been an important guide enabling the newer believers to avoid some of the serious tactical errors of earlier Pentecostals. The interpenetration of the older classical stream with the newer stream of charismatic belief may be further demonstrated in the rise of intentional communities and home fellowships within the movement.

Notes

1. Pentecostal-Holiness church historian Vinson Synan observes: "For many years dismissed as the fanatic fringe of the fundamentalist movement, little interest was shown in the holiness-pentecostal churches by serious scholars beyond passing references to "holy rollers" as interesting relics of the nation's primitive frontier past. Perhaps there was a tendency on the part of traditional Protestantism to ignore these groups because they were an embarrassing reminder of what had been true of themselves a generation or two earlier" (Synan 1971, p. 7). It appears that this same process may be taking place in some segments of Pentecostalism today. Grateful for the respectability that middle-class and upper-middle-class Neo-Pentecostals have given to the movement, there is a persisting fear of "extremes" and "fanaticism" of newer recruits. Seventy-five years after the origins of the Pentecostal movement, some charismatic congregations differ very little from other evangelical congregations.

2. I am following Synan's thesis in tracing Pentecostalism back to Holiness roots. Messerano (1966), on the other hand, contends that Pentecostalism has broader origins than the Holiness movement, including the teachings of nineteenth-century evangelists D. L. Moody, R. A. Torrey, and A. B. Simpson. Moreover, Pentecostalism was rejected outright by most established Holiness groups at the time of its inception.

3. The following are lists of denominations included in Synan's (1974, pp. 11–12) typology, with updated membership reports from the "Statistical and Historical Section" of the 1980 *Yearbook of American and Canadian Churches* (Jacquet 1980, pp. 218–27). (Synan's typology is also given on page 108 of the *Yearbook* as a way of grouping Pentecostal denominations.)

Category I. Holiness-Pentecostal	Church	Membership	Year Reported
The Apostolic Faith	45	4,100	1978
The Church of God	2035	75,890	1978
The Church of God (Cleveland, Tenn.)	4847	392,551	1978
The Church of God in Christ	4500	425,000	1965

Church of God in Christ, International	1041	501,000	1971
Church of God of Prophecy	1791	65,801	1975
Church of God of the Mountain Assembly	105	3,125	1977
Congregational Holiness Church	147	4,859	1966
Full Gospel Church	n.a.	n.a.	n.a.
International Pentecostal Church of Christ	105	11,659	1977
The (Original) Church of God	70	20,000	1971
Pentecostal Fire-Baptized Holiness Church, Inc.	41	545	1969
Pentecostal Free-Will Baptist Church, Inc.	128	12,272	1978
Pentecostal Holiness Church, Inc.	2340	86,103	1977
United Holy Church of America	470	28,980	1960

Category II. Baptistic-Pentecostal

Assemblies of God	9410	1,293,394	1978
The Bible Church of Christ, Inc.	5	2,300	1979
Christian Church of North America, General Council	101	12,000	1979
Elim Fellowship	70	5,000	1973
Full Gospel Assemblies, International	105	2,800	1978
Independent Assemblies of God, International	136	n.a.	1962
International Church of the Foursquare Gospel	714	89,215	1963
Open Bible Standard Churches	280	30,000	1979
Pentecostal Church of God	1189	110,670	1977

Category III. Unitarian (Oneness)-Pentecostal

Apostolic Overcoming Holy Church of God	300	75,000	1976
Bible Way Church of Our Lord Jesus Christ, World Wide, Inc.	350	30,000	1970
Church of Our Lord Jesus Christ of the Apostolic Faith, Inc.	155	45,000	1954
Pentecostal Assemblies of the World	550	45,000	1960
United Pentecostal Church	2830	450,000	1979

"According to Dr. Synan, 'Holiness-Pentecostal' bodies are those that teach the three stages theory of Christian experience (i.e., conversion, sanctification, baptism of the Holy Spirit). 'Baptistic-Pentecostal' denominations are those that teach a two-stage theory (i.e., conversion and baptism of the Holy Spirit). 'Uniterian-Pentecostal' bodies deny the traditional concept of the Trinity and teach that Jesus Christ alone is God" (Jacquet 1980, p. 108).

4. The degree to which a church government is congregational or centralized can vary within as well as among denominations. For example, the United Pentecostal Church, International, reportedly views itself as a federation of ministers rather than churches, with the minister rather than the church having the vote. Despite the relative autonomy of the pastor in most United Pentecostal Churches, in some states (including Texas, Louisiana, and Mississippi) the denomination has been firmly established and has a stronger centralized government than in other regions.

5. It is one thing to legislate and another to implement policies. For example, while the Assemblies of God relaxed some of their "holiness" standards in the 1950s (e.g., regarding movies, mixed swimming, length of women's hair, etc.), the Church of God strongly reaffirmed such standards. It was apparent to me that although they are still very much a part of the church's doctrine of morals, such standards are not enforced, except in some isolated rural areas of the country. They are liberally "reinterpreted" in most urban areas. Although the church may have the power to enforce such standards, to do so would inevitably alienate some pastors and congregations.

6. David du Plessis, a Pentecostal evangelist to the mainline denominations for nearly twenty years, was recently reinstated as a minister of his Assemblies of God church. *Charisma* (1980) described the situation leading to his dismissal as follows: "Du Plessis was censored by many in the pentecostal movement for taking the message of the Baptism in the Holy Spirit to so-called liberal, ecumenical leaders of the World Council of Churches and to the Roman Catholic Church. In the early 1960s both groups were considered 'apostate' churches by many pentecostals. When du Plessis refused to stop his ecumenical activities, the Assemblies of God terminated his recognition as an ordained minister in 1962" (*Charisma* 1980, p. 19). Du Plessis's reinstatement is a recognition of how much relations have changed between the Assemblies of God and both the mainline Protestant denominations and the Catholic Church.

7. This assistance has not only been rendered nationally but also internationally. *New Covenant* (1978, pp. 11–13) reported that in 1976 Cardinal Leon Joseph Suenens of Brussels, Belgium, invited Steve Clark and Ralph Martin to work directly with him and his staff in fostering the growth of the international charismatic renewal. In September, 1976, Clark, Martin and his family, and ten other members of the Word of God Community moved from Ann Arbor, Michigan, to Belgium. Since then twenty others from the Word of God have moved to Brussels.

8. For an analysis of one formerly transparochial prayer group that appears to be moving toward a parish model see Neitz (1981).

9. For an account of the early renewal within St. Mark's Episcopal Church in Van Nuys, which Bennett communicated to St. Luke's in Seattle, see *Nine O'Clock in the Morning* (Bennett 1970). The book also explains why the Episcopal Church has been hospitable to the charismatic movement.

10. In all six of the accounts the author read dealing with the history of a renewed Episcopal parish, it was the rector, rather than the congregation itself

who sparked the movement. The accounts include the following: Church of the Redeemer (Houston, Texas) in Pulkingham (1972); St. Paul's Episcopal Church (Darien, Connecticut) in Slosser (1979); St. Luke's Episcopal Church (Seattle, Washington) in Bennett (1970); St. Luke's Episcopal Church (Bath, Ohio) in Irish (mimeo); St. Ambrose Episcopal Church (Claremont, California) in *Acts 29* (April, 1980); St. John's Episcopal Church (Kissimmee, Florida) in *Acts 29* (May, 1980).

11. Oral Roberts (1971), who belonged to a small Pentecostal Holiness sect for twenty-five years, reported having difficulty accepting the position of some Pentecostals that all tongue speakers should be channeled into Pentecostal churches. "I began to feel that God was leading me to transfer to the Methodist Church. To my mind, the Methodist Church was more than a denomination. It represented all the diverse elements of historic Christianity. In its membership and ministry were deeply committed evangelicals. Yet it had radical liberals, too. More importantly, it had maintained a free pulpit. Methodist ministers could preach their convictions" (Roberts 1971, p. 131).

12. Perhaps one of the most intriguing accounts I read while preparing this book was former Mennonite minister Gerald Derstine's (1980) *Following the Fire*. In 1955, during a Pentecostal outpouring in his Mennonite congregation, Derstine was repeatedly given the following prophecy: "Gerald, you are to be separated from the Mennonite Church, but do not fear for I shall give you a greater ministry. I am going to take you to the outer edges of the Mennonite communities. You shall minister and teach many of your people the things of my Spirit. Gerald, the Mennonites will not understand now, but they shall later. I am going to send you into the cities—from city to city you shall go, and you shall minister to multitudes and thousands of my people, teaching them about the things of my Spirit" (Derstine 1980, p. 3). Now twenty-five years later, Derstine is president of Christian Retreat and Gospel Crusade and far from his little church in Strawberry Lake, Minnesota: the prophecy has been completed. Derstine was forced to leave the Mennonite Church in 1955 because of his charismatic experiences. He moved to Florida, where he became a national charismatic evangelist. During 1972 the last phase of the prophecy began, as Derstine gradually came to a reconciliation with the Mennonite Church. Significantly, a Mennonite bishop wrote the introduction to *Following the Fire*.

CHAPTER 7

See How They Love One Another: The Charismatic Movement and Intentional Communities

> They devoted themselves to the apostles' teaching and to the fellowship, to the breaking of bread and to prayer. Everyone was filled with awe, and many wonders and miraculous signs were done by the apostles. All the believers were together and had everything in common. Selling their possessions and goods, they gave to anyone as he had need. Everyday they continued to meet together in the temple courts. They broke bread in their homes and ate together with glad and sincere hearts, praising God and enjoying the favor of all the people. (Acts 2:42–46)

One of the fruits of the charismatic movement has been the rise of intentional communities among a small but significant number of believers. While the origin, purpose, and structure of these communities vary, members share a commitment to each other that goes beyond ordinary church membership and involvement. Like other intentional communities, those of the charismatic movement are based on a mutual commitment of members that focuses on an organic conception of society in which the whole is greater than its member parts (Bouvard 1975, pp. 9–10). The vast majority of such communities, like the early Christian community in Jerusalem, have been shaped by religious values. In recently formed charismatic communities, as in other religious communities throughout the history of Christendom, a common religious consciousness transforms the community into a vital organism.[1]

Charismatic intentional communities appear to be indebted in many ways to the Roman Catholic Church, which has had an unbroken history of intentional communities within its larger structure. Five "ages," overlapping yet somewhat distinct, have been identified within Roman Catholic religious history: the age of the desert monks (ca. 200–500); the age of monasticism (500–1200); the age of mendicant orders (1200–1500), during which community members left the security of the monastery to live in poverty and to beg for their daily needs; the age of apostolic orders (1500–1800), when members of communities became involved in social outreach to the sick and the poor; and the age of teaching congregations (since 1800) (Cada et al. 1979, p. 13). Each of these ages represents a shift in the dominant image of community life, although the other forms continued to exist alongside newer ones. These shifts "seem to occur when there are major societal changes astir and when the Roman Catholic Church too is undergoing major changes" (Cada et al. 1979, p. 45). Given the important role that religious communities have played in the history of Catholicism, it is not surprising that Catholic charismatics are at the forefront in the rise of charismatic intentional communities and may be heralding a new age of religious life within their own church.

The development of intentional communities is not, however, limited to Roman Catholicism. Although less prominent in the Protestant traditions, community has played a role in some of the older Protestant denominations, particularly in some recent attempts to rediscover community life.[2] Well-known to students of intentional communities are the histories of now defunct Protestant communities, including the Zoar community and the Shakers, as well as the successful ventures of the four centuries of Hutterite community life and the twentieth-century development of the Bruderhof. With the notable exception of the Shakers, Protestant religious ventures have often been family based, while Catholic religious orders and the Episcopalian orders patterned after them have been celibate. Catholics involved in intentional communities in the charismatic movement may be more numerous, but non-Catholic communities in the past and present day adoptions and adaptations are also significant.

For the purpose of discussion, charismatic intentional communities may be divided into three broad groupings: (1) denominational, usually congregation based; (2) interdenominational or ecumenical; and (3) non-denominational.[3] We will consider representative communities from each of these categories, noting differences in origin, purpose or goals, and organizational structure.

Denominational Charismatic Communities

Roman Catholic Charismatic Communities. The charismatic movement has touched Catholic communities through individuals within traditional religious orders who have brought charismatic renewal into existing congregations and through the development of new communities.[4] As communal religious life experienced a crisis of declining membership in a post-Vatican II Catholic church, many who opted to remain in or to join such communities sought individual spiritual renewal.[5] Sisters, brothers, and priests found their way not only to Catholic charismatic prayer meetings, but also to nondenominational Full Gospel Businessmen's Fellowship meetings and to nondenominational charismatic workshops and conferences. Many received the Baptism of the Holy Spirit and in turn spread the word about the charismatic movement within their communities.

While no major Catholic religious community would call itself "charismatic" or "neo-Pentecostal," some have been influenced by charismatics and are instrumental in promoting the movement. The Jesuits, for example, who represent an historically important Catholic religious order, function largely as a teaching community and direct houses of prayer throughout the country. Individual Jesuits at both retreat houses and in schools may actively promote charismatic experiences, although no Jesuit organizations identify themselves as charismatic. Another illustration may be found in Franciscan priest Father Michael Scanlan's work for the charismatic movement. Scanlan, while a member of his religious community, has spearheaded the changes in the largely charismatic University of Steubenville of which he is president.[6] He has also been actively involved in the development of a charismatic intentional community in Steubenville, the Servants of God's Love, of which he is a founding member. Thus traditional Catholic religious communities are influenced by the charismatic movement and its members may be contributing to the movement without the existing community becoming part of the charismatic formal organizational structure.

A Community Venture into "New Monasticism".   The Order of St. Benedict, commonly known as the Benedictines, traces its history to the "age of monasticism," which began nearly 1,500 years ago. Pecos Benedictine Monastery's own history goes back to 1955, when three monks from a Wisconsin Benedictine abbey launched a new community in Pecos, New Mexico. In common with Catholics everywhere the new abbey at Pecos experienced the effects of the Second Vatican Council— "changes which came so thick and fast in the mid-sixties, without sufficient preparation, that a sense of confusion caused many people to lose perspective" (*Pecos Benedictine* 1980). The monastery suffered as attendance at retreats, the monastery's principal mission and source of revenue, dropped considerably.

At the same time, however, the charismatic movement was developing within the Catholic Church. Four monks who had previously been involved with the charismatic movement came to Pecos in 1969 and gave it a decidedly charismatic thrust. This not only spared the abbey from closing, but through retreats, missions, and a publishing house (Dove Publications) the Pecos Abbey has furthered the spread of the movement within the Catholic Church.

Although the Pecos Community is viewed as a single, integrated unit, it is juridically a male-Benedictine community that includes a covenant community made up of single men and women, both lay and sometimes religious. All members are celibate, whether they are the Benedictine monks (approximately twenty) or part of the larger covenant community of men and women (approximately thirty). This community, in turn, founded an offshoot mission in 1974, the nearby Holy Trinity Monastery, which admits married couples and children.

By admitting women and founding Holy Trinity, the Pecos Community has departed from the traditional all-male or all-female Catholic religious orders. One member who had been part of a women's religious community for over twenty years before coming to Pecos noted:

Certain negative aspects of communities, either of all men or all women, are lessened in a mixed community. The women become less petty and the men become softer. The sensitivity of women to pain, loneliness, and unhappiness makes community life less harsh for men; and men are able to lessen the tendency of women to focus on the foibles of other women. Certainly the women in this community have helped to bring out the gentleness of men. (Fracchia 1979, p. 125)

The Roman Catholic Church, together with its Eastern rites, and the Orthodox churches have the longest history of religious orders, but religious life in the Church of England experienced a revival in the mid-nineteenth century (Heidi 1980, pp. 19–20). Now the Anglican and American Episcopalian churches have religious orders similar to the Catholic ones. The Community of Jesus in Orleans, Massachusetts, is an Episcopalian community that bears a structural resemblance to the Pecos community. This charismatic community contains a religious order for single men, one for single women, and a community for families and singles who choose not to commit themselves to a religious order, all within a single structure known as the Community of Jesus. The brotherhood and sisterhood are integrated with the single men and women and the married couples to form a single community. "The brothers and sisters, however, maintain a conscious and intentional tie with the monastic-religious tradition of the historic Church" (Heidi 1980, p. 21).

All of these communities are rooted in the monastic tradition of the Catholic Church and high-church Episcopalians. They represent a blend of tradition and the modification of traditional monasticism that permit extensive contact with and commitment to nuclear families (as in the Jesus Community), as well as male-female relations (as found in Pecos).

Community as a Subgroup within a Parish.   Several attempts have been made to develop an intentional community within local Catholic parishes. Members of such communities contribute varying degrees of time and financial resources to the community while living within the larger parish organization. The specific living arrangements, the degree of financial support, and the community organization vary both among such communities and within a single community over time. Those who choose to covenant in such communities do so largely for the greater spiritual support that is available from members whose religious values are central to their lives and for the opportunity to engage in some type of collective service.[7]

One of the earliest of such Catholic communities developed in St. Patrick's Parish in Providence, Rhode Island (Randall 1973). The charismatic community was devoted to the larger church and was determined to avoid any potential rifts between charismatic and noncharismatic members of the parish. Because many community members (both married and single) lived in extended households and shared financial resources, money was available for projects that benefited both the entire parish and the surrounding community. One such project was the reopening of the parish school to serve members and other interested persons in the declining neighborhood where the parish was located.

St. Patrick's Parish continues its charismatic thrust while working to serve others in the surrounding neighborhood. Some members remain committed to living in communal households in order to use their resources collectively, while others make lesser commitments of time, person, and finances. "St. Pat's" operates a food cooperative and secondhand store, has a social service ministry, and works with other secular leaders to improve the neighborhood. The social action end of the ministry is integrated with the prayer meetings, religious sharing groups, and the parochial school.

Spin-off communities from "St. Pat's" have helped renew other parishes in the region. Father Randall, the founder of the original community, is now at another inner-city church that is plagued by the same problems that St. Patrick's faced in its precharismatic renewal days. He and his community are committed to revitalizing St. Charles Boromeo's Parish in Providence and to engaging in active Christian evangelism. Immaculate Conception, in nearby Cranston, has also felt the rippling impact from the original charismatic fervor of "St. Pat's."

The Son of God Community in Cleveland, Ohio, provides another less successful illustration of this type of community. Early in their history members felt called by God to move from suburbia to a declining neighborhood on Cleveland's near-west side. The community has gone through a number of transitions during its nine-year history (including a loss of nearly two thirds of its membership a little over a year ago) and presently is struggling with issues crucial to its survival. The twenty adults remaining in the Son of God Community are convinced that they are in need of more than a parish or large prayer group to meet their spiritual needs and consider the community essential to their lives as members of an inner-city Catholic parish. They no longer live in households or hold a common purse, limiting their present involvement to meetings and extended-family type social gatherings.

New Jerusalem, a 325-member Catholic community in Cincinnati, Ohio, provides an excellent example of successful integration of community and parish life. Its founder, Franciscan priest Richard Rohr, describes the community as "extra-parochial," because approximately 175 members belong to St. Bernard's Parish, while the remaining members belong to various other Cincinnati parishes and are expected to support their home parishes both financially and through service. (New Jerusalem comprises over half the regular membership of St. Bernard's.) It is conceivable that in the future other parishes may follow St. Bernard's example in establishing close relations with a religious community as greater numbers of community members cluster in a single parish.

Every member of New Jerusalem must belong to one of the "Circles of Spiritual Companionship," which constitute the core of personal relations in the community. These circles consist of six to ten members who meet weekly for prayer and fellowship. Some circles take the form of households that share living expenses while others do not. The degree of involvement and commitment may vary from circle to circle, but New Jerusalem members see their circle involvement as a vital link to the larger community. Members are also called to serve in various community ministries, each of which is headed by a coordinator who is responsible to the parish administrator. Such ministries meet diverse community needs, including evangelization, counseling, initiation into the community, clerical and office tasks, and religious gatherings.

Rohr expresses the desire for the community to be "transferable and imitable"—a goal the community appears to be realizing. He wants it to be a "means for a renewal of the Church," rather than an end in itself. At present, potential members may go through the initiation process, make a commitment to New Jerusalem a year later, and eventually leave the community. Rohr believes this is in accord with the community's purpose. New Jerusalem has a large committed core group, some members of which intend to spend their lives in the community. Others have come to New Jerusalem, learned about church renewal and personal spiritual growth, and have left the community. Training of those who may not elect to remain in New Jerusalem appears to be an integral part of its ministry.

While these three Catholic communities share a common heritage, there are differences among them as well as similarities. With the aid of Cincinnati's Management Design Inc., a Christian firm assisting and advising in the development of group structure and goals, New Jerusalem has created an organization that is exemplary in balancing group and individual needs. Son of God Community is older than New Jerusalem, and, in spite of historical similarities, appears to be in danger of folding. It has shared with St. Patrick's and New Jerusalem the full support of its respective local bishop, but unlike its two sister communities, it has lacked priest leadership. Priest leaders appear to play a key liaison role between community and parish that lay leaders may be unable to fill. Lay pastors have been more successful in establishing transparochial communities.

Transparochial Communities.   In books and articles on charismatic communities the term "covenant community" appears to be most frequently associated with Catholic transparochial communities and ecumenical communities originally led and founded by Roman Catholics. The covenant community thus represents one stream within the Catholic charismatic renewal (the other consists of more loosely knit prayer groups). These covenant communities frequently developed out of prayer groups as members desired to share more of their lives and commitments with one another (McDonnell 1978). Most transparochial communities are ecumenical, but one that is not illustrates the adaptation of the charismatic renewal to the Catholic Church.

Mana Community's development until 1978 has been described elsewhere (Poloma 1980).[8] Unlike many other covenant communities, Mana did not stem from a charismatic prayer group but rather from the vision of its founder. It became a charismatic community and an important force in spreading the charismatic movement in its locale only after it began as a community. The leader saw the need for a greater power to equip him and other community members for the service of the poor, and the charismatic movement was seen as a means of attaining that power through prayer.

While Mana Community has failed during its ten-year history to attract many non-Catholics, its Catholic membership has risen steadily. At the request of the local bishop, Mana changed from an ecumenical community to a Catholic one, although in reality it was always nearly entirely Catholic. Its members belong to local Catholic parishes, but, at present, participation in the parish is practically nil. The entire emphasis is on the community that has effectively replaced the local parishes. With the permission of the bishop, Mana has its own priest, its own Sunday service, and weekday gatherings. In every way it performs the functions of a parish.

The present arrangement is considered temporary until members are better trained for service within a parish. Members tend to move to one of three neighborhoods in the city, each within a different parish. As Mana Community outgrows the space it rents for Sunday worship community members may become involved in those parishes. This transition would not be without difficulty. Despite the support of the local bishop of the diocese, a parish might resent the influx of a tightly knit, highly structured community that could cause divisions in the parish. The present rigid style of leadership at Mana may not be compatible with the larger, more loosely knit, and increasingly democratic parish congregations. It is also possible that Mana may become the Catholic charismatic "parish" of the area, which in fact would probably change this community to one patterned after some religious or lay Catholic order. This second option would take Mana out of the mainstream of parish life and also limit its impact on the larger Catholic Church.

Non-Catholic Denominational Communities. Non-Catholic charismatic communities within a single denomination develop within a congregation as some individuals desire to make deeper commitments to each other. The attempt to move the church from an organization of secondary relationships to a community of primary relationships can be found within both Episcopalian parishes and Assemblies of God congregations. That effort, in turn, is influencing other Pentecostal and neo-Pentecostal ventures in community.

Neo-Pentecostal denominational communities, Catholic and Protestant alike, have been influenced by the Episcopalian Church of the Redeemer in Houston, Texas.[9] The story of its development and the role of the charismatic gifts in its success has been told elsewhere (Harper 1973; Pulkingham 1972; Schiffmayer 1979) and need only be summarized here. In the early 1960s Graham Pulkingham accepted an assignment to serve as rector of an Episcopalian parish in a declining neighborhood of Houston. His ministry there was largely ineffective until he received the Baptism of the Holy Spirit through the prayer of Pentecostal minister David Wilkerson, founder of Teen Challenge and author of *The Cross and the Switchblade*. Over the next few years, the Church of the Redeemer in Houston was transformed. Parish members often left comfortable suburban homes to cast their lots with the poor surrounding their church. Sharing their lives and resources, they combined their efforts to serve residents of this area in Houston. In describing the history of the community, Schiffmayer (1979, p. 1) notes its move from being "a dead parish in a decaying neighborhood" to being a "lively congregation of 800 today." He attributes this growth to the evolution of a concern for the needy, the open manifestation of gifts of the Spirit, and a structured leadership that shares the responsibilities with the rector. It has not only served the community in Houston, but Church of the Redeemer has sent out leaders to other communities in different parts of the world.

The Church of the Redeemer has been a model for a number of other Episcopalian communities, including the Community of Celebration (Denver, Colorado), the Church of the Messiah (Detroit, Michigan), and St. Paul's Episcopal Church (Darien, Connecticut). Modifications and adaptations have freely taken place, with numerous changes occurring in the Church of the Redeemer community as well.

The Assemblies of God have also developed smaller communities within larger congregations as a means of dealing with rapid growth in membership. Influenced by the ministry of Dr. Paul Yonggi Cho, pastor of a 200,000 member Assembly of God congregation in Seoul, Korea, a few Assemblies of God ministers have adapted this model for their own churches. Roy Harthern, former pastor of the rapidly growing Calvary Assembly in Winter Park, Florida, concluded that discipleship and home fellowship group ministry had to begin with him before it could be started in the larger congregation.

My wife and I began meeting on a regular basis with other ministers and wives and staff members and wives. Although we had worked together for several years, we still did not have the committed interpersonal relationships I knew God desired for us. We needed to get to know each other, to accept each other and serve each other. As we met, we began to be open with each other, to share our deep personal needs and desires; and to become of one heart and one mind. We discovered that we didn't need to hide behind ''religious masks.'' We could take off those masks. (Harthern 1979, p. 37)

From this beginning, members of the original group reached out to encourage and train others to form new groups. Today there are several hundred fellowship groups meeting throughout central Florida. The success of Dr. Cho and the Reverend Harthern have provided a model of community for Pentecostal congregations as Catholics and Episcopalians have for neo-Pentecostals.[10]

Ecumenical Charismatic Communities

One of the traits of the charismatic movement is the frequent extension of fellowship across denominational lines. Prayer groups developing outside formal church structures are often interdenominational, and it is not surprising that communities spawned by such prayer groups retain an ecumenical flavor. While many of these communities were founded under the leadership of lay Catholics, those joining from other denominations were encouraged to maintain their denominational ties. The largest and perhaps best-known of such communities is the Word of God Community in Ann Arbor, Michigan, with over 2,000 members, approximately 60 percent of which are Roman Catholic. It is from the Word of God Community that many of the teachings used in affiliate communities originate.

A covenant community, such as Word of God, does not represent an attempt to establish a new church. In part the goal of such communities is to aid in the reconciliation of various denominations by furthering understanding among community members. Its emphasis is on creating a type of religious suprafamily that helps members enrich their lives as Christians while maintaining membership ties with established churches.

Many covenant communities, particularly those receiving their teachings from the Word of God Community, are highly structured. The degree of regulation has created some controversy, but from the community's perspective, a highly structured group allows for the most effective use of resources and for the maintenance of order within. Each community affiliated with the Word of God is well structured internally, and some covenant communities are being unified through a network of national and international leadership. There are differences from community to community, McDonnell (1978, p. 24) observes, "but there is a conscious attempt to build one style of life so that a member of one community could be transferred to another community, live there, and be quite at home with the pattern of life."

Life-styles within the community vary. Some members remain single while others marry; some live in extended households, while others reside in nuclear family arrangements. Regardless of the particular living arrangement, all members develop intense interpersonal relations with each other. Robert Hawn, an Episcopalian priest and a member of the Word of God Community, describes the commitment required of members as follows:

In making this commitment one agrees to first love and serve Jesus and secondly to love and serve his brothers and sisters and to live out the life of the community. One agrees to support brothers and sisters spiritually and, if need be, materially. This is also a commitment to be willing to serve in the community as the need arises, to support the community financially, and to participate by faithful attendance in community activities. (Hawn 1979, p. 53)

The ecumenical charismatic communities are interdenominational rather than nondenominational. Although members retain their traditional denominational ties, primary group support may come from Christians of another denomination. Such communities seek to demonstrate the feasibility of maintaining denominational identifications while at the same time participating at the grass roots level in activities that transcend these differences. Whether such communities can continue to exist over time remains to be seen. Members tend to worship within denominational groupings and to have less ecumenical contact as the community grows in size. Ecumenical in theory and perhaps in leadership, such communities must make a concerted effort to maintain a genuinely ecumenical base while at the same time upholding denominational differences.[11]

Nondenominational Communities

Both the denominational and ecumenical communities remain linked to established churches. Each community seeks to spread the charismatic movement within its church. Members of nondenominational communities, on the other hand, tend to view the community as their church. It appears that many such communities have developed, thrived for a time, and disappeared as quietly as they appeared on the scene. The most likely to succeed are those which have a specified ministry that provides members with a common goal. Often such communities are small, with fifteen or fewer adults, but their efforts, resources, and very lives are joined together to further what they perceive to be an important Christian cause.

One such community, consisting of about forty adults, is Sojourners Community in Washington, D.C. Its life-style and ministry reflect a reaction to the materialism and political conservatism that has infiltrated parts of the charismatic movement. The charismatic belief in an active God who intervenes in the affairs of men and women sometimes turns God into a "bellhop in the sky," who provides abundantly for believers who know the right formula.[12] The "prosperity doctrine," which emphasizes God's material blessings, is not as likely to be expounded in mainstream or Pentecostal churches as it is in the media, but it turns up in several independent ministries of the charismatic movement. However, political conservatism based on (actually an interpretation of) biblical theology characterizes many charismatic churches as well as the broader

spectrum of evangelical Christian forces. The God of the political conservative is often depicted as a God who blessed a faithful America of
yesterday, but whose wrath is about to fall on a militarily weak nation that
has gone soft on communism and is plagued by sexual license. For such
groups, perhaps best illustrated by the noncharismatic evangelist Jerry
Falwell's Moral Majority, conservative politics is a requisite for Christian
righteousness.[13]

Sojourners represents an antithesis to both the prosperity doctrine and
to conservative politics. Taking seriously Jesus' admonition that it is
easier for a camel to pass through the eye of a needle than for a rich man to
enter heaven, Sojourners' members live a simple life-style in the slums of
Washington, D.C. Their complete sharing of resources and frugal living
allows them to devote their resources to services, both locally and
nationally, through their monthly magazine, *Sojourners.* The magazine
not infrequently challenges believers to biblical interpretations that are at
odds with both the prosperity doctrine and conservative politics.

Sojourners Community could date its beginning to 1971 and to the
publication of *Post-American,* forerunner to *Sojourners.* The tabloid was
a result of the efforts of a few young seminarians in Chicago who shared
orthodox Christian beliefs and a concern for social justice. Jim Wallis,
editor of *Post-American* and now of *Sojourners,* explains how living in a
community developed out of a search for a new way to live out religious
beliefs and social concerns:

We became aware of the broad historical tradition of communities committed to radical discipleship. Just as we were coming to know that we
were not alone in the present, so we were realizing that throughout
Christian history all of the convictions and the commitments that were
beginning to shape our life had been present in the life of other believers
before us. . . . It was very immature and embryonic, but there was a
strong sense among us that to talk of the church meant to talk of
community. We shifted from a feeling of opposition to the church to a
sense of commitment to rebuild it: to transform its form and life. We had a
growing sense of not being able to totally reject the church, and we began
to talk about new ways of being the church. (*Sojourners* 1977, p. 16)

Sojourners Community has continued its commitment to a simple
communal life-style through the ups-and-downs of its brief history.
Contact with the Catholic charismatic movement in Chicago was one
source of deepening the spirituality of the Community, and the Church of

the Redeemer (Houston) served as one model to develop its pastoral dimension. The Post-American Community and magazine became Sojourners in 1975 when a group of about twenty persons moved to Washington, D.C., where their ministry continues.

Despite the obvious Catholic and Episcopalian influenced in Sojourners worship, the community remains nondenominational. One might be surprised to find that Sojourners' members, most of whom come from various nonliturgical church denominational backgrounds, place much emphasis on Eucharist (communion) as being central to their worship. When asked about this anomaly, one member responded, "The more we came to understand about community, the more communion came to mean to us. We presently have communion services twice a week, but are praying about doing so daily." The communion service, structured much like a Catholic or Episcopalian mass, provides time for shared prayer and less formal worship as well. Worship is central to community life, but their "church" bears no denominational label (Wallis 1981, pp. 21–27).

The Gathering of Believers in the Washington, D.C., suburb of Wheaton, Maryland, represents another successful venture into community living. The Gathering, currently about 500 in number, seeks to live out what they regard as biblical imperatives: "the church is to be an alternate society to the surrounding pagan environment" (Moore 1980, p. 7). Living in neighborhood clusters allows members to share tools and garden equipment, have spontaneous get-togethers, care for each other's children, and share cars. The community has its own Christian school as well as its own food cooperative. Members gather for a corporate meeting one Sunday a month with other Sunday worship services being held at four different locations simultaneously to facilitate free and spontaneous worship. The Gathering of Believers is a worshipping, recreating, working, sharing, and serving community whose members value their interdependence upon one another.

I have personally observed the rise and fall of two other nondenominational communities in the Akron, Ohio, area. It appears that this type of community is especially vulnerable due to the lack of a common value-base. A strongly stated and supported goal or purpose (not simply the desire to be a community), as provided by both Sojourners and the Gathering of Believers, appears to be a necessary basis for unity. While both denominational and ecumenical communities have, at least to some degree, shared values and a common goal of renewing existing churches, the nondenominational community faces the problem of creating a shared religious vision and a community simultaneously. It can be done, as Sojourners and other such communities demonstrate, but a common vision is an even more important ingredient for nondenominational communities than for other religious communities.

The Dilemma of Social Structure

It is impossible to do justice to the many diverse religious communities spawned by the charismatic movement. Not only do they differ in structure according to the typology presented, but they differ in degree of communal sharing, use of communal residences, unifying goal or purpose, allocation of work roles, and numerous other structural factors. Each community struggles with the dilemma of using charismatic gifts to build a community without succumbing to the tendency of social groups to legislate, codify, and bureaucratize. In order to supplement the brief structural descriptions already provided, I will describe some of the dilemmas faced by communities as they struggle to preserve the organic nature of their beliefs in the face of the increasing complexity of their organizations.

Personal Freedom versus Authority. Biblical references, the source of most charismatic community teachings, may be found to support the concept of individual freedom as well as the development of hierarchical rule. Without freedom, a community ceases to be a viable organism; without authority, anarchy results. The degree to which each ingredient is present appears to depend on the stage of community development as well as the model chosen by the community.[14] At present there are two networks of communities in the United States, each representing a different emphasis and providing a different model.

The Federation of Covenant Communities, led by the Word of God and People of Praise communities, have a highly structured authority system resembling many other religious intentional communities (Kanter 1973). In such covenant communities the leaders, usually community founders and others selected by them, are responsible for the community as a whole and, therefore, "also have responsibility for people's personal lives to the degree these lives are put in common." Steve Clark, one of the founders of the Word of God Community, states:

I think there are a number of reasons why people would want to have relationships involving headship and submission. One is that headship enables the body to function in unity. The more a particular group or community wants to act in a disciplined, unified way, the more likely the members are to want some kind of authority.

A headship relationship also provides a context in which formation can take place. A disciple enters into a master-disciple relationship in order to be formed. By agreeing to submit to the person who is doing the formation, the disciple's growth in the Christian life can take place more quickly and effectively. (Clark 1975, p. 24)

Followers may have to submit to the leader's authority in serious matters such as marriage, attending college, changing jobs, or purchasing a house, as well as in less consequential matters, such as style of dress, scheduling daily activities, and socializing with people outside of the community. In many respects the authoritarian model resembles the rules and regulations found in Catholic religious orders prior to the Second Vatican Council and appears more frequently in Catholic communities.

Another model, found in both Catholic and Protestant charismatic circles, provides for looser structures and broader parameters which grant members a wider range of acceptable behavior. Members must make decisions daily that are not covered by rules and which always have the potential to disrupt community life.

Affiliates of the Community of Communities (Sabath 1980) are less likely to follow an authoritarian pattern than their counterparts in the Federation of Communities. Many of these communities passed through a period of extreme regimentation but found themselves stifled by their own rigidity and consequently relaxed their authoritarian standards. Sojourners, Son of God, New Jerusalem, and Church of the Redeemer are some of the thirteen Community of Communities affiliates that experienced such a period of rigidity. Like other communities before them, they learned that authoritarianism does not guarantee success (Kanter 1973).

It appears that there is a direct relationship between group rigidity and community growth. Those following Federation of Communities standards appear more likely to increase membership but at the expense, perhaps, of decreased intimacy and fellowship among members. Participation in such communities is well-defined and contractual, rules are clear, leadership undisputed. Much of the community's effort goes into forming such a structure, leaving little energy and few resources for any outside ministry. Communities that have a mission in the outside world, as Sojourners and Church of the Redeemer, have found the rules and regulations detrimental to the very task the communities have set for themselves. For them, community is not an end in itself but rather a means to serve the world around them.

A simple example may illuminate this difference. In the highly structured Mana Community, members are expected to resign from jobs such as teaching or social work if they are unable to maintain the commitments required of members. Any conflict between community expectations and job requirements is resolved at the expense of the job. In New Jerusalem, Son of God Community, and Sojourners Community—all affiliates of the Community of Communities—members are allowed to resolve conflicts between work and community commitments on their own. Service-oriented jobs are viewed as extensions of the community and not in competition with its needs. Outreach and service outside of the community is considered desirable for members. It appears that inwardly directed communities are more likely to limit personal freedom and to develop bureaucraticlike structure than are outwardly directed communities. However, the conflict between personal freedom and authority—a conflict that can easily lead to community disbanding—is more active in the latter groups. Bureaucratization adds stability and can foster growth, but at the expense of personal freedom and familiallike community features.

Role of Women in Charismatic Communities. Another dilemma facing charismatic communities and the larger charismatic movement as well is the appropriate role of women in the church. Again, the more structured communities resolve the dilemma while the less structured communities allow the dilemma to exist rather than seek an arbitrary solution.

The role of married women in affiliates of the Federation of Communities is clearly in accord with traditional values. The husband is the authority and provider; the wife is the homemaker, submissive to her husband. Married women with children are discouraged from seeking work outside the home. This hierarchical model of marriage and gender roles applies also to the role of women in the larger community. Women expect men to be the community leaders and men expect to lead. In this respect such communities reflect the traditionalism of conservative

Christian churches, which ignore or downplay the contributions of women. They pay lip service to the equality of all Christians in Christ, but
the hierarchical patterns which exclude women from positions of leadership in such covenant communities mirrors the Apostle Paul's own
ambivalence about the role of women in the church.

The Community of Communities is more likely to allow the dilemma
of the role of women to remain alive. Sojourners is committed to sexual
equality in practice as well as theory. Married couples in Sojourners share,
domestic tasks, including child care. A father may be expected to decrease his occupational involvement just as the mother does so that both
may care for small children. In the larger community structure, women as
well as men serve as community leaders. Sojourners may be more
committed to sexual equality than other members of the Community of
Communities, but all affiliates show a willingness to treat men and
women equally.

Personal versus Institutionalized Religion. The institutionalization
of religious experience is another problem that faces both charismatic
communities and the charismatic movement. The late humanistic psychologist Abraham Maslow (1964) suggested that the attempt to institutionalize experiences of God results in the subsequent loss of that
experience for the individual. This he saw as an age-old problem of
established churches. For Maslow, the great religions of the world and
their sacred writings were the work of those who had experienced a sense
of the Ultimate. The danger arises when individuals who have had the
experience try to define it in writing, and represent it through symbols.
Idolatry, the worship of the sacred symbols, "has been the curse of every
large religion."

Charismatic communities, like other religious institutions, can easily
resolve the dilemma of personal religious experience versus institutionalization through idolatrous practices. The charismatic renewal
claims a fresh outpouring of the Holy Spirit, which touches and transforms individual lives. Establishing a personal relationship with God
through Jesus by the power of the Holy Spirit is central to its ideology.
The movement allows Christians to see the Scriptures not as a dry
historical document but as an expression of God's love, which all Christians may experience. As social beings, however, people do not live by
feelings alone. Coming together in groups, men and women attempt to
develop theology and social structures based on the personal religious

experience. In the case of charismatic communities, instructional programs are often used to introduce interested persons to the structure and presumably the experience. The promotion of community structure and growth without a concurrent emphasis on the experience of the Holy Spirit may lead to idolatry.

An open, flexible approach to these problems allows a community to remain a viable and organic institution. Rigidly structured groups arbitrarily resolve or suppress conflict-laden issues, rather than allowing them to be a source of life and growth.

The term "community" is overworked in both social science literature and in colloquial usage. In religious literature, "community" implies committed familylike relations among members. Graham Pulkingham (1976), founder of the influential community at the Church of the Redeemer, suggests that the term "community" should be replaced with "extended family" in order to convey the naturalness and depth of commitment required of members. Those involved in intentional communities believe that, in one form or another, such communities are the only source of church renewal. Nevertheless, the possibility remains that many attempts to revitalize the church will deteriorate into lifeless bureaucracies.

There appears to be a great deal of truth in the observation made by Virgil Vogt, one of the founders of Reba Place, a Mennonite community in Chicago: "Whenever community is really taking place, it is a gift which comes to us from the Lord, rather than something which we have been able to create through our own wisdom and strategy" (Vogt 1976, p. 29). Some religious communities seem to bear a resemblance to Erving Goffman's "total institutions," which attempt to subjugate members completely. The similarities appear more pronounced among some newly developed communities that sprinkle military analogies in their teachings. Mana, for example, which derives its teachings from the Federation of Communities, often refers to the community as an "army of God," which follows "the general into battle," and where strong soldiers must be disciplined. Such groups possess the stability but lack the family orientation of less regimented communities. The success of those few that are closer to the familial ideal enjoy a fragile and elusive gift.

Notes

1. Zablocki (1980, pp. 266–67) distinguishes between "communal" and "associational" commitments in observing that the former requires 100 percent commitment—99 percent will not do. Most of these communities, although not all, represent associational rather than communal bonds, although in some cases, both types of bonds are found within a single community.

2. For a discussion of the relationship between historical Protestantism and communal life, see Bloesch (1974). In this well-written book, the author treats the recent rise of Protestant communities patterned after the religious orders rejected by Protestants during the Reformation as well as recent experiments with communal life both in America and abroad. Bloesch considers these evangelical religious communities to be an important alternate form of Christian discipleship and as a "new vanguard in the church's mission."

Zablocki's (1980) comprehensive analysis of the communitarian movement also takes note of Protestant religious communities that have developed through the centuries. His discussion (particularly in chapter 1) hypothesizes that such communities are "a social response to the los of larger-scale consensus brought about by cultural proliferation of choice alternatives" and as such appear unevenly throughout history.

3. Not all newly emergent Christian communities, particularly non-Catholic ones, are products of the charismatic movement. It appears, however, that many, if not most, have not only been touched by this religious revival but may have been formed as a response to it. Well-known communities that are not discussed in this chapter because they both developed before the rise of the charismatic movement and because they would probably not identify with the movement include Reba Place (Chicago), Koinonia (Americus, Georgia), and the Church of the Savior (Washington, D.C.). From the author's point of view, however, all three of the communities reflect the spirit of the charismatic movement.

4. Catholic priests may or may not belong to a religious community, whereas brothers and sisters do. Priests who serve a diocese directly under a local bishop are not members of religious orders and are primarily involved in parish work. Religious orders of priests (and nonordained brothers), including Jesuits, Franciscans, and Dominicans, may be involved in parish work or, more often, in

teaching high school and college students in schools founded by their respective orders.

5. Cada et al. (1979, p. 183), based on their well-researched and analyzed discussion of the current state of Catholic religious communities, note: "The task of revitalization is centered around the question of a community's rootedness in Christ and in the spirit of the founder. Contemporary adaptations in forms of service and lifestyle can only be productive to the extent that this radical transformation is an ongoing process." Based upon countless testimonies from members of Catholic religious communities, that the charismatic movement has been the medium through which individual community members have themselves become "rooted in Christ" and through which these same individuals are effecting changes within their own religious orders.

6. See Scanlan (1980) for a discussion of changes brought about in the college since his arrival as president.

7. For a discussion of the process of initiating persons into such a community, see Giordano and O'Brien (1978) and Glynn (1980). The subject of the first article is the parish-type community of the Community of God's Love (Rutherford, New Jersey); the second is an account of the stages of initiation in New Jerusalem (Cincinnati, Ohio).

8. In writing the original article on Mana Community (Poloma 1980), the author honored the founder's request that the community not be identified by name. In keeping with this original request, I continue to use the pseudonym for the community that appeared in the original article.

9. Both the Catholic communities of Son of God and New Jerusalem were also greatly influenced by Graham Pulkingham and the Houston community he founded at Church of the Redeemer.

10. For an account of the move toward community within another Assembly of God congregation (Full Gospel Tabernacle, Orchard Park, New York), see Tommy Reid's *The Exploding Church* (1979).

11. People of Praise (South Bend, Indiana), with about 950 adult members (Leggatt 1978, pp. 23–30), is a sister community of Word of God. Together they have had a great influence on the development of other similar communities. Particularly through the publication of a monthly magazine, *New Covenant,* and through a publishing house, Servant Publications, the teachings of Word of God and People of Praise are readily available to others seeking to establish communities.

12. The religious spirit that is central to the American cultural heritage is an individualistic and materialistic one. As Wills (1978, p. 80) notes: "This side of evangelical belief is the sanction of, and a stimulus to, individualism in its course's manifestations. It is the religion of success, of Horatio Alger, of 'live wires' and millionaires." Lehmann (1979), in his criticism of "rich religion" has provided a good synopsis of this spirit, which is taught in various ways among charismatics: "God is a giver! He loves us and wants us to experience the abundant life (John 10:10). Material prosperity glorifies Him and shows His blessing in our lives, whereas poverty is a curse. He desires 'above all things that you may prosper. We're King's Kids, and if we're not prospering financially, then

Satan is robbing us of our inheritance in Christ.' The secret to prosperity is this: 'Give and it shall be given to you . . .' (Luke 6:38). If you give to the Lord, He promises you a hundredfold return in this life (Mark 10:30). Invest in God, and be prosperous for His glory!'' Lehmann emphasizes that the point of his article criticizing the ''Gospel of Prosperity'' is ''Not that poverty is godly or that God can't multiply finances. . . . This is an appeal from those of us who have seen what the prosperity doctrine and others like it have done to the American Church. It has produced a brand of self-centered Christians who believe that God and all of His universe revolves around their own personal comfort and happiness'' (Lehmann 1979, pp. 11).

13. The relation of politics to the larger charismatic movement is discussed at length in chapter 11. Conservative Christian politics appears to favor defense spending and school prayer and to oppose communism, the ERA, abortion, and homosexuality. The same few issues are repeatedly raised as constituting threats to Christianity. Politicians who differ in opinion, even those claiming Christian commitment, are considered undeserving of the ''true'' Christian's vote.

14. This particular dilemma, often referred to in charismatic circles as the ''discipleship controversy,'' has importance not only for communities but for the larger charismatic movement as well. Editors of the charismatic publication *New Wine* and leaders of the two leading ecumenical charismatic communities emphasize the hierarchical pattern of submission to authority, while other charismatics teach that Christians are called to a ''mutual submission,'' more in line with the democratic tenets of American culture. It appears that those who have developed a ''discipleship'' or ''eldering'' model, including *New Wine* editors Bob Mumford and Charles Simpson and Catholic charismatic movement leaders Steve Clark and Kevin Ranaghan, are having a decided impact on resolving the dilemma in favor of strongly regulated communities. This is not occurring without opposition. Ranaghan's community, People of Praise, has been singled out for special criticism for allegedly ''brainwashing'' members. Complaints have been lodged by former members to the Catholic Fort Wayne–South Bend Diocese for the bishop's investigation (McClory 1980, pp. 1, 4). Whether the offenses are as serious as alleged remains to be seen, but the controversy shows the degree to which personal freedom in decision making is limited by formal and informal community rules and regulations.

CHAPTER 8

You Shall Be My Witnesses: Strategies of Recruitment and Initiation

> The notion that religion tunes human actions to an envisaged cosmic order and projects images of cosmic order onto the plane of human experience is hardly novel. But it is hardly investigated either, so that we have very little idea of how, in empirical terms, this particular miracle is accomplished. We just know that it is done, annually, weekly, daily, for some people almost hourly; and we have an enormous ethnographic literature to demonstrate it. But the theoretical framework which would enable us to provide an analytic account of it . . . does not exist. (Geertz 1973, p. 90)

In the previous chapters I attempted to develop the salient historical, ideological, and structural features of the charismatic movement. There can be no question that Pentecostalism has moved beyond the fringe status it occupied for nearly the first half of this century to a full-bloomed religious movement with the potential to change the shape of Christianity. While I have focused mainly on the objective features of the movement (historical, structural, etc.), it is apparent that these objective features exist in dialectical relation to subjective ones.

Sociologists Peter Berger and Thomas Luckmann (1966) have provided a theoretical model that may be useful in exploring strategies of recruitment within the charismatic movement. Following those sociologists and anthropologists who have studied the reality of social

157

structure, Berger and Luckmann acknowledge that there is an objective reality that may be viewed in terms of social institutions, norms, and social status. This objective reality, however, is not static and is constantly affected by human action. The movement today has very different structural features than it did in 1920. It is larger and more organized, and it has entered the mainline denominations and crossed social class lines. The changes have been brought about through the externalization process by which both the movement and the larger social order have been expanded through personal interactions. It is easy to see how key figures such as David du Plessis and Demos Shakarian have participated in this externalization by helping to spread the charismatic movement to the mainline denominations, but Berger and Luckmann's thesis further assumes that each and every participant in the movement is involved in the process of externalization and, to some degree, has affected the social order.

At the same time, there are institutional constraints on individuals. Each of us is born into a social order that determines the extent to which we are free to externalize. The classical Pentecostals, for example, despite their desire to reform the mainline churches, were unable to exert much impact when Pentecostalism first developed during the turn of the century. Developments and changes in the social order, shaped in part by the establishment of Pentecostal denominations, have enabled Pentecostalism to influence mainline churches. Having considered in previous chapters the externalization process with respect to the charismatic movement, I will now consider what Berger and Luckmann (1966) refer to as the process of internalization (or socialization). How are new members recruited into the Pentecostal movement and how, in turn, are they themselves altering the structure of the movement? The dialectical relationship between this process of socialization and the existing charismatic structures will be the focus of this chapter.

The Process of Commitment and Socialization

In their study of social movements, Gerlach and Hine (1970, p. 97) observe that, regardless of the social or psychological factors facilitating the rise of the movement, "the key to its spread is to be found in the process of face-to-face recruitment by committed participants." This type of commitment has been empirically studied by Gerlach and Hine (1970) in their research on classical Pentecostals, and by Harrison

(1972), McGuire (1977), and Neitz (1981) in their work on Catholic neo-Pentecostals. The literature and religious services of other charismatic groups also reflects the commitment.

The first step in the process of promoting participation in the movement is to expose a potential convert to a witness of how the charismatic experience makes religion more meaningful and helps to close the gap between Christian ideals and day-to-day living (Gerlach and Hine 1970, pp. 110–17). The potential convert then verifies the witness by seeing changes in the life of a friend or relation or by meeting individuals in the movement who display an admirable sense of assurance and depth of faith. As the interest of the potential convert grows, he or she receives training in spiritual matters through group interaction and teachings relevant to the charismatic experience. This is followed by a conscious decision to surrender an "old identity" and to allow God to take control of one's life. The charismatic experience, through which a person receives baptism in the Spirit, precipitates the commitment that separates the person from his or her past. For most charismatics, glossolalia is the pivotal experience that authenticates the commitment.[1]

Both Pentecostal and neo-Pentecostal groups have been relatively effective in developing and maintaining commitment. In fact, research suggests that charismatics as a group may be more committed to their churches than noncharismatics. McGaw (1979), for example, in comparing a charismatic with a noncharismatic upper-middle-class Presbyterian congregation, found that in terms of both ideology and ritual, religiosity is stronger in the charismatic church. This commitment may also be reflected in financial contributions to the church, as well as the giving of time and talents to further religious outreach. Such commitment undoubtedly helps to further the spread of the movement.

There are a number of vehicles through which the commitment process operates. The electronic church (see chapter 9) helps to create the "psycho-social state" leading to such commitment. The Full Gospel Businessmen's Fellowship has also been an important vehicle. Its banquet meetings provide guest speakers who give witness, group praise and prayer, and specific prayer for individuals wishing to receive baptism in the Spirit. Some converts have been moved to commitment through the reading of accounts in religious books and magazines. Perhaps the single most significant vehicle for commitment is the religious service. Religious ritual, especially formal and informal prayer gatherings, furthers the commitment process—not only the initial baptism in the Spirit, but also a deepening and renewing of commitment to the charismatic movement by those already involved.

Types of Charismatic Religious Ritual.   Prayer gatherings range from small informal groups with close interaction among members to large camp meetings that bring together believers from a number of congregations (Wood 1965, p. 64). They include cottage prayer meetings (small meetings in private homes), weekly prayer meetings (termed "evangelistic services" in some congregations), Sunday services (morning worship), local revivals, and camp meetings. These services appear to have slightly different functions and vary considerably among congregations.

Prayer meetings in private homes, also called Bible and prayer sessions, may take place with or without church sponsorship. Some of these meetings reflect an evangelistic strategy, which recognizes that it may be easier to get a potential convert to visit a private home than a Pentecostal church. Through such gatherings, potential members may be introduced to charismatic prayer and worship, as well as to the spiritual gifts available outside the larger, more formally structured church. At times such gatherings are encouraged and supervised by the church pastor, who may be convinced that small gatherings are important as a means of exposing nonmembers to witness and of building deeper commitments within the church. One minister explained that he rarely has an altar call (a practice of most Pentecostal and neo-Pentecostal prayer meetings, in which the potential convert comes forward for prayer at the invitation of the minister) at his services because commitments are usually made in small home gatherings. He encourages members to bring potential converts to home prayer meetings before inviting them to attend formal services.

It appears that such home gatherings are in the process of being reintroduced into the formal structure of some Pentecostal congregations. This is being done both for the benefit of church members who desire close and informal fellowship to supplement larger church services and for evangelistic purposes. Such meetings also occur in neo-Pentecostal circles, and may in fact be the medium through which many of the larger church-sponsored prayer groups have come into being.

Weekly prayer meetings or evangelistic services also take place in both Pentecostal and neo-Pentecostal churches. They assume particular importance for neo-Pentecostals, whose churches may not have a charismatic Sunday worship service. In most Pentecostal churches the prayer meeting is less formal than Sunday worship but more formal than home meetings. The prayer meeting allows time for individual members to lead congregational prayer, for the giving of personal testimonies and witnesses, and for individuals in the congregation to share particular Scripture passages and give brief lessons. Neo-Pentecostal prayer meetings generally include enthusiastic singing and worship, witness, and prayer, as well as some form of altar call for personal prayer needs and an opportunity to make a deeper commitment. They are perhaps the most important single means of introducing new persons to the movement.

In Pentecostal churches, the Sunday morning worship is more formally structured than prayer meetings but actually contains many elements from the prayer meeting. Because many members do not attend the evening or midweek service, the Sunday morning service provides the opportunity for spiritual gifts to be manifested just as the prayer meeting does. However, the sermon, generally followed by an altar call, tends to be the focal point of morning worship. Liturgical denominations, including Catholics, Episcopalians, and many Lutherans, make the liturgy the center of Sunday service, even if the gathering is attended only by charismatics. Even when the ritual includes such charismatic elements as an occasional prophecy or prayer for healing (if it is a service for neo-Pentecostals), it is, for the most part, liturgically centered and quite formal.

Revivals in Pentecostal churches usually feature an outside evangelist who comes to minister to the local church. Through a week of such ministry, commitments may be renewed and new commitments made. Both local revivals and the intercongregational camp meetings are usually aimed specifically at getting church members to make a deeper commitment. Camp meetings bring together members of different congregations and function as a means of strengthening the values within Pentecostalism (Wood 1965, p. 64).

In neo-Pentecostal churches and denominations, "Life in the Spirit" seminars, workshops, and conferences serve much the same purpose as revivals and camp meetings in Pentecostal circles.[2] Usually held on weekends, allowing people to travel some distance in order to attend, they are a means of recruiting new members and deepening the knowledge and experience of charismatic phenomena for old members. Workshops or conferences may concentrate on a special topic such as inner healing, healing of diseases, or deliverance. Guest speakers with a particular spiritual ministry often attend.

Revival services may also be held by independent charismatic evangelists who, often for reasons of idiosyncratic doctrines (e.g., on divine healing or on eschatology) may not enjoy the favor of any mainline or Pentecostal denomination. These evangelists rent public facilities, advertise in local papers, and utilize mailing lists to promote their meetings. They promise, in their advertising, that those who come will see and experience miracles. My personal observations of such revivals suggest that they may be more overtly charismatic than those sponsored by denominations, but that they may also be less responsible in insuring order. For example, at one independent revival meeting, a woman lay dying and no one came to her assistance. Those around her assumed she had been "slain in the Spirit." Dramatic deliverances from demons and demonstration of psychic powers are part of the religious presentation that draws spectators and believers alike. A tension exists between such independent revivalists and ministers of most local congregations. Local ministers accuse the revivalists of fostering excesses similar to those which caused difficulties in early Pentecostalism and the revivalists charge that local ministers are stifling the power of the Holy Spirit.

Charismatic Symbols and Commitment

In chapter 4, on charismatic ideology, I referred to some of the terms or symbols that are meaningful for participants in the movement. Following anthropologist Clifford Geertz (1973, pp. 87–141), I maintain that understanding the meaning of such symbols provides a key to the socialization process through which members commit themselves to the movement.[3] That commitment, in turn, affects the objective nature of the movement, as members seek to communicate the charismatic experience. In other words, the key symbols serve both to explain and to change the movement.

From my discussion of ideology we learned that the experience of Spirit baptism, accompanied by spiritual gifts, is the basis of the charismatic movement. "Spirit baptism" is a biblical concept (see Acts 8:14, 10:44) that is crucial to a literal interpretation of the Scriptures. Where many charismatic believers part company with other fundamentalist and evangelical Christians is in their understanding of the nature of this baptism and the importance of the spiritual gifts (especially glossolalia) as a manifestation of it. But the symbolism of the baptism has changed even for classical Pentecostals. New interpretations have emerged as second and third generation Pentecostals have risen to leadership. For example, while some early Pentecostals would have asserted that baptism of the Holy Spirit, with the accompanying evidence of speaking in tongues, is the source of salvation, most contemporary Pentecostals steadfastly deny that a Christian can be saved only through Spirit baptism (with glossolalia). In part this stance has become necessary because a large number of classical Pentecostals do not speak in tongues, not as the result of any official doctrinal change in their churches but because those of the second and third generations may not desire the experience.[4] This leaves the Pentecostal denominations with the dilemma of either changing emphases (redefining the symbol) or of losing members. Most have chosen the former.

It is through symbols— both symbolic words and deeds—that order is achieved in social interaction. As Duncan (1968, pp. 22–23) observed, these symbols must inspire belief in their capacity "to consecrate certain styles of life as the 'true' source of order in society" if they are to be powerful in organizing social relationships. Those symbols which depict a battle between good and evil, between the gods and the demons, are the most powerful ones in organizing social relationships. Duncan demonstrates how symbols are used to create and maintain communities, including worship communities. This ongoing socio-drama represents an effort to maintain authority: "a struggle by those in power, or those seeking power, to control symbols that are already powerful." Within the drama there will be a struggle between good and evil out of which order is born. The struggle will be reflected in the individual psyche as well as within the community structure. The structure of the socio-drama involves the stage or situation in which the act takes place; the kind of act considered appropriate to upholding order in the group life; the social roles which embody social functions; the means of expression used in the act; and the ends, goals, or values which are believed to create and sustain social order (Duncan 1968, p. 67).

Pentecostal and neo-Pentecostal services are perhaps the single most important structure through which charismatic experience remains viable for believers and becomes a reality for those who seek it. The various forms of service permit members of the congregation to participate collectively and individually in worship. Such gatherings require more than a minister's stage performance, although the minister's role, particularly in Pentecostal services, is often crucial to the service. The ritual, however, is contingent upon interaction between the congregation and the leaders of the worship service.

Setting the Stage. Whether charismatic worship takes place in a Catholic cathedral or a living room, a storefront church or a stadium, an auditorium-type church or the church's social hall, the congregation believes that God is present. The leaders of the congregation set the stage for the ritual by making worshippers aware of God's presence and their common purpose of praise. The prayer group leader or the minister enthusiastically conveys the message that it is a joy to come together to worship. The group responds through songs and prayer. The situation is thus defined as an active worship service in which clergy, laity, and choir work together to stage the production.

Appropriate Action. Despite the seeming spontaneity of charismatic gatherings, most are eventually structured, and regular participants become aware of the kind of conduct that is appropriate to maintaining this structure. There is a wide range of behavior that may be considered charismatic, but the activities at a specific gathering may be quite limited. In addition to prophecy and glossolalia, other more or less common practices include "being slain in the Spirit" (or "going down with the power"), "singing in the Spirit," the "holy jerk," and "dancing in the Spirit." Such practices, believed to be initiated by the power of the Holy Spirit, would be bizarre at a noncharismatic service. A person "slain in the Spirit" lies seemingly unconscious on the floor as the rest of the service continues. "Singing in the Spirit" involves a chorus of glossolalia, often with musical instruments performing extemporaneously. Those doing the "holy jerk" walk up and down the aisles with spasmodic bodily movement. "Dancing in the Spirit" includes dancing in place or sometimes in the aisles during congregational singing.

There are other variations in behavior that are evident among charismatic congregations. In some congregations there is open wailing as the service progresses; in others such behavior is never manifested. Some congregations take pride in the length of their services, which may go on for hours, allowing "the Spirit to move as He will." Others limit themselves to the one and a half or two hours allotted for the service. Through regular attendance at a gathering the new participant soon learns the appropriate behavior for that gathering. No formal rules are generally given, but there is the unspoken example and the hand of the leader to assure a smooth production in accordance with house practice. Participants in Pentecostal gatherings soon learn that prophecy generally takes the form of tongues, followed by interpretation, whereas in many neo-Pentecostal gatherings prophetic utterances need not be preceded by glossolalia. Some prophecies come in a short sentence, while others go for a minute or longer, and they may be expressed in King James or contemporary English. In some services prophetic messages may be sung; in others they are not. Frequency of prophetic utterances varies from congregation to congregation. In some groups they occur only a few times a year; in others numerous prophecies are delivered during each service. Like most other practices in charismatic services, the forms and uses of prophecy vary widely.

Some practices may be considered exuberant worship in one group but may be viewed as bizarre behavior in another. The custom of interjecting "amens" into a preacher's sermon, for example, would be regarded as rudeness in some congregations. Dancing during songs may be encouraged in one gathering and never seen in another. Although even the most sedate of charismatic services is more active and enthusiastic than most ritualistic services of mainline denominations, the spontaneity is far more controlled than perhaps many participants realize.

Roles Involved in the Action. In classical Pentecostal gatherings the role of the minister (or ministers) is not unlike that of other churches. The congregation is encouraged to participate actively, but the minister must keep the performance going. This seems to be especially true of Pentecostal churches with upwardly mobile congregations, which are in danger of becoming passive in worship as are mainline denominations of similar status. The minister's sermon is the focal point of the service, and his preaching is an important tool for engendering a desire for commitment among the congregation.

Roles appear more diffuse in many neo-Pentecostal groups than in middle-class Pentecostal gatherings. Although leaders keep the service flowing, teachings, prayer, and Scripture readings are likely to be delivered by anyone in the congregation at the appropriate times. It also appears that these newer groups may be more open to frequent prophecy than are more established Pentecostal churches. In many ways, charisma is more routinized in well-established, middle-class Pentecostal congregations than in the newer neo-Pentecostal groups and perhaps even the lower-class Pentecostal gatherings.[5]

Means of Expression. Duncan's (1968, p. 69) general observation regarding the means of expression used to legitimize authority applies especially to charismatic worship. It is the duty of the leader to inspire a positive response from the audience to her or his leading. Symbolic phrases ("Don't you just feel the presence of the Holy Spirit here tonight" or "I sense that God is going to do great things for us in this service"), usually delivered in a manner that will evoke congregational response, are often used to provide audible indication of such approval. The audience is eager for an experience of the Holy Spirit and is, in varying degrees, willing to promote the leadership that has demonstrated the ability to bring it about. Past performances give the leader or minister the authority "to create attitudes of obedience, loyalty, and devotion" in staging the religious drama.

The key role of the minister in Pentecostal prayer gatherings receives reinforcement from the religious symbolism that is meaningful to the believer. For example, the committed believer is familiar with the gift of wisdom or knowledge and may have experienced it in his or her own personal life. The believer also accepts the Scriptural dictum that some men were specially "anointed" by God. It is not unusual for a Pentecostal minister to begin his sermon by reminding his congregation that he is "divinely anointed" and that his sermon topic has been "given by the Lord." By using expressions that are familiar to charismatics, he reinforces his position of authority in the church.

Leadership must become stronger and more centralized for a newly organized neo-Pentecostal gathering to develop and grow. Sermon references to biblical passages emphasize the need for authority and order in gatherings. For example, in the prayer group I attended for more than five years, an increasingly hierarchical structure circumvented participation in the gathering. Worship was exuberant, with little visible leadership and much congregational participation, but anyone wishing to lead a prayer, share a Scripture passage, or give witness, had to notify assistants who in turn checked with the leader of the prayer meeting. Those in the "Word-Gifts Ministry" have more freedom to share their prayers, but they too must receive permission to deliver prophecies. The result is that a small group of persons under the authority of a single leader are working together to elicit response from the larger congregation.[6] These are the persons who control the meaningful charismatic symbols at prayer gatherings and who have the power to use these symbols to attempt to bring about desired behavior.

Values that Create and Sustain the Social Order. The most significant values articulated in the charismatic movement are personal holiness and fraternal love among believers. Both have facilitated the rise of the movement, and both find different modes of expression in different groups. All Christians share these values. The first is the message of the Great Commandment: "Love the Lord your God with all your heart and with all your soul and with all your mind." Jesus expressed the second value when he said, "Love your neighbor as yourself" (Matt. 22, 37–40). If charismatics are more successful as a group in living these values, it is perhaps due to their belief that the Holy Spirit has released a new power in those receiving the Baptism. A charismatic Christian is taught to believe that he or she has a new power and to act in accord with it.

Most classical Pentecostal churches have relaxed their original holiness standards, which insisted on the need to maintain external behavior standards that reflect the changed inner lives of believers. Pentecostals of an earlier time, for example, were prohibited from attending movies or going swimming in mixed bathing areas, and women were not permitted to cut their hair or wear jewelry. Such practices served to separate Pentecostals from other Christians, but such regulations became more difficult to enforce after Pentecostals began to acquire middle-class status. Like many evangelical Christians, most Pentecostals still refrain from the use of alcohol and tobacco, and encourage discretion in pursuing "worldly amusements," but external "holiness standards" no longer followed in most Pentecostal groups.

Both Pentecostals and neo-Pentecostals value the changed life brought about by conversion, by being born again or by accepting Jesus as one's personal savior. Rather than emphasizing hellfire and brimstone, however, the message is more likely to be the need to experience God's love through a personal relationship with Jesus Christ. Conversion is one step in this relationship; a deeper relationship may come through Spirit baptism. Even though spiritual gifts are an important ideological tenet, the emphasis of charismatic teachings is on the Giver, not the gifts: "Speaking with other tongues is not the Baptism, nor should people seek for this gift. Jesus Christ is the Baptizer; by drawing close to Him in prayer, worship, and yieldedness, one prepares himself for the Lord to baptize him in the Holy Spirit'' (Harris 1973, p. 122).

As the Great Commandment of Jesus teaches, there is a close relationship between love of God and love of one's neighbor. This love of neighbor is manifested in many Pentecostal and neo-Pentecostal communities. Empirical research on both Pentecostals and neo-Pentecostals has substantiated the importance of such ties, which cannot be separated from the belief that God works in and through the believers. In his study of classical Pentecostals, Wood (1965, p. 23) notes: ''I have established that to the Pentecostal person ethical character and close group relationships are necessary for extensive activity by the Holy Spirit in a congregation.'' He found a strong belief that it was only through the activity of the Holy Spirit, however, that such ethical behavior and close interpersonal relations were possible for the believer.

McGaw's study of neo-Pentecostals also found that for charismatics, personal holiness includes Christian fellowship. Beliefs are important, but so is a sense of belonging. McGaw (1980, p. 297) concludes that it is the ''meaning system [that] provides the rationale and justification for the group.'' A sense of belonging was found to be much stronger in the charismatic churches than in the mainline denominations under study. It is this interdependence of members in a believing community that seems ''to be the strength and forcefulness of its meaning system for its members.'' Many charismatics recognize that believers cannot believe in isolation. The strength of their belief and the operation of the gifts of the Holy Spirit are contingent upon fellowship. This holds true for both Pentecostal and neo-Pentecostal groups.

Thus the ideology of the charismatic movement includes values that give meaning to life by making the presence of God a reality for believers, but only through love, service, and fellowship with others can that presence be realized. While members and congregations alike are flawed, charismatics are committed to living out the ideals of the Great Commandment.

Notes

1. McGuire (1977, p. 165) is correct in observing that witnessing or giving testimonies is a better indicator of commitment than glossolalia for neo-Pentecostal Catholics. She asserts that "Although glossolalia may serve as a symbol of commitment, testimony is a greater commitment mechanism since it includes both acts of involvement and abandonment." My own observations of both neo-Pentecostal and Pentecostal prayer gatherings also suggest that such testimonies are an important commitment mechanism for both groups.

2. Life in the Spirit seminars consist of a weekend of concentrated teaching and prayer of eight weekly sessions designed to lead to a conversion experience and/or baptism in the Spirit. For a discussion of the use of these seminars in the Catholic charismatic movement, see Harrison (1972) and Neitz (1981).

3. Geertz's (1973, p. 90) definition of religion and the key role that symbols play in it is worth noting here: religion is "(1) a system of symbols which acts to (2) establish powerful, persuasive, and long-lasting moods and motivations in men by (3) formulating conceptions of a general order of existence and (4) clothing these conceptions with such an aura of factuality that (5) the moods and motivations seem uniquely realistic." This definition of religion, with its emphasis on symbols in the creation of social reality, seems especially appropriate in considering the religion of the charismatic believer.

4. Conn (1977) reports a 1967 survey sponsored by the Church of God (Cleveland, Tennessee) that found only 61 percent of its members spoke in tongues. On the basis of conversations with Pentecostal pastors, I would venture to guess that anywhere from 25 to 50 percent (depending on the congregation) of classical Pentecostals do not speak in tongues, despite the significant place of glossolalia in Pentecostal theology.

5. Classical Pentecostal Womack (1968, p. 17) has made a poignant observation about what sociologists might term "routinization of charisma": "A gradual domestication and control of what began as a spontaneous burst of life is like a blight upon us; and the increasing ingraftations of nonapostolic teachings, methods and attitudes make it more and more difficult to discern the fruit of Pentecostal Christianity in our children." I have observed, however, that a local revival may wake a sleepy Pentecostal church from the threat of routinization.

One church with which I am quite familiar had reportedly developed a church service and ministry that was not very different from other nonliturgical Protestant denominations. The routinized ritual seemed to defy its professed Pentecostal beliefs. After the minister had an intense personal religious experience, he reintroduced some Pentecostal practices, including an altar call during which hands were laid on each person coming forward. The first Sunday he began this practice, numerous people came to the altar, many of whom were "slain in the Spirit." As the minister reported to me: "I had been a minister for over 25 years. I was determined that my services would never find persons laying on the floor after prayer, and never had anyone been slain in the Spirit when I prayed with them. This Sunday I would no more begin to approach a person at the altar when he would 'go down under the power.'" According to the minister and the congregation, this was the Sunday that revival began. Three years later many Pentecostal practices have been reintroduced, including less formal services, frequent prophecies, glossolalic prayer, and singing in common.

6. While maintaining order is a concern in Charismatic worship, there is a delicate balance between the danger of overstructuring and the danger of chaos. It appears that charisma is easily routinized and hard to maintain as a viable force. Bert Ghezzi's recollections and comments about the first international Catholic Charismatic renewal conference (1967) are telling in this regard:

As I recall it, the whole weekend was uninhibitedly Pentecostal. On Saturday morning, with his typical fire, Ralph Martin preached about Jesus. Saturday night witnessed what must have been one of the longest and least structured—to put it mildly—prayer meetings ever held in the Catholic charismatic renewal. We assembled at 7 o'clock in the evening in an oversized classroom under the Golden Dome and did not straggle out until 2 o'clock Sunday morning. About 200 people jammed into the room, including guests, the curious, some skeptics, and one priest-psychologist who took notes furiously all night long. What a wonderful evening of charismatic chaos! At one point I surveyed the room—groups praying all over the place, others giving instruction, still others wandering in and out. To this day I wonder what the priest-psychologist noted when I assembled a group and prayed rather loudly (read: shouted) in tongues over each for some particular healing. *After 13 years of experience, none of us would let that prayer meeting happen again, but all of us who were there would not want to have missed that night.* (Ghezzi 1980; my italics)

CHAPTER 9

Go and Tell the World: The Charismatic Movement and the Media

Then the eleven disciples went to Galilee, to the mountain where Jesus had told them to go. When they saw him, they worshipped him; but some doubted. Then Jesus came to them and said, "All authority in heaven and on earth has been given to me. Therefore go and make disciples of all nations, baptizing them in the name of the Father and of the Son and of the Holy Spirit, and teaching them to obey everything I have commanded you. And surely I will be with you always, to the very end of the age." (Matt. 28:16–20)

The evangelical Christian's use of the media is a joke to the skeptic and a scandal to the nonevangelical Christian. Comedians parody the more flamboyant evangelical performers, while liberal church people decry the cheap grace being peddled through the razzle-dazzle of the electric church. What both groups fail to appreciate is the commitment of many evangelicals to spread the gospel—or, in the words of one media evangelist, "to reach the lost, at any cost." It is the commitment of believers to evangelism that motivates leaders of the electric church and produces dollars from the faithful. Many evangelists view this mission as a matter of special urgency, particularly in light of the prophecies claiming that humankind is in its last days and that Jesus is coming soon.

Charismatics are evangelical Christians. Their first task is to preach the necessity of being "born again"—a message of repentance from sin, conversion, and accepting Jesus as one's personal savior. Baptism in the Holy Spirit and its accompanying gifts are only for believers who have already made this commitment to Jesus Christ. The charismatic experience comes after salvation.

While the evangelical electric church has been growing rapidly, the charismatic media campaign has been even more successful.[1] PTL, CBN (Christian Broadcasting Network), and TBN (Trinity Broadcasting Network), the three Christian television networks in the United States, are solidly evangelical and charismatic. M. G. "Pat" Robertson's *700 Club* and Jim and Tammy Bakker's *PTL Club,* two of the best-financed Christian television programs, are more open to the display of the "gifts of the Holy Spirit" than the best-known charismatic evangelist, Oral Roberts. Toronto's *100 Huntley Street,* hosted by David Mainse, preaches the same charismatic gospel to a Canadian television audience. Evangelical television has come of age, and charismatic evangelical programs now lead the way.

The phenomenal growth of evangelical broadcasting can only be understood in terms of the commitment of these believers to spread the gospel and their original exclusion from the electric church. A firm purpose and favorable conditions combined to enable evangelicals, much to the chagrin of their adversaries, to capture much of the religious audience.

The Founding of the Electric Church

Radio as a Precursor.   Since the airing of its initial program on Pittsburgh's KDKA in 1921, Christian radio has reportedly grown to nearly 800 stations devoted chiefly to religious broadcasting (Sloan 1980, p. 124). More than 500 out of 4,600 AM stations and 280 out of 5,200 FM stations are committed to the radio church. Approximately half of a sample of the American adult population reported listening to religious radio programs either often (20 percent) or occasionally (28 percent), and most listeners are already affiliated with churches (Johnstone 1971, p. 101). Radio is a relatively inexpensive and effective medium for reaching a mass audience with a Christian message (Hale 1974).

The radio audience of evangelical preachers is estimated to be about 114 million Americans, who listen to one or more religious radio programs in an average week (Bethell 1978). Despite competition from television, the radio audience is believed to be eight times larger than that of the television evangelists (Armstrong 1979, p. 122). The radio programs feature teaching, inspiration, and religious news at a fraction of the cost of television programs. Religious radio has survived the popularity of television and continues to prosper.

While radio continues to be an important medium for the evangelical message, it lacks the glamor and excitement offered by television. The stars of evangelical radio, including Charles E. Fuller ("Old Fashioned Revival Hour") and Walter A. Maier ("The Lutheran Hour"), have been replaced by television's Oral Roberts, Pat Robertson, and Jim and Tammy Bakker. The Bakkers are multimedia performers whose programs are carried on both radio and television, but in general, the stars of national renown are those whose faces and voices may be seen and heard over television networks reaching hundreds of cities both here and abroad.

Television as a Medium of Salvation. One of the first to use television as a medium of evangelism was the former traveling preacher Rex Humbard. Leaving his parents' team ministry in 1952 to establish a church in Akron, Ohio, Humbard began his television career by starting a weekly program for shut-ins on an Akron television station. From these modest beginnings, Humbard's syndicated program has come to be broadcast over 360 television stations, coast to coast and overseas (Humbard 1975).[2]

It was Humbard who encouraged Oral Roberts, already a well-known healing evangelist, to launch his television program in 1954 (Armstrong 1979, p. 86). Roberts's own religious background, like Humbard's, was classical Pentecostal, but he tended to be more controversial because of his practice of divine healing. Due to this controversy, Roberts was eventually denied air time on network television but continued his healing ministry on nonnetwork stations. Unlike Humbard's more familiar evangelical program, Roberts gave his viewers a chance to see Pentecostal faith in action.

By the mid-1960s, Roberts abandoned his tent evangelism and changed his style. In 1969 he returned to television as president of the new Oral Roberts University with a sparkling new television presentation. Gone were the dramatic prayers for healing and witnesses of cures; added were attractive young people, contemporary music, and a less-Pentecostal Oral Roberts, preaching a more typical evangelical message.[3] Although he professed to maintain his Pentecostal tenets, Roberts left his Pentecostal Holiness sect in 1968 to become a member of the United Methodist Church (Roberts 1971). His new format in part reflected this change in his religious status. The change was also accompanied by an improved technical production, enabling Roberts to supplement the weekly church-like programs with hour-long specials in prime viewing time that reportedly drew a nationwide audience of up to 50 million viewers (Armstrong 1979, p. 87). Roberts's annual revenue from viewers was estimated at about $60 million in 1978 (McWilliams 1979, p. 552), substantially more than Humbard's $25 million (Maust 1980). The new Oral Roberts and Rex Humbard have a similar evangelical message, a similar style, and probably a similar audience.

Television evangelists like Humbard and Roberts—like their colleagues in radio—cannot rely on public service time donated to religious programming. Public service time is monitored by the National Council of Churches, which understandably caters to the established denominations. This has meant that Humbard, Roberts, and those who followed them have had to rely on private donations to subsidize their use of the media. The public has supported such religious programs with contributions exceeding $600 million in 1979, double the sum received in 1977, and twelve times the level of ten years ago (Sloan, 1980, p. 116).

Denial of the free public service network time to evangelicals has thus served as a blessing in disguise. The evangelicals believed their biblical and fundamentalist message of salvation was not being delivered by mainline church programs aired on public service programs, so they were willing to subsidize programs on both radio and television that delivered the message. Today the evangelical Christians can claim a communication system with an organization, National Religious Broadcasters, that speaks for their interests. Its messages are less susceptible to reinterpretation by the commercial media simply because its own system of communication is formidable enough to stand alone[4] (Rifkin 1979, p. 104).

The church of radio and television continues to grow. Ben Armstrong (1979, p. 100), the executive director of National Religious Broadcasters, reports that more than thirty Christian television stations are presently in operation, along with hundreds of all-religious channels on cable television and new stations growing at the rate of one per month. While some of the stars of these programs are not charismatic (notably Jerry Falwell, James Robinson, and Robert Schuller, among others), many do have ties with the charismatic movement.

Charismata and the Electric Church

Five of the ten syndicated television ministries reported on by Martin (1981, p. 15) are professed charismatics. Their combined audience (based on Nielsen Company data) exceeds six million persons, and their programs are carried on scores of television stations across the nation. Included in this top ten are Oral Roberts with a total audience of 2,351,000; Jimmy Swaggert, an Assemblies of God minister, with a viewing audience of 1,780,000; Bakker's *PTL Club,* reaching 1,050,000 persons; Robertson's *700 Club* with 705,000 viewers; and independent charismatic Kenneth Copeland with a viewing audience of 381,000. Other national but lesser-known charismatic television personages include Kenneth Hagin, Richard Hogue, David Mainse, Don Stewart, and Ernest Angley, with numerous other local preachers filming broadcasts televised only in their particular regions.[5] These programs range from talk shows to healing services, from those that focus on formal preaching to those that attempt systematic teaching.

Recent and popular American and Canadian charismatic television programs have assumed a talk-show format. The hosts of these shows have perhaps learned more from Johnny Carson than Rex Humbard. Interviews and musical entertainment takes place on a cozy living room studio set. The host, however, is the focal point of the show.

One of the best-known hosts is M. G. "Pat" Robertson, whose television ministry began in a decrepit station in Portsmouth, Virginia, in 1962. In the 1970s Robertson's show was televised nationwide and now provides him with a multimillion dollar enterprise known as the Christian Broadcasting Network (CBN). The rival nationwide program with a similar format is hosted by former CBN stars Jim and Tammy Bakker, whose own PTL Network is rapidly gaining on CBN's. CBN reportedly grossed $70 million in 1979, while PTL reportedly grossed $53 million; CBN claimed to reach about eight million households, while PTL claimed some four million viewers.[6] The *700 Club* (CBN) is carried by 150 stations while PTL Club is carried by 235 stations.

A similar program is "Praise the Lord," hosted by Paul and Jan Crouch, on the Trinity Broadcasting Network. After leaving CBN, the Bakkers, together with the Crouches, established TBN and initiated the "Praise the Lord" program. Following a disagreement over appropriate denominational affiliations (the Bakkers are committed to nondenominational television programming), Jim and Tammy Bakker left TBN to the leadership of Paul and Jan Crouch and established PTL in Charlotte, North Carolina. Based on the West Coast, TBN claims to reach about 2.5 million viewers and grossed $17 million in 1979. TBN is attempting to expand its operation. In addition to the base station in Los Angeles, TBN owns stations in Phoenix, Oklahoma City, and Miami (Hadden and Swann, 1981, p. 38).

Canada's version of a charismatic Johnny Carson is David Mainse, of *100 Huntley Street,* a program originating in Toronto. It is reportedly seen on twenty-five stations across Canada for a potential viewing audience of over three fourth's of Canada's population. Mainse, a Pentecostal Assemblies of Canada minister, hosts the show with the assistance of a United Presbyterian, an Assemblies of God, an Anglican/Episcopalian, and a Methodist minister as well as a Jesuit Catholic priest. In 1978, Mainse established Crossroads Christian Communications, Inc., which produces programs that are seen throughout Canada, the United States, Italy and the United Kingdom.[7]

While the Crouches and Mainse have the potential of reaching millions of viewers, *PTL* and the *700 Club* are better-known programs and may be used to demonstrate how the media is used to spread the charismatic movement and to reinforce the beliefs of its followers.

Pat Robertson and CBN.   Pat Robertson, a Phi Beta Kappa with a Yale law degree and son of a United States Senator from Virginia, is representative of the neo-Pentecostal phenomenon that has touched the lives of middle and upper-middle-class Americans. Neither his Southern Baptist upbringing nor his wife's Roman Catholicism led him to become a charismatic spokesperson. He started on the road to committed Christianity through the witness of a missionary evangelist by the name of Cornelius Vanderbreggen. It was Vanderbreggen who brought Robertson to an acceptance of Jesus Christ as his personal savior, causing a dramatic change in Robertson's life from "swinger to saint" (Robertson 1972, chap. 2). Shortly after that born-again experience, Robertson enrolled in Biblical Seminary in Manhattan, where he learned about the baptism of the Holy Spirit from a Korean student, Su Nae Chu. Robertson and others prayed for this Pentecostal experience, which he had quietly at home later that year.

Following his Pentecostal experience, Robertson began "consulting the oracles of God" (Robertson 1972, chap. 3) by seeking God's direction in prayer. Like many other practicing charismatics, Robertson discerned what he believed to be the voice of God guiding his life. In response to that voice, after graduating from Biblical Seminary, Robertson sold virtually all of his and his wife's possessions and contributed the money to help with orphanage work in Korea. Penniless and still seeking God's plan for his life, Robertson experienced the poverty of ministry in a Brooklyn slum before going to Virginia, where he began his television ministry: "The seventy dollars in my pocket comprised all our earthly wealth, and as we prayed I felt the Spirit of God upon me again, and I repeated the cryptic prophecy the Lord gave: 'I am sending you into a wasteland. Do not be taken by the wasteland. Look only to me'" (Robertson 1972, p. 103).

Robertson claims to have been led to Virginia and to the television station. Money came to him from diverse sources to meet his personal and ministerial needs, and God told him how much to pay for the station. In February, 1960, Robertson's mother reported a vision to her son:

And I saw a vision. I've had only two other visions before. This time I had been on my knees praying for you when I saw heaven opening. I saw you kneeling in prayer with your arms outstretched toward heaven. As you prayed, I saw a packet of bank notes floating down out of heaven into your hands. I looked closely and saw that they were made up of large denominations. I didn't know how much money it was, I just knew it was a lot; and it was as if you were kneeling under the open windows of heaven and God was pouring out his wealth upon you. (Robertson 1972, p. 123)

What Robertson and charismatic believers term "divine providence," the "voice of God," "prophecy," and "visions," a nonbeliever might term "coincidence," "self-delusion," and "hallucinations." The fact remains that a man, reduced to near-destitution by giving away all he had, listened for what he believed to be the direction of God and now heads a multimillion dollar television ministry. The pieces of this success story have been fitted together to form a founding myth that remains sacred to Pat Robertson and to the "partners" of his ministry without whose contributions it would not exist.[8]

The Bakkers and PTL. If Pat Robertson is typical of the educated neo-Pentecostal, his one-time colleagues, Jim and Tammy Bakker, represent the classical Pentecostalism of the common man. The differences in their backgrounds have produced different styles of presentation, but the charismatic ideology of the two networks is more similar than dissimilar.

Jim Bakker was brought up as a Pentecostal, although his parents allowed him to enjoy more of the ''worldly'' pleasures than did many Pentecostal parents in the 1950s. His conversion experience occurred at age eighteen, when a child his car had struck was ''miraculously'' healed as a result of prayer offered by members of his church. After being born again, Jim Bakker left his home town of Muskegon, Michigan, for North Central Bible College in Minneapolis. It was at a church in Minneapolis that Bakker received the baptism of the Holy Spirit. It was also in Minneapolis that he met and married another Bible College student who was to become his partner in ministry. Since the college did not permit students to marry while attending school, Jim and Tammy began their ministry in Minneapolis without a Bible College degree.

The Bakkers began their careers as traveling evangelists by conducting revivals. God directed them to each stop along the way, and the Bakkers continually sought His guidance. On the evangelistic circuit they developed two special talents: fund raising and a puppet show for children. Both were put to use at CBN by Pat Robertson, as Jim and Tammy produced a children's show and assisted with telethons that enabled CBN to develop during the 1960s (Bakker 1976).

Jim Bakker credits Robertson with giving him ''an opportunity to learn all I know today about Christian television'' (Bakker 1976, p. v), but he resigned his position at CBN in response to God's direction:

Within thirty minutes, I was seated in Pat Robertson's office. We chatted briefly and then I spoke up. ''Pat,'' I began faltering, ''God has told me to leave CBN.''

Pat seemed amazingly calm. ''If God has told you, I can't argue with that. In my heart, I don't want you to go. In fact, the board of directors has just voted you a salary increase.''

I tried to smile, but it was difficult for me. ''I have to leave. I don't know what God has in mind for us, but I know He's speaking to me to resign.'' (Bakker 1976, p. 107)

After an extended vacation the Bakkers met with Paul Crouch, a former assistant minister from Jim's home church in Muskegon, who also felt led to television ministry. Paul Crouch was to run the business end of the newly formed Trinity Broadcasting Network in California, and Jim and Tammy were to produce the shows. Buoyed by the success of CBN, the Bakkers and Jan and Paul Crouch pooled their resources and were "daily believing God for a miracle to raise up the new television ministry." On PTL's first California program viewers promptly responded with financial contributions which enabled the purchase of new equipment and the expansion of the ministry (Bakker 1976, p. 124).

TBN soon experienced internal problems, leading the Bakkers from this network they helped to found. Criticisms from local pastors about the appropriateness of "ministering in the Spirit over television" were leveled against the Bakkers. When the TBN board of directors decided to establish the ministry under a single denomination, the Bakkers left California. Still believing they were called into the television ministry, the Bakkers again began to do revivals. After conducting a revival in Charlotte, North Carolina, the Bakkers found the doors were open for a new television ministry that flowered into the highly successful PTL Network during the 1970s.

The human figures in both PTL's and CBN's founding myths see God as their producer. Prophecies, "miraculous" timings, and "leadings" of the Holy Spirit are central to both accounts. While an organizational analyst would undoubtedly explain their success differently, both Bakker (1976, 1977) and Robertson (1972) use the charismatic language of faith in the supernatural to describe the development of efficient, bureaucratic, modern television operations.

If the language of these myths is an anomaly in a rational and empirical social world, so are the programs themselves. Using the natural medium of television, both shows attempt to demonstrate the reality of the supernatural. Through their programs, the charismatic beliefs and practices are shown to millions of viewers. Unlike the noncharismatic evangelical program, the charismatic shows are presented as evidence that the supernatural is alive and well in Christian religion and that the "miracles" recounted in biblical history are relevant for today.

Charismatic Television Format. Robertson, the Bakkers, and other charismatic show persons are committed first to the basic evangelical doctrine of the need for Christian salvation and only secondarily to promoting the charismatic movement. Robertson explains that: "We would preach Christ crucified, and while not denying the work of the Holy Spirit, we would not try to force the baptism upon anyone" (Robertson 1972, p. 69). However, circumstances brought Robertson's *700 Club* closer to the charismatic movement. The incident that turned the tide occurred one evening late in 1967, when Bakker was still affiliated with CBN. During the last fifteen minutes of a typical show, there was a decided "move of the Spirit," as the program's guest wept through his testimony, a worker at the station began "to dance in the Spirit," and reports of miracles in the viewing audience jammed the telephone lines. The program went on unscheduled through the night.

God was rousing people from their sleep to turn on their televisions. Many people called their neighbors and told them about the all-night program. Others dressed hurriedly and came down to the studio to see what was happening. . . . By five o'clock, hundreds of people had called to say they had given their hearts to Christ. (Bakker 1976, p. 71)

From that point the *700 Club,* and later Bakker's own *PTL Club,* was open to manifestations of the charismatic gifts of the Spirit over the airwaves. On both programs, virtually all of the gifts are manifested "as the Spirit leads." Persons on the show give witness to "miracles" of being saved from fatal accidents, or of divine healings.

Perhaps the most dramatic gift from the home viewer's perspective occurs when a host or guest on a show receives word of divine healings in the viewing audience. On such occasions, usually as host and guest pray together on the set, someone will receive a revelation from God.

There is someone in our television audience who is being healed of diabetes. Don't quit taking your insulin, but go to your doctor. You'll find you won't need it anymore. I see someone who sustained a back injury in an automobile accident. God is healing you right now. There are several people in our viewing audience who are being healed of arthritis. Praise God!

The revelations of healing go on and on. Some people will call or write the station later to affirm a cure, occasionally with a doctor's confirmation.

Such manifestations of charismatic gifts are supposedly not written into the script, but the host of the program is open to them. Those who have never had the experience of attending a charismatic service or conference where the gifts of the Holy Spirit appear have the opportunity to witness the experience in their living rooms. As in the live charismatic prayer service, however, planning is very much a part of the television program. The gifts are a welcome surprise in a well-planned program consisting of teaching and preaching, interviewing and witnessing, some film clips, Christian entertainment, and television living room fellowship. In addition, the talk show format is supplemented with telephone counselors who soften the impersonality of the television medium as viewers call the number on their screens for personal prayer and counsel.

Robertson versus Bakker: Patrician versus Common Man. In terms of both secular and religious education, Robertson's formal training greatly exceeds that of Jim and Tammy Bakker. The product he produces reflects this formal learning as Robertson plays the political and religious expert, teaching his viewers his conservative politics and theology with the poise of a skilled college professor. Robertson's co-host, Ben Kinchlow, appears to represent the audience, sitting at the master's feet, drinking in his words of political and economic wisdom, posing the common man's questions to the trained and learned expert. The message is typically simplistic, especially to those who have learned there are two sides to any political or economic issue, but Robertson skillfully presents his one-sided lecture on humanism, the arms race, or government spending, apparently to the satisfaction of his television audience. Among Robertson's guests are other degree-holding experts in psychology, economics, or history with political and social views similar to his own. Robertson apparently sees his television ministry as devoted to educating viewers in conservative political-economic thought.

Bakker's opinions are probably similar to Robertson's, but his talents differ. He and Tammy are most effective playing a "man in the street" role, rather than standing aloof as teachers. Tears and cheers alike are more apt to be expressed openly and unashamedly on the *PTL Club* than on the *700 Club*. The Bakkers pride themselves on letting the Spirit lead the show, which means that at times a scheduled guest fails to appear and cameramen remain uncertain of what may be next. Tammy and Jim's exuberant down-home manners, language, and style, complete with co-host "Uncle Henry" Harrison, produce a show that is more homespun than the *700 Club*.

Criticism and Controversy: Unrest in the Kingdom

Evangelical Christian television in general, and the highly successful *PTL Club* and *700 Club* in particular, have been targets of criticism and controversy. Some objections stem from secular sources, but more often the dissent comes from religious writers. Under recent attack is the particular type of Christianity sold through the media and its inability to "reach the lost." Three other criticisms of the electronic church are its potential effect on local congregations, its political effects, and the methods of the television pastors (Hadden 1980).

Heresy on Television: The Trivializing of Christian Belief. Television often depicts a simple world of beautiful people in glamorous settings who live happily after every episode. It is designed as an escape into a fantasy world from the doldrums of daily living. It gives the appearance of reality without being too real. It may depict mundane problems of life, but without depth. It plays at being informative, but not intellectual. Successful programs must appeal to the widest possible audience.

The electric church has necessarily developed a popular Christianity that has prompted viewer support. It has, in the words of one critic (Yancey 1979), created the illusion of "a superculture, a realization of the very best the world has to offer." Television, particularly charismatic television, has been used to promote a heresy of health, wealth, and prosperity that fits the thriving medium. One non-Christian, curiously a regular viewer, is reported to have said, "If their God is so benevolent, why does he allow death and suffering? The Bible can't be as polyannaish as it seems on PTL" (Yancey 1979, p. 31). The television church, according to its critics, is guilty of "trivializing the Christian faith," making it a "consumer religion" and a source of "instant gratification" (*Charisma* 1980, p. 17).

Converting the Heathen: Who is Left to Save? It is difficult to refute the criticism that many popular Christian programs paint an ingenuous picture of life. Some of the stars themselves acknowledge that the message is simplified to fit the medium. Many of them apparently have more complex beliefs and a less simplistic conception of God than what they preach on the screen; but the theory seems to be that if you get them watching you get them saved. There are, however, indications that most of the viewers are already professed Christians (Hadden and Swann 1981). The television message may actually turn off more potential converts than it turns on. Whatever the validity of this criticism, there can be no doubt that the saved are in fact contributing millions of dollars per year to reach the unsaved.

Jim Bakker of PTL claims that 30,000 persons call in annually to report to telephone counselors that they have been "born again" through his program (Kehl 1980). Critics, however, have accused Bakker and others of misusing their own figures to encourage financial contributions. Martin Marty (1979, p. 991), a church historian and critic of the electronic church, wryly remarks that "After a decade of weekly and even nightly claims that so-and-so-many thousand pagans have hit the electronic sawdust trail and that therefore more than 100 percent of the population should be church members, church membership has not grown." Who is left to convert, Marty seems to argue, if the figures are indeed reliable?

Undoubtedly the vast majority of viewers of these shows are conservative Christians. Certainly the "faith partners" who support these shows with a twelve or fifteen dollar monthly contribution to the evangelists of their choosing are the ones whose favor must be curried. The ideology and fund-raising tactics always focus on the "end days" and "saving the lost." In reality, these programs may represent the viewers' desire for a comfortable and nonthreatening Christian message.

Living Room Church, Empty Pews. Some critics, usually from liberal denominations whose churches are suffering membership drain, have accused the electronic church of "sheep stealing," but there is little evidence to substantiate that claim. Both *PTL Club* and the *700 Club* often work through local churches to staff their telephone counseling lines, and new converts are directed to join local churches. The evangelists themselves, moreover, insist that the electric church is not a replacement for local congregational participation.

Critics may also worry about empty collection plates that accompany the empty pews. Believers who are entertained by Christian television send their dollars to support the media, it is argued, rather than support local congregations. Armstrong (1979, p. 151) rebuts this criticism by citing media-sponsored studies that suggest that only a small percentage of viewers (probably less than 5 percent) send financial contributions regularly. Those viewers who support the Christian media are more than likely supporting local churches as well. He concludes, "After carefully studying the major published reports, I find little to substantiate the fear that the electric church is draining money away from local churches."

Political Effects: The Conservatization of America. Another common criticism of the electronic church is that it is part of an evangelical effort to reshape American culture—a criticism that is "absolutely true" (Hadden 1980, p. 612). The television churches tend to espouse conservative politics and a lost culture that never really existed. The prime-time television stars of the electric church are sure that something has gone wrong with America, and the political liberals and secular humanists are the culprits. And they are sincerely convinced that God and the common man are on their side.

The politics reflected in charismatic television preaching is undoubtedly conservative. Robertson, who more than any other charismatic television minister expresses the sentiments of the Moral Majority, often presents an overly simplistic analysis of world affairs. Wall (1980) expresses a concern over the possible effects of his "teachings" that is shared by other critics: "Preachers like Robertson who poison the airwaves with right-wing views couched in biblical-prophecy language do not need to run for public office. They may be able to influence public debate to such an extent that all politicians are forced to pay them some homage, despite the distortion of political reality of which they are guilty." Robertson makes world leaders appear as pawns of a God who agrees with his own conservative approach to world politics. The way to avoid God's wrath is to be born again and presumably accept a conservative political stance (which is assumed to be biblical). Wall concludes that "what we have in some segments of the electronic church is not just competition with the institutional church but a serious threat to public discourse and potential for bigotry aimed at anyone who is not a 'born-again' Christian."

God as Capitalist: Mass-Marketing Christianity. If American evangelicals have in fact "mass-marketed" God, as critics say, charismatic television may be leading the way. Its demonstration of the gifts of the Holy Spirit, especially healing and prophecy, provides a spiritual drama that noncharismatic evangelical shows lack. Both groups, however, share in the creation of a colorful church on television that few local congregations can match. As one Australian observer has noted, "It is impossible to separate the techniques of capitalism from the U.S.'s current religious revival" (Smark 1978). God is packaged in the best wrapping Madison Avenue has to offer and sold to a viewing public with no apologies offered.

In addition to the methods of producing a message that fits the medium, the electronic church's methods of soliciting funds have also come under fire. The computerized letter that promises its recipient personal prayer, love, and concern is a sham to those who know it is impossible for Oral Roberts, Rex Humbard, or Pat Robertson to respond personally. The false intimacy created by the religious media speaks, perhaps, to the need for human love, warmth, and concern. The "we love you" and "we care" cooed over television and reaffirmed in computerized letters is better, apparently, than no word at all.

The Printed Word and the Charismatic Movement

There is definitely a reciprocal relationship between the development of the charismatic movement and the dissemination of its ideology through the communications media. This chapter has focused on the electric church as a means of promoting movement growth, but the printed word has also been an effective medium.

Publishing houses dealing primarily in charismatic literature have been doing well. In addition to the classical Pentecostal publishers, including Gospel Publishing House (Assemblies of God) and Pathway Press (Church of God), newer houses have developed to capture the growing market. These include Servant Publications, Dove Publications, and Fleming H. Revell Company, which are responsible for the bulk of the charismatic literature published.[9] Book exhibits are a feature of nearly all charismatic conventions and conferences and of many prayer meetings as well. Authors are regularly featured as guests on charismatic talk shows. Advertisements and book reviews in charismatic magazines alert readers to publications that are of potential interest.

The 1970s also witnessed the birth of several magazines for the charismatic believer. Perhaps the four best-known are *New Covenant, Catholic Charismatic, New Wine,* and *Charisma* (which recently incorporated *Logos Journal*). *New Covenant* and *Catholic Charismatic* are directed primarily toward a Catholic audience. *New Covenant,* which began in 1971, is a monthly publication which professes "to foster the charismatic renewal in the Catholic Church and to serve that church as an instrument of its renewal." Until *Catholic Charismatic* began in the spring of 1976, *New Covenant* was the voice of the Catholic charismatic movement. *New Covenant* represents a trend toward tightly organized, hierarchical covenant communities, theological conservatism, and minimum attention to Catholic tradition (e.g., Mary and the saints or the sacraments). *Catholic Charismatic,* as the title suggests, is oriented toward a Catholic audience and specifically seeks "to relate charismatic experience to the wealth of Catholic tradition." Perhaps paradoxically, it is more likely to take a liberal and humanistic stance on topics relevant to interpersonal relations than the morally authoritarian *New Covenant.*

Articles in *New Covenant* tend to be directive while those in *Catholic Charismatic* are less exhortive and more suggestive (Neitz 1981, pp. 132–35).

New Wine, the oldest neo-Pentecostal magazine, began publishing in 1968 and continues to be available without a subscription charge. (To remain on the mailing list, it is necessary only to correspond with the editor to assure continued interest in receiving the publication.) The magazine is directed by a board of four charismatic leaders who, as independent charismatics, were concerned about the lack of accountability enjoyed by many leaders. Reportedly to safeguard against their own leadership abuses, the four men pledged accountability to each other. *New Wine* reflects concern for strong leadership with the kind of accountability the board members have built into their relationships. *New Wine,* like *New Covenant,* tends to publish directive and exhortive articles.

In October, 1981, two formerly independent charismatic magazines merged: *Logos Journal,* established in 1970, was incorporated into *Charisma,* published since 1974. Both magazines appealed to a similar audience of evangelical charismatic Protestant believers. Unlike the more directive *New Wine* or *New Covenant, Charisma* editors note that "the views expressed in *Charisma* are not necessarily those of the editors of the magazine." Articles may be on controversial topics and care is taken to present different sides of such issues. *Charisma* (as had *Logos Journal*) tends to capitalize on the diversity within the charismatic movement and presents a wide range of opinions on topics such as healing, prosperity of believers, and various controversial charismatic ministries which are of interest to a charismatic audience.

Other evangelical and secular presses and magazines have published materials that serve to disseminate information on the movement. Early Pentecostals found that the only way to get their writings into print was to establish their own publishing houses. These publishing houses continue to serve Pentecostal denominations, but others have joined them to spread the ideology of the movement. Denominational materials are supplemented by nondenominational books and magazines.

The media are available now, as never before, to publicize the movement. According to some, this is the major difference between this religious renaissance and earlier ones (Zarctsky and Leone 1974). These media, in turn, advertise teaching cassettes, records, and conferences which further reinforce the message. The rise of the charismatic media, supported by believers, is a sign that there is a viable alternative to liberal, rationalized Christianity. The charismatic movement, complete with its myth and mystery, is not only surviving media technology but has employed it to advantage.

Notes

1. In analyzing Nielson Company viewing data for February and November, 1980, Martin (1981, p. 11) contends that the religious viewing audience may have reached its peak and may now be shrinking. He observed a decrease in the percentage of households viewing none out of ten of the most popular television ministries during that time period. Both Martin's analysis of Nielsen data and Hadden and Swann's (1981) use of Arbitron data suggest that the potential pool of religious viewers is limited and may not be able to support the expanding facilities. As this book was going into print, a more recent news announcement stated that, according to Arbitron data, "1981 was the biggest year in history for viewing religious broadcasting." The viewing audience increased from "slightly more than 15 million households" for November, 1980 to "almost 16 million households" for November, 1981 (*Charisma* 1982, p. 17).

2. Although Humbard's parents were Pentecostals, Humbard's own Akron church, the Cathedral of Tomorrow, has always been nondenominational and non-Pentecostal. During the 1950s and 1960s, the Cathedral appeared more Baptist in doctrine than Pentecostal. Its teachings were evangelical but it avoided controversial Pentecostal emphases. The rise of neo-Pentecostalism brought a charismatic minister to serve the Cathedral for a time during the 1970s, and neo-Pentecostals continue to be welcome as members, but neither the Cathedral nor the larger Humbard television ministry could be called charismatic. Humbard is sympathetic to the charismatic movement (for example, FGBMFI's Akron chapter holds its monthly meetings at the Cathedral-owned restaurant), but he himself has chosen not to promote Pentecostal ideology through his ministry. Just as he remains neutral on political issues, Humbard has attempted to remain neutral on the charismatic issue that has caused controversy among evangelicals.

3. Mariani (1978) describes the shift as a role change "from screeching faith healer" to that of the "Ed Sullivan of the Evangelical network." An illustration of the shift in Oral Roberts's emphases comes from a former dean of Oral Roberts University, Bob DeWeese, in a talk he delivered at a FGBMFI's (Akron) monthly meeting in Spring, 1980. DeWeese had suffered a heart attack and his chances for survival were slim. As Roberts was leaving DeWeese's hospital room, he met

DeWeese's young granddaughter and expressed his regret that "it doesn't appear as if your grandfather is going to make it." The young woman began to cry, saying "Brother Roberts, why don't you go in and pray the kind of prayer you *used* to pray with him." Roberts, according to DeWeese, immediately went back into his hospital room and prayed the kind of "faith-filled" prayer for which the evangelist had become famous. DeWeese recovered, to narrate his story to believing charismatic audiences across the country.

4. The power of National Religious Broadcasters to mobilize viewers to respond to perceived threats from the Federal Communications Commission may be observed in the response to the Milam-Lansman petition in 1975. The FCC reported nearly four million pieces of mail, most of it opposed to the petition that threatened to eliminate "the proclamation of the gospel via the airwaves in America." Milan and Lansman were opposed to the growth of religious broadcasting, but their petition requested an investigation to determine whether or not the religious licensees in the educational category were really living up to the standards set for educational television (Plowman 1975, pp. 44–45). The fact that the petition was not correctly understood by letter writers and that it would not have halted religious broadcasting is less important than the response of the viewers to a perceived threat to televising religious programs.

5. For a description of some of the distinguishing features of a few lesser-known evangelists see Andrews (1978) and Hadden and Swann (1981). Most of these men are involved in writing and speaking to mass audiences, as well as in radio and television ministries.

One evangelist who appears in the top five programs according to both Nielsen and Arbitron data, but who has not been featured in articles on the electric church by either secular or religious magazines, is Assemblies of God minister Jimmy Swaggart. A cousin to rock musician Jerry Lee Lewis, Swaggert is "an old-fashioned camp meeting preacher with a Nashville flair for music" who has earned several gold records (Hadden and Swann, 1981). The Jimmy Swaggart Evangelistic Association owns eight radio stations and produces a television program that is syndicated to 222 stations.

6. Using viewing data supplied by Nielsen and Arbitron, Martin (1981) and Hadden and Swann (1981) cast serious doubts on the size of the audiences claimed by television preachers and uncritically reported by the press. According to Arbitron data, *PTL Club* (in February, 1980) attracted only 668,170 viewers while the *700 Club* attracted 380,460. No program, according to Nielsen data, was viewed by more than two percent of the potential viewing audience for any single show.

7. For an account of *100 Huntley Street* see Mainse (1979). Mainse, a leader in the development of Christian television in Canada, has pioneered in children's programs which have found their way into commercial stations as well as Christian networks.

8. Pat Robertson is now setting his sights on family-centered networks to compete effectively with NBC, CBS, and ABC. In a mailing to viewers during the summer of 1980 and in preview presentations in September of that year,

Robertson called for "programs to change the world." The problem, according to the mailing, is that "the giants of television are flooding our homes with moral garbage and shaping America's lifestyle for evil rather than good." CBN now produces a daytime soap opera ("Another Life") and has purchased several other shows from independent producers (e.g., "This Week on Wall Street," "Romper Room," National Geographic specials, and movies produced by Billy Graham's evangelistic association's Worldwide Pictures), aimed at a diversified audience (Spring 1982).

9. The largest of the charismatic publishers, Logos International Fellowship (LIF), recently filed for bankruptcy. LIF had published some of the most popular charismatic books as well as the bimonthly *Logos Journal*. Its downfall was due reportedly to its unsuccessful attempt to publish a national Christian newspaper *(National Courier)* from 1975 to 1977, which left LIF $5 million in debt (Buckingham 1981, pp. 48–55).

PART III

Impact of the Movement

CHAPTER 10

Warming the Fires: The Charismatic Movement and the Mainline Churches

> The church has lost any vision for its life. Without that
> vision, the people are perishing. The vocation of those
> committed to rebuilding the church must therefore be to
> hold forth the vision of a renewed people in a church that
> no longer has the capacity to see it for itself. . . . We must,
> like the prophets, call God's people back to an
> understanding of who they are and to whom they belong.
> (Wallis 1980, p. 15)

One of the criteria used to distinguish a religious sect from a church is the state of tension that exists between the religious group and the social environment in which it exists (Stark and Bainbridge 1979). The early Pentecostals, who rejected worldly values and emphasized a fresh spiritual outpouring, were one among a number of evangelical groups who opposed the ways of the world, preferring to be singled out for their "puritanical" standards and "fanatical" worship rather than yielding to secular values. As Pentecostals joined other Americans in leaving behind the doldrums of the depression years for the economic growth and relative prosperity of the post–World War II era, many abandoned the external signs of Pentecostalism. Changes in dress and life-style, coupled with organizational changes such as more structured worship, indicated a routinization of the charisma that characterized early Pentecostalism. Pentecostal churches experienced a typical organizational transformation from a charismatic sect in conflict with a rationalistic and materialistic world to a bureaucratic structure adapted to this larger social order (Zald and Ash 1964). The movement of Pentecostalism away from its charismatic emphases was observed some fifteen years ago by British sociologist of religion Bryan Wilson (1966, pp. 220–21): the early enthusiasm of the Pentecostalists was abandoned as they came to recognize "that their particular teaching and practice was no more than an added blessing to the evangelical fundamentalist tradition in which it arose." There is little doubt that by mid-century Pentecostalism had come of age as an institutionalized church and that the tensions between its values and those of the larger social order were diminishing. Without the development of neo-Pentecostalism as a force of renewal for the charismatic movement, Pentecostalism was well on its way to becoming simply another orthodox Christian denomination.

Neo-Pentecostalism has been an important source of renewal and strength for upwardly mobile Pentecostals. This benefit of the charismatic movement has not always been recognized by those Pentecostals who have worked with these newer members of the movement. The manifest goal of those working in the neo-Pentecostal circles of the movement has been to spread the charismatic gospel to the mainline churches. The charismatic movement has thus served to reinforce the tenets of early Pentecostalism as well as to attract adherents in mainline denominations.

The Charismatic Movement and Classical Pentecostalism

Early Pentecostals may best be remembered for their unusually lively worship and puritanical life-style, but they were also steeped in a religious ideology that valued miracles and mystery. Many other evangelical and conservative Christian churches tenaciously defended the miracles recorded in the Bible, but few taught that such miracles could occur in a modern Christian's life. This belief in miracles conflicts with the dominant secular and rationalistic orientation of Western culture; but religious groups have, perhaps unwittingly, bought into such thinking to varying degrees—a trend that began long before the twentieth century (Berger 1967). Pentecostals proved to be vulnerable to the strong pull of rationalistic thought in contemporary culture. The early experiences of the Pentecostalists, like those of numerous groups before them, appeared in danger of disappearing.

The fires of Pentecostal experiences, however, appeared to be rekindled as members of established denominations began to give witness to the reality of Pentecost in our time. At first, such witness was viewed with hostility and suspicion, and Pentecostal leaders who associated with neo-Pentecostals met with opposition. Such feelings seem to be on the decline. Visits to numerous Pentecostal churches, conferences, and revivals suggest that the congregations that are most alive with fresh enthusiasm and growth are those whose leaders have some contact with neo-Pentecostalism. This contact is readily available to all through charismatic television programs, books, and magazines, as well as through nondenominational efforts such as the Full Gospel Businessmen's Group International.

A recent conference attended by the author serves as a good illustration of the sentiment of the largest Pentecostal denomination in America, the Assemblies of God. It supported the author's impression of a new openness toward neo-Pentecostalism on the part of this denomination and gave additional insights into the influence that neo-Pentecostalism may be having on classical Pentecostalism.

Conference on the Holy Spirit: A Case Illustration. In the fall of 1980, the Charismatic Committee of the Assemblies of God (AG) called for seven conferences on the Holy Spirit to be held in different locations in the country. The leaders of the AG Church, including the general and assistant general superintendents, the executive presbyter, the general secretary, and other high ranking church officers, were included among the speakers and panel participants. The audience appeared to be composed predominantly of AG ministers, although it was open to anyone who wished to attend. Included on the program attended by the author was David du Plessis, who had been defrocked as an AG minister in 1962 as a result of his activity with the World Council of Churches.[1] Only a few months prior to this 1980 conference, du Plessis had been reinstated as an AG minister, and the first of the conferences in Oak Park, New York, provided his first opportunity in nearly twenty years to participate in an AG-sponsored program.

One of the highlights of the two-day conference was the address given by du Plessis to the denomination that had once expelled him. As he shared with the audience his personal conviction of his God-given mission to witness to non-Pentecostals, even at the expense of being forced out of the denomination he loved and had served, the audience responded with a standing ovation!

The AG denomination, strongly suspicious and even hostile to neo-Pentecostalism during the 1950s and 1960s, has since become more sympathetic and supportive. Particularly noteworthy has been the change in attitude toward the Roman Catholic Church, once viewed as the "harlot church" of Revelations. It was perhaps primarily because du Plessis's ministry embraced not only Protestants but also members of the Catholic Church that he found himself cut off from AG fellowship. The suspicions and indictment of earlier years appeared to be totally absent among the fifteen men who participated in this program.

Some of the former opposition turned up in a few questions asked by some of the ministers in the audience following different panel presentations. Of particular interest were those revolving around charismatic practices such as "dancing in the Spirit" and "being slain in the Spirit," which are not part of traditional AG charismatic experiences, as well as some of the teachings made popular by charismatic television ministers that appear "unbalanced." The answers to such inquiries were open-minded and conciliatory. Leaders of the conference urged the audience not to limit the power of the Holy Spirit.

Most impressive to an outsider was the emphasis on working for the spread of the gospel, including the Pentecostal message, rather than on denominational loyalty or recruitment. In the face of difficult and potentially divisive questions, the AG church leaders and other panel participants exhibited a deep commitment to the Christian church, without any traces of the elitism that was apparently widespread at the onset of neo-Pentecostalism.[2] The host congregation, Full Gospel Tabernacle in Oak Park, New York, reflects an openness to neo-Pentecostalism. Undoubtedly there are AG pastors who still harbor old resentments and prejudices, but the leadership has clearly moved beyond this stage toward fellowship with newer converts to the charismatic movement.

As a denomination the Assemblies of God seems to have come closer to official approval of neo-Pentecostalism than some Pentecostal churches, but the AG is not alone in viewing neo-Pentecostalism as a fresh outpouring of God's Holy Spirit. The influence of this denomination and its stance on neo-Pentecostalism is reflected in the fact that the 1972 position paper on the charismatic renewal drafted by the AG has been adopted by other Pentecostal bodies as well (Synan 1979, p. 12). This position paper states: "We do believe in the institution of the Church. We trust the Holy Spirit to bring the members of Christ's Body into a true unity of the Spirit. If there is yet a truth to be revealed to the Church, it is the essential unity of the Body of Christ which transcends but does not destroy organizational bounds."

It appears that congregations which open to the more recent developments of neo-Pentecostalism tend to enjoy enthusiastic congregational worship, to experience prophecy frequently, to advocate and experience divine healing, and to express support for other charismatic gifts and practices such as receiving words of knowledge and being slain in the Spirit. The groups that are steeped in Pentecostal traditions and fearful of neo-Pentecostal developments, which they view as counterfeits of the "genuine" movement of the Holy Spirit, are in danger of routinizing charisma and appear to be petrified in terms of growth and influence.[3]

The Charismatic Movement and Non-Pentecostal Churches

Almost every Protestant and Orthodox denomination, as well as the Catholic Church, has been touched in one way or another by the charismatic movement. In most mainline denominations, some degree of organization has developed to publicize the movement's activities. In a few denominations, particularly some independent Baptist congregations and some districts of the Missouri Synod Lutherans,[4] opposition has developed to the charismatic movement. I am familiar with churches that have expelled charismatic members who practice glossolalia in private prayer. One church requests members who teach Sunday School, sing in the choir, or serve on boards, to sign a form professing that they do not speak in tongues. For the most part, however, such opposition is localized.

The opposition to neo-Pentecostalism has been similar to opposition to Pentecostalism in the early twentieth century, but its influence is much more limited. Extremists charge that the charismatic movement is the "work of Satan," while more moderate critics contend that it misguides otherwise good and sincere people. This opposition generally does not extend to the social structures that exist in all major denominations to facilitate the spread of the movement.

David du Plessis has observed with regard to the Pentecostal revival that throughout the world a similar pattern may be observed: fundamentalist churches are most likely to oppose the charismatic movement, evangelical denominations are moderately tolerant of it, while the liberal mainline denominations are the most supportive of charismatic efforts (du Plessis 1970, p. 28). This observation is basically accurate but requires some qualification. The terms "liberal," "evangelical," and "fundamentalist" are difficult to define. Most mainline churches, for example, have both evangelical and liberal wings. Quebedeaux (1978), in discussing the evangelicals, notes both liberal and more orthodox components in such denominations. The distinction is further blurred by the rise of evangelicalism in so-called liberal churches and also in the Catholic Church. It appears that those churches that insist on a verbatim and literal interpretation of the Bible are unwilling to allow for any phenomenon that does not support their predefined understanding. The more liberal denominations, already influenced by modernist thought, are more likely to admit the fresh insights of the Pentecostal experience. The difficulty in analyzing the evangelical mid-ground position is that liberals may tend to become more evangelical after a Pentecostal experience.

Second, the move away from liberal or modernist interpretations of the Bible by charismatic believers has, in turn, influenced the thinking of so-called evangelical churches. Within the past decade, evangelicals have apparently been greatly influenced by the charismatic movement. As du Plessis observes, fundamentalists may continue to oppose the movement, but it is often difficult to sort out the charismatics from the larger evangelical milieu. The decreasing significance of extreme fundamentalism to the American religious scene leaves the moderate evangelicals as the potential opposition to the charismatic movement. Such opposition has not developed in any cohesive form from evangelical circles and it is not likely to do so.

In general, any opposition movement has been overshadowed by a wide tolerance of charismatic teachings.[5] Individuals among the clergy and laity may not be in sympathy with the goals of Pentecostalism, but the leadership in most churches has given tacit acceptance to many of its teachings and activities. Opposition to the charismatic movement lacks the proponents' organizational strength, although it may surface with some strength in individual congregations.

The charismatic movement has affected the biblical teachings of the denominations it seeks to reshape. One of the factors responsible for congregational growth appears to be an evangelical approach to the Bible. Methodist or Presbyterian ministers who preach a "demythologized" Scripture or whose sermons are capsules of the week's news are not experiencing church growth.

The charismatic movement has also promoted both interdenominational and intradenominational unity among orthodox believers of different denominations.[6] This unity, however, must not be confused with organizational unity. Most charismatic ecumenists respect organizational boundaries and politics but emphasize a unity of spirit, in which common religious experience and belief join believers in a spiritual fellowship of harmony and cooperation. This desired unity is at present more an ideal than a reality, but there are numerous concrete signs that the ideal is being actively promoted.[7] The charismatic movement also fosters intradenominational unity. Religious "families" of Lutherans, Baptists, Mennonites, etc. are not necessarily related or cooperative in spirit or organization. Frequently, hostility occurs not only among denominations but within them as well. Charismatic service committees of different denominations tend to be organized as "Families" (simply as Lutheran, Baptist, Orthodox, etc.) rather than according to any more specific organizational tie (American Baptist, Southern Baptist, National Baptist, etc.).

Intradenominational Unity: Three Cases

The Episcopal Church: Ideological Pluralism. In its theology and practice, the Episcopal Church is both "Catholic" and "Protestant." Like the Roman Catholic Church, its strong episcopal form of government has prevented many of the splits and schisms that have beset other denominations. The Episcopal Church has demonstrated an ability to absorb certain differences rather than force their proponents to establish new denominations. The result is a distinct pluralism in belief and worship styles. At the same time, the bishops show various theological leanings that have led to a more heterogeneous episcopate than that of the Roman Catholic Church in America. Churches thus range from "low" Episcopalian (very Protestant in character) to "high" Episcopalian (very Catholic in worship and belief). Officially, there is but one Episcopal Church, but the internal variations are numerous.

Charismatic Episcopalians are reluctant to recognize such internal divisions. Issues addressed in the *Acts 29 Newsletter of the Episcopal Renewal Ministries* (formerly the *Episcopal Charismatic Fellowship*) are most likely to center on biblical teachings rather than intradenominational differences. Charismatic Episcopalians appear to adopt beliefs and practices from the entire spectrum of denominational inclinations. The Protestant component appears in the emphasis on the Bible rather than on Episcopal traditions (e.g., the Book of Common Prayer or the sacramental system). At the same time, the charismatic experience may lead members to a new appreciation of the Catholic roots of their tradition, including the practice of all seven sacraments (baptism, penance or confession, holy communion, marriage, ordination, confirmation, and sacrament of the sick), as opposed to the two (baptism and communion) practiced by the "low" church. Both the celebration of communion and the sacrament of confirmation, linked in both Episcopal and Roman Catholic theology to the Holy Spirit, may assume a deeper meaning for charismatic Episcopalians than for noncharismatics. Sunday morning worship may be "high church" Episcopalian, with some charismatic manifestations, but prayer meetings and praise services are also an indispensable part of the renewed Episcopal parish. Charismatics may form new divisions within the Episcopal church—and in some cases charismatic beliefs and manifestations have divided local parishes—but there is also evidence that charismatics contribute to the unification of the pluralistic beliefs of Episcopalians.

The Lutheran Synods: Structural Pluralism. Unlike the the organizationally unified Episcopalians, Lutherans are represented by some fourteen denominations. Some of these groups have been reluctant to fraternize and may be openly critical of Lutheran congregations with different emphases. The charismatic movement has been viewed by some of these leaders as another potential source of division. The Missouri Synod of the Lutheran church published a cautionary report in 1977 that was followed by a stronger statement in the *Lutheran Witness*: "Pastors who propagate neo-Pentecostal doctrine in Lutheran congregations often divide the church and thereby give offense to their flocks. Therefore, they must take seriously the possibility of coming under church discipline" (cited in Jungkuntz 1977, p. 3).

Such opposition has been met organizationally through the Lutheran Charismatic Renewal Services (LCRS), which serves all denominations of the Lutheran family. It attempts to interpret neo-Pentecostalism within Lutheran theology and thus facilitate the growth of neo-Pentecostalism. For example, Lutheran theologian R. T. Jungkuntz (1977, p. 4) acknowledges that the Pentecostal theology of the baptism of the Holy Spirit is not in accord with the Lutheran Confessions. However, he claims that this baptism is in accord with Lutheran theology:

In this view baptism in the Holy Spirit is understood not as an event "beyond" sacramental baptism in the sense of "separate from," but as an event "within" sacramental baptism and yet an event to be "distinguished'' from its initial expression with water. Such a view in no way diminishes the significance of sacramental baptism, but merely speaks of the manner by which, according to God's promise, the benefits of sacramental baptism might be more fully released and manifested in the life of the believer.[8]

The attempt to explain charismatic phenomena in accord with the Lutheran Confessions has brought together members of different Lutheran congregations and has enabled them to put aside other divisive issues, while at the same time affirming Lutheranism. One of the aims of the Lutheran Charismatic Renewal Services is to make "better Lutherans." Delbert Rossin, a leader of the LCRS, said of his own congregation (Faith Lutheran Church–Missouri Synod): "We are better Lutherans now as far as appreciating our Sacramental and liturgical heritage than we were before the renewal began" (Matzat 1977, pp. 3–4).

A further split within Lutheranism may create a charismatic denomination, but such a schism is not the goal of Lutheran charismatics. They do not seek to be recognized as a ''mission group'' because that would lessen the impact of the charismatic movement on the institutional church. Lutherans want "the renewal's spiritual life to have a dynamic impact on the church and to be integrated into the church" (Vaagenes 1980, p. 8).

Orthodox Charismatic Renewal: Ethnic and Structural Pluralism. The divisions among Orthodox Christians have been more a result of ethnic than theological differences. The Albanians, Armenians, Bulgarians, Ukranians, Romanians, Russians, Greeks, and Syrians have been fragmented in the Orthodox tradition by cultural and linguistic differences. The Service Committee for Orthodox Charismatic Renewal has brought together Orthodox charismatics to further the movement within the Eastern churches, regardless of ethnic origin.

Theosis, the Newsletter for Orthodox Charismatic Renewal, emphasizes the charismatic renewal's adaptation to Orthodox tradition and theology. Father Boris Zabrosky, a leader of the Service Committee for Orthodox Charismatic Renewal, commented that "The charismatic experience is not only harmonious to our Orthodox tradition, but it is the very expression of the life to be found in the church." *Theosis* features articles that explain the consistency of Orthodox piety and tradition with the baptism of the Holy Spirit and the accompanying gifts.[9]

Each of the three groups considered provides an illustration of how the charismatic movement has contributed to intradenominational unity in different types of religious structures. The Episcopalians are united organizationally but divided ideologically. The biblically conservative charismatic ideology provides a common ground for "high" and "low" church believers. The Lutherans represent an organizationally fragmented denomination. Again, a conservative biblical theology and shared charismatic experience serves to unify different Lutheran denominations. The American Orthodox churches have been historically divided by Old World ethnic differences. The charismatic movement provides an ideology that transcends historical divisions and a purpose for coming together in fellowship.[10]

Interdenominational Unity

The spirit of unity among charismatics bridges both denominational and interdenominational differences. Charismatics have participated in conferences jointly sponsored by Catholics and Protestants, as well as in those of particular denominations other than their own. The International Charismatic Conference, held in Kansas City in 1977, included over 40,000 participants from all denominations.[11] Newsletters and journals serving a particular denomination regularly feature charismatic events and personalities of other denominations.

The leader of charismatic Roman Catholics, Cardinal Suenens of Belgium, views the charismatic movement as heralding a third Christian millennium. The first millennium saw an almost undivided Christian church; the second was marked by the Orthodox Roman Catholic schism of the eleventh century and the Protestant Reformation of the sixteenth century. Suenens sees the charismatic movement as one of "certain signs dawning on the horizon . . . that the restoration of visible unity is at hand" (Suenens 1978, pp. 107–8). While not all charismatics agree with Suenens's prognosis of "visible unity," most concur with the spirit of the statement.

Many differences and divisions, however, still exist both among charismatics and between charismatics and noncharismatics. The potential divisions and disharmony over doctrinal issues may be viewed as an inevitable part of the movement and may even be a sign of vitality. A unity that respects individual differences is precarious but essential to organizational life. Furthermore, competition or conflict may actually be a force for needed institutional changes.[12]

Gathering Storms: Some Areas of Conflict

The unity being furthered by the charismatic movement is also a potential source of conflict within denominations—perhaps particularly within so-called liberal denominations. Denominations such as the United Church of Christ (formerly the Congregationalist-Christian and the Evangelical and Reformed Churches), the United Presbyterian and the United Methodist Churches, where modernist (nonorthodox) Christian theology had made great inroads, are also experiencing the charismatic influence. The movement tends to support conservative theology that is closer to the fundamentalist end of the belief spectrum than the modernist. Within these denominations, the old battle lines are being redrawn between modernism and fundamentalism (actually a more moderate *evangelical* position), with the charismatics situated firmly in the evangelical camp.[13]

There are several interrelated areas of disagreement plaguing liberal churches. The first is the conflict between the evangelical approach to Scripture as the literal word of God and the modernist tendency to "demythologize" the Bible. This difference in biblical interpretation leads the charismatics into fellowship with other evangelicals who support orthodox denominational creeds. The need for salvation, acceptance of Jesus as the Son of God and the redeemer of the world, and belief in the virgin birth are orthodox beliefs contained in church creeds but not necessarily held as tenets by ministers or members.[14]

The conservative biblical trend raises other related issues. The role of social action (often referred to as the "social gospel") in the church is a second area of disagreement, particularly with regard to the type of programs to be funded by churches. The role of women in the church and the status of homosexuals are also areas of conflict. Both the ordination and leadership of women and especially the ordination of homosexuals are critical issues that have led some charismatics to break with their denominations.

The United Presbyterian Church: A Case Illustration.   As early as 1969 the United Presbyterian Church demonstrated a sympathetic attitude toward the charismatic movement. The committee appointed to report on neo-Pentecostalism acknowledged and approved of the worldwide growth of Pentecostalism and the newly emergent charismatic movement in the mainline churches. It further stated:

The committee is grateful to observe the rapid breaking down of barriers that have separated Protestant denominations from our brethren in the Roman Catholic and Greek [sic] Orthodox Churches. Similarly, we are glad to note the beginning of a breakdown of the barriers that have deprived us of fellowship with Pentecostal denominations. Believing that both of these are the result of the work of the Holy Spirit, we call on United Presbyterians to be sensitive and responsive to the insights and experiences of fellow Christians within all traditions. (Report of the Special Committee on the Work of the Holy Spirit, 1970, p. 1)

Despite the official recommendation of this committee, the execution of policy rests in the hands of the local presbytery.[15] While the presbytery may reflect the sentiment of local ministers, it is also possible to have, in effect, a "tyranny of the majority" operating against minority views. Reportedly, this happened to two congregations within the liberal Denver, Colorado, presbytery, leading to their secession (in late 1979) from the United Presbyterian Church.[16]

The seceeding congregations were theologically conservative and experiencing rapid growth. They might have been able to live and let live within the denomination, but attempts were made to divert the churches from evangelical causes to those approved by the Presbyterian Church. This move, coupled with an earlier attempt to force another Denver congregation to appoint women and minorities to the church board, led to increased tension over the funding of Presbyterian causes. ordination of women, and the feared ordination of homosexuals.

In response to this "resistance to renewal," the general secretary of the Presbyterian Charismatic Communion and editor of *Renewal News* wrote:

We had earlier informed the denominational hierarchy that the United Presbyterian Church has lost tens of thousands of charismatics during the past decade because of the subtle and not so subtle intimidation of many pastors, many sessions, and many presbyteries. There may be at least 100,000 of us still persevering. We believe we have been commissioned to pray, to fast, to love, to work, to witness, to contribute toward renewing the Presbyterian and Reformed churches. It is a difficult assignment which cannot be accomplished apart from the power and the wisdom of God's Holy Spirit nor apart from submitting totally to the Lordship of Jesus. (Bradford 1980, p. 4)

The extent of such tensions in Presbyterian and other denominations is difficult to evaluate. The events in the Denver presbytery certainly demonstrate the existence of unresolved tension leading to conflict between charismatic and noncharismatic Presbyterians. Only the passage of time will reveal the direction the movement will take. The desire for unity expressed by both sides of the charismatic issue may lose out to the kind of divisiveness that occurred in Colorado.

Vision for the 1980s

On the basis of the current situation we can predict some of the likely effects of the charismatic movement on mainline churches in the future. There will be signs of greater unity among orthodox Christians with less emphasis on the term "charismatic" and more emphasis on translating charismatic phenomena into the language of existing doctrine of the Holy Spirit in an attempt to reach others who may be charismatic in spirit but not in name. The rift will continue to grow between liberal and conservative Christians, but the latter will likely hold greater power, due to the greater personal and financial commitments of the theological conservatives. Tension will also grow between the more conservative churches and the social order over the promotion of values that are believed to be at odds with conservative Christian principles. This is particularly evident in the rising opposition to secular humanism which is viewed by many evangelicals, including charismatics, as the "false religion" of America (see Gordon 1980).

The charismatic movement differs from most earlier religious movements in its ecumenical scope. It cannot be traced to a single leader and has thus transcended denominational barriers (Hocken 1979). Hostility and suspicion between Protestants and Catholics as well as among different Protestants themselves has largely prevented the spread of revivals across denominational lines. Some of the old hostility and suspicion lingers, but evangelicals appear more willing to give credit to the charismatic movement "for a breakthrough in spiritual reality and power," which is presently "a missing dimension" in many evangelical churches (Pinnock 1981, p. 16).

Thus the charismatic movement is likely to increase unity among denominations, promote theological conservatism (although not necessarily political conservatism) within so-called liberal denominations, and conflict increasingly with the secular values of society. Believers are bound together by a shared personal experience that transcends denomi-

national lines—an experience they are committed to transmit through
personal and collective evangelization efforts. The revival fires are
burning, and charismatics expect them to spread throughout the Christian
world.

Notes

1. Du Plessis's tenure with the Assemblies of God, U.S.A., was relatively brief. It was only in 1955, perhaps before the AG realized the depth of his commitment to ecumenism, that du Plessis's ordination papers were transferred from South Africa's Apostolic Faith Mission to the AG in the United States denomination. (See du Plessis 1970, 1977 for an account of his activities.)

2. When the author reported the events of the conference to a minister involved with neo-Pentecostals in another classical Pentecostal denomination, the minister commented, "The hierarchy of my church certainly has not come that far! What is encouraging to me, however, is the attitude of many younger ministers who are not now in the hierarchy and the evidence I see of shifts in our voting patterns at our last general conference." Different Pentecostal denominations may be at different stages in their acceptance of the neo-Pentecostal movement, but the move appears clearly to be one toward acceptance rather than rejection.

3. In talking with an AG minister who had previously been affiliated with another denomination, I inquired about his opinion as to why that denomination does not seem to be benefiting from overall Pentecostal growth. He cited his former denomination's elitist attitudes toward other Pentecostal denominations and neo-Pentecostalism. Such isolation, whether self-imposed or forced, leaves these groups out of the charismatic movement, although they may be nominally part of its structure.

4. The report of the Commission on Theology and Church Relations of the Lutheran Church, Missouri Synod, issued in April, 1977, stopped short of condemning the charismatic movement. It recognized that there were both charismatic pastors and members within the denomination and chose to be critical of select teachings rather than denouncing the entire movement. Its caution about "practices and theological tenets of this movement that conflict with Biblical doctrine" nevertheless included the core Pentecostal teaching of "baptism in the Holy Spirit." The manner in which it is written allows the document to be used by some synod leaders to stifle the movement in their districts or to quietly permit it to develop (*Charisma* 1981, p. 20).

5. I recently attended a conference on the Holy Spirit sponsored by the East Ohio Conference of the United Methodist Church which illustrates a tacit acceptance of charismatic phenomena not widely experienced among Methodist churches of this particular district. While there was no manifestation of the controversial charismatic gifts of healing, tongues, or prophecy, the basic teachings were in agreement with the charismatic movement. One minister expressed a concern about "charismania," but he appeared equally concerned about "charisphobia." The large turnout was completely unexpected by conference organizers. Over 800 persons attended, and a couple hundred more were turned away for lack of space. I see this particular conference on the gifts of the Holy Spirit as paving the way for subsequent gatherings with an open display of the gifts.

6. Social science studies of religion and those utilizing religion as a background variable have generally failed to distinguish *among* Lutherans, Baptists, Orthodox, etc., in effect treating these denominations as undifferentiated wholes. The *Handbook of American and Canadian Churches* lists 23 different Baptist bodies, 6 different Brethren churches, 20 "Eastern" churches, 14 Lutheran, and 12 Methodist bodies. The editor further notes: "It is not to be assumed, however, that all denominations under one family heading are similar in belief or practice. . . . The family categories provided one of the major pitfalls of the church statistics because of the tendency to combine the statistics by 'families' for analytical and comparative purposes. *Such combined totals are almost meaningless,* although often used as variables for sociological analysis (Jacquet 1980, p. 106; my italics).

7. This conception of unity bears distinct resemblance to Robert Park's conceptualization of the process of assimilation. For Park (1950, p. 257) assimilation need not eradicate individual differences, nor does it permanently eliminate competition or conflict. What assimilation does assure is enough unity of experience to allow a "community of purpose and action" to emerge.

8. Jungkuntz's theology of the baptism of the Holy Spirit corresponds to that of other liturgical denominations, including the Roman Catholic, Orthodox, and Episcopal churches. It appears that less sacramentally oriented (and less liturgical) churches may be more likely to accept a Pentecostal theology of the baptism.

9. Munk's (1978, pp. 1–3) article, "The Charismatic Experience in Orthodox Tradition," demonstrates that tradition is a source of authority that exists along with the Bible. While Protestants emphasize the Bible as the sole source of revelation, both Roman Catholic and Orthodox Christians regard sacred tradition (council decisions, writings of early fathers of the church, history, etc.) as an equally important source of faith. While neo-Pentecostal Protestant writers concentrate on the biblical evidence of charismatic experience, both Orthodox and Roman Catholics also interpret such experiences in light of church tradition.

10. See McDonnell (1981), a three-volume collection of over 100 documents published on the charismatic movement by major Christian denominations between 1960 and 1980.

11. For more details on the 1977 Kansas City Conference see articles in *New Wine* (October, 1977) and Manuel (1977). The latter is a book-length personal

account of the planning of the conference and the charismatic groups that formed as a result of it.

12. See Lewis Coser (1956) for an excellent discussion of the effects of conflict on organizational structure. Coser's work specifies conditions under which conflict is beneficial in promoting group cohesion and in identifying boundary lines of groups.

13. Regardless of one's theological preferences, it appears that the only way to strengthen the institutional church is by returning to conservative theology. Contemporary society has tended more toward heterogeneity and specialization, and some recent church theologicans have attempted to vary church goals. An institutionalized church that is godless and goalless, that seeks to duplicate social and governmental services, is not likely to flourish in a specialized social order. Evidence for this thesis may be found in declining church membership among those churches that have moved furthest along the continuum toward secularization and toward replacing religious theology with humanistic philosophy.

14. See Glock and Stark (1965) for a comparison and contrast of major denominations of such orthodox beliefs.

15. In questioning Dr. Brick Bradford, the general secretary of the Presbyterian Charismatic Communion, about what I perceived to be a more limited growth of the charismatic movement in the Presbyterian church than in some other denominations, Dr. Bradford wrote: ''You are correct in concluding that the charismatic renewal has not moved as rapidly within the Presbyterian denominations as it has within the Episcopal and Roman Catholic. This may be partially due to the form of government in which we are confronted with a 'corporate bishop' rather than a single person. This can be both a safeguard and a hindrance.''

16. For a newspaper account of the secession of these two Presbyterian congregations see Virginia Culver's article in the *Denver Post* (November 9, 1979); it is reprinted in *Renewal News* (January–February, 1980).

CHAPTER 11

Power and Politics: Charismatics on Social Issues and Political Action

> On my arrival in the United States, the religious aspect of the country was the first thing that struck my attention; and the longer I stayed there, the more I perceived the great political consequences resulting from this new state of things. (Tocqueville 1945, p. 308)

Alexis de Tocqueville, the famous nineteenth-century French observer of American democracy, admired a religion that was politically liberal yet morally conservative (Stout 1974, p. 315). In contrast to the conservative political flavor of contemporary evangelicalism, the perspective of many early Americans was precisely this blend of conservative theology and liberal politics admired by Tocqueville. Bible-believing Protestants promoted far-reaching change, particularly through the abolitionist and feminist movements. Tocqueville was convinced that such action-oriented religion was a major force "which powerfully contributes to the democratic republic amongst the Americans" (Tocqueville 1974, p. 378).

The pre–Civil War forerunners of evangelicalism were instrumental in initiating change. Men like Jonathan Blanchard, the founder of the evangelical Wheaton College (Illinois), and Charles G. Finney, the famous nineteenth-century evangelist, were outspoken opponents of slavery (Dayton 1976). Oberlin College, once an evangelical stronghold, was a center of abolitionist, integrationist, and feminist activity. The first

American conference for women's rights in Seneca Falls, New York, was held in a Wesleyan Methodist church in 1848. The evangelicals, who urged abolition and equal rights for women, faced the theological conservatives of established denominations who used biblical exegesis to oppose both social movements, much as some of the descendants of these evangelicals now use biblical exegesis to oppose the contemporary civil rights and feminist movements.

Evangelical activists calling for equal rights for blacks and women represent a position quite different from evangelical politics of the twentieth century, which, for the most part, have either been indifferent or opposed to these and other social reforms. Billy Graham, perhaps the best-known evangelical spokesman of today, expressed his political indifference when asked to use his friendship with President Nixon to stop the bombing in Vietnam: "I am convinced that God has called me to be a New Testament evangelist, not an Old Testament prophet. While some may interpret an evangelist to be primarily a social reformer or a political activist, I do not!" (cited in Dayton 1976, p. 8). Many present-day evangelicals do, however, defend political conservatism from a supposedly biblical point of view. *Christianity Today,* a leading evangelical publication, at one time supported "voluntary segregation," accused Martin Luther King's pro-integration stance of being implicitly communist, and defended the war in Vietnam. Unlike their nineteenth-century predecessors, who were leaders in controversial areas of social reform, present-day evangelicals have tended to "alter their position only in response to a reversal of popular consensus or official national policy" (Oliver 1975).

More recently, an openly political position has emerged as a potent force within the evangelical fold in the form of the conservative Moral Majority. While many evangelicals still remain apolitical, and some may have liberal political ties, many others openly equate the God of Abraham, Isaac, and Jacob with capitalism, democracy, and conservative politics. They claim to have made a decisive impact on the 1980 national elections and promise to restore morality to the American fiber.

Conservative politics dominate evangelicalism, but there are some evangelicals who favor liberal social and political action similar to that of the first half of the nineteenth century. This minority speaks for the poor and underprivileged, for Christian feminism, against the economic oppression of Third World countries, and against nuclear weapons. The liberal evangelicals, however, have few of the media resources of their conservative brothers and sisters.

Evangelical Christians, including their theological kin in the charismatic movement, thus span the political spectrum from conservative to liberal, although conservatives are a decided majority. This conservatism is an American phenomenon, rooted in the late nineteenth- and twentieth-century history of the United States. It differs from the charismatic-evangelical political stance of Latin America or Africa. In order to understand the relationship between conservative politics and evangelicalism, we must begin with the pre–Civil War evangelical's tendency toward political liberalism.

Evangelicalism, Pentecostalism, and Politics in Historical Context

The forerunners of evangelicalism took liberal and even radical stands on social issues, including abolition, racial integration, and feminism. A shift began to take place by the 1870s. There is an ebb and flow between periods of creative vitality and periods of stability which consolidate and institutionalize gains. The latter period, to some extent, includes a reaction against the reforms. We have seen this ebb and flow in the United States with a liberal emphasis in protecting rights of the poor and minority groups during the 1960s which in turn led to new legislation. The early 1980s is witnessing a reaction to this legislative reform and the rise of political conservatism. Similar shifts occurred in evangelical politics after the Civil War as the pendulum swung from liberalism toward conservatism.

Several reasons have been provided for this shift in evangelical politics. Intense social struggles are difficult for a group to sustain over long periods of time. The shift may also be related to generational differences in attitude with the second generation reacting to the intense activism of their parents (Dayton 1976, p. 122–24). Furthermore, new religious movements often turn to the poor and disinherited for support, demanding high ethical and moral involvement. The upward mobility of social reforms and their followers tended to conservatize them as they struggled to maintain their newfound status (Niebuhr 1929). Whatever the exact socio-historical reasons, the post–Civil War evangelists became more concerned with "personal purity" than social reform. It was within this context that the Holiness movement, the direct forerunner of Pentecostalism, was spawned.

During this time two definite camps began to form within American Protestantism: fundamentalism and modernism. The theologically liberal or modern camp was attracted to newly developing scientific thought, which they attempted to integrate with their theology. The more conservative wing adopted an antiscientific stance and a conservative biblical theology. Tutle (1978, p. 66) astutely notes that "the Holiness Movement overreacted. The personal gospel had been severed from the social." In contrast to the social conscience exhibited by earlier revivalists, the great preachers of the latter half of the nineteenth century failed to address themselves to emerging social concerns. They never seriously challenged such concepts as laissez faire capitalism or the rights of organized labor (Jorstad 1972, p. 121).

The two major twentieth-century attempts of evangelical-fundamentalists to influence a large, more pluralistic United States with their conservative morality were failures.[1] The movement for fundamentalist education met defeat in the famous Scopes "Monkey" Trial of 1925, and the repeal of Prohibition ended temperance activism (Stout 1974). Thoroughly defeated, the evangelicals regrouped to proclaim the "radical nature of sin" and to warn against "treating the symptoms as the source of difficulty" (Inch 1978, p. 123). The evangelicals were ready to leave social action to the liberals who, they felt, were neglecting the Bible, and to take upon themselves the task of spreading the gospel. There was a renewed emphasis on an imminent second coming of Jesus, from which followed the corollaries that there is nothing worthwhile in contemporary society and that sin must increase for the biblical prophecies to be fulfilled (Jorstad 1972, p. 77). The evangelical's task was to save as many souls as possible during these "last days."

The neo-Pentecostal movement emerged from this apolitical evangelical milieu during the 1950s and 1960s. Church historian Martin Marty (1975, p. 224) observes that the demise of numerous Christian social action movements in the late 1960s was "contemporary with the rise of the new pentecostalism." However, the neo-Pentecostals, many of whom had been involved in Christian social action, were appalled by the seeming indifference to social issues of many charismatics from Pentecostal or evangelical backgrounds.

Given the diverse roots of the charismatic movement, it is not surprising that no single political perspective has emerged. Many remain apolitical. Evangelical-charismatics who have taken positions on politics and social action, have tended to emphasize "personal morality" issues, such as homosexuality, pornography, and abortion. A smaller group has asserted that moral issues include social concerns. Charismatics from liberal mainline churches may be more likely to align with the latter group in emphasizing social justice, freedom from hunger, and human rights.

In order to contrast these two positions, one representing an offshoot of early nineteenth-century evangelicalism and the other demonstrating a later-day evangelical conservatism, I will discuss a representative of each camp. The politically conservative position is perhaps best represented by Pat Robertson, founder of CBN television network and host of the *700 Club*. Jim Wallis, the editor of *Sojourners* magazine and a founder of the Sojourners Community, is a voice from the liberal minority.[2]

Two Approaches to Christian Political Action

Pat Robertson: Moral Majority in Charismatic Dress[3]. Pat Robertson, the son of a senator from Virginia, grew up surrounded by politics. His conversion to charismatic Christianity led him into full-time gospel work through television, but politics are inseparable from his mission. Through the Christian Broadcasting Network and through the *700 Club,* Robertson disseminates conservative politics through his teachings on the *700 Club,* through its newsletter, *Pat Robertson's Perspectives,* through CBN news coverage, and through rallies. As host of the *700 Club,* Robertson is a teacher, preacher, and prophet, as well as economist, historian, and social commentator. Some programs may focus on religious topics such as prayer, healing, or the dangers of religious cults, but others are clearly (and increasingly) political in nature. For example, his shows from May 12 to 23, 1980, revolved around the theme of "Good News for a World in Crisis." (The eruption of Mt. St. Helens provided a "divinely ordained" confirmation of the message that the world is entering its final days.) Through selected Bible passages and an even more selective use of history, political analysis, and natural science, he explained world events and their relation to the end of the world. Robertson shows similar skills in topics as diverse as today's inflationary economy and how to have a happy and well-adjusted family.

Two frequent targets of Robertson's wrath are "secular humanism" and "big government." He presents secular humanism as a new religion taught in schools to compete with Christian moral principles. Humanism, with its culturally relativistic beliefs, is a direct attack on the absolutes of the Bible.[4] A film made by CBN for general distribution, denounces secular humanism for its goal of providing a "good life" here and now rather than preparing for external life.[5] Big government supports secular humanism through such measures as funding programs to develop "values clarification" courses in elementary schools and legalizing abortion. If secular humanism is the religion, big government is God. As Robertson expresses it:

The basic problem in politics is: either God is God, or government is God. Now if government is the court of last resort, if government is womb to tomb . . . we're going to have all-encompassing health insurance, all-encompassing medical protection, all-encompassing work laws, and so forth. Well now, the problem is only God has unlimited resources. But the government doesn't have unlimited resources. (Williams 1979, p. 20)

Robertson's conservative politics seem to call for laissez faire capitalism while maintaining that God provides for the poor.[6]

Robertson's conservative politics are not only disseminated on the airwaves but are also available in print for faithful contributors. Each "member" of the *700 Club* who contributes fifteen dollars or more per month to CBN receives a monthly report called *Pat Robertson's Perspectives*. These reports take a clear-cut stand on almost all political issues. An analysis of the content of issues from February, 1977, through June, 1979, produced the following list of positions: (1) opposition to the Panama Canal treaty; (2) strong support for the use of nuclear power as an answer to the energy shortage; (3) support of Israel and opposition to a Palestinian state in the region; (4) abolition of public education; (5) opposition to the recognition of Red China; (6) belief that President Carter is an honest, decent man, but inept as president; (7) prediction of a "Great Depression" in 1982; (8) need for a balanced federal budget; (9) need for lower taxes and less government intervention in state, local, private, and business affairs; (10) opposition to homosexual rights legislation; (11) support of a tough military line against all communist countries; need for heavy military build-up for the U.S.; (12) opposition to the Equal Rights Amendment; (13) opposition to a national health insurance plan and any form of "Keynesian economics" or "state socialism" like welfare, workfare, etc.; (14) belief that more Christians should get involved in government; opposition to complete separation of church and state; (15) belief that nuclear war will be an inevitable part of God's judgment in the "end times," possibly soon; (16) belief that the U.S. government should support the white governments in Africa; favoring the recognition of Rhodesia and backing of the existing coalition government; (17) belief that the U.S. should increase arms sales to anti-Communist countries; (18) belief that the government and individuals should operate on a minimum of credit; (19) favoring the draft for all male youth at age eighteen or upon finishing high school; (20) belief that big oil corporations are secretly backing the antinuclear power movement (see Williams 1979, p. 18).

With continuing crisis in the Middle East, the end of inflation not to be seen, and the national debt greater than ever, *Pat Robertson's Perspectives* has continued to expound many of these positions throughout the 1980 volume. Robertson cites earthquakes, weather conditions, and localized military conflicts in support of his eschatology, causing him to sound more like an Old Testament prophet than a modern evangelist.

Robertson usually stops short of endorsing any particular political candidate or party. In a statement made in the August, 1980, issue of *Perspectives* he asserts that *"whatever happens, Christians should not get too excited that this election will bring any great change"* (Robertson 1980, p. 4). Due to years of mismanagement of world affairs, limitation of presidential powers and an indecisive Congress, and a powerful "Eastern establishment," Robertson believes that a significant change in policy is unlikely by either the Democratic or Republican parties. Robertson's politics are more "issue oriented" than "politician" or "party oriented."

Robertson has expressed a clear commitment to CBN's coverage of the news. The network plans to expand into a full news coverage over the next ten years to prepare viewers to make their political choices. Robertson himself does not develop the news broadcasts, but he hires writers and producers with a political philosophy akin to his own. The news, as presented by CBN, has a biblical slant in accord with Robertson's politics and religion.

Pat Robertson accepted an invitation from John Gimenez, a relatively unknown charismatic minister from Virginia Beach, to serve on the

sponsoring committee of the 1980 Washington for Jesus Rally. Robertson's chairmanship of the program provided the momentum for the rally,
which attracted over 200,000 persons (Hadden and Swann 1981, pp.
127–28). The expressed purpose for the rally was to attract persons to
Washington, D.C., "to pray and to repent." The rally was backed by
both charismatics and evangelicals, a fact leading Hadden and Swann
(1981, p. 128) to observe: "In fact, the Washington rally was the first
time that charismatics and evangelicals had ever cooperated on anything
of significance."

Although Robertson denied the political nature of the rally, its site as
well as the content of addresses given were politically conservative.
Three primary problems were reiterated that demonstrated the plight of
America: military weakness, destruction of the family, and economic
disintegration (Shenk 1980). In addition to the one hundred speeches,
many of which had political overtones, the political thrust of the rally was
demonstrated by a widely distributed "Christian Declaration" contain-
ing explicitly political and economic views and a letter sent to some
senators and congressmen urging them to attend the rally to learn "how
we want you to vote" on various issues (Hadden and Swann 1981, p.
129).

Jim Wallis: Radical Politics in Christian Attire[7].   While Robertson
and Wallis share basic evangelical theology and a conviction that Christians must be politically active, Wallis's emphases are very different from
Robertson's. As a student at Michigan State University and Trinity
Evangelical Divinity School (Deerfield, Illinois) during the late-1960s,
Wallis was haunted by the needs of the poor and the seeming indifference
of evangelical Christians to their plight. Influenced by the works of Karl
Marx, Wallis reached a point at which it was either "Marx or Jesus"—
either he would remain a Christian or become a Marxist. He decided to
give the gospel another reading. In doing so he was struck by Jesus'
concern for the poor and a gospel that told His followers they were to
share in this concern. This teaching, however, was not being lived out in
many evangelical circles. Wallis and others with a similar desire to
reconcile Christianity with social action began to publish a tabloid called
the *Post-American,* later changed to *Sojourners.*

The spiritual dimension of Wallis and Sojourners continued to deepen
during the 1970s, particularly as a result of its fellowship with a group of
charismatic Catholics in Chicago, before Sojourners moved to Washington in 1975. Graham Pulkingham and the neo-Pentecostal Church of the

Redeemer shared Sojourner's vision of spiritual life wedded to social action.

Wallis's most complete statement of the relationship between politics, social action, and evangelical Christianity may be found in his book, *Agenda for Biblical People* (1976). In it he clearly states his commitment to Bible-believing Christianity, but he is critical of religious liberals as well as conservatives who represent what he terms "establishment Christianity":

Establishment Christianity has made its peace with the established order. It no longer feels itself to be in conflict with the pretensions of the state, with the designs of economic and political power, or with the values and style of life enshrined in the national culture. Establishment Christianity is a religion of accommodation and conformity, which values realism and success more than faithfulness and obedience. It is heavily invested in the political order, the social consensus, and the ideology of the economic system. (Wallis 1976, p. 1)

Wallis believes the cost of true discipleship involves a "rejection of the greed, the racism, the violence, and the aggressive nationalism that have come to characterize the life of the nation and its institutions" (Wallis 1976, p. 9).

Wallis criticizes much of contemporary evangelicalism for its lack of a social conscience, but he simultaneously chastises liberal Christianity for ignoring its biblical roots and spiritual resources. Numerous articles in *Sojourners* have attacked establishment churches for peddling a "cheap grace" that overlooks the social dimension of sin and breeds complacency (Wallis 1979). Wallis, a thoroughly committed Christian believer, views the Bible as the Word of God and refuses to "demythologize" it as many liberals have done. Wallis calls for a Christianity that is theologically conservative but politically radical in seeking changes in the sociopolitical system through the guidance of prayer and deep faith (Wallis 1979).

Wallis challenges not the larger secular world but rather those who claim to be committed Christians, and he calls for action as well as belief. Modern evangelism emphasizes "getting one's heart right with Jesus" but omits *social* responsibility:

The "saving" of individuals apart from the radical allegiance and living witness to the kingdom of God takes the heart out of the gospel. Conversely, a belief in the kingdom apart from the transformation of persons in Christ and through the power of the Holy Spirit is a false hope that loses the empowering dynamic of the gospel. (Wallis 1976, pp. 29–30)

Wallis's call is neither to a new political party nor to a new ideology; rather it is a call to a new way of life for Christians. For Wallis, commitment to a community of believers who actively engage in ministry to the world is the basic call of discipleship (Wallis 1976, pp. 136–39). He has a vision of the church as a "new society" in which the ethic of individualism, so prized in our culture, is replaced with an individuality that finds its expression through a church body. The Sojourners Community seeks to be a cultural alternative to the materialism and individualism that it believes permeates the American church and holds it captive.

Sojourners is devoted to the basic life struggles of the poor. Its members have chosen to live a simple life-style among the poor in Washington, D.C. The community has organized a food cooperative, a tenants' rights group, a day-care center, and other services for area children. Its inner-city ministry thus provides a testing ground for personal commitment, and its magazine publicizes this living experience. In both practice and ideology, Sojourners is committed to the furthering of social justice.

The articles featured in its magazine demonstrate Sojourners' concerns. Many deal with laying spiritual foundations through prayer, commitment to Christian community, and discipleship. Others focus on issues, including global concerns such as world hunger and human rights, as well as social injustices in the United States, such as poverty, racism, and sexism. *Sojourners* magazine issues a nonpartisan challenge to "radical evangelicals" to establish an alternative social order based on their understanding of basic biblical principles. In this sense, Sojourners is less political than prophetic.

Its prophetic position can be seen in its views on national defense. *Sojourners* is less concerned with being "realistic" than in being faithful to biblical admonitions. Influenced by the anabaptist tradition, Sojourners represents a prophetic voice calling for Christians to be peacemakers rather than weapon-builders. Conversion, being born again, must be related to the present historical situation, just as the revivals that peaked in the 1830s and 1840s were linked to the abolition movement:

Like slavery, the danger of nuclear holocaust is not simply a political matter; it is an issue that tests the very credibility of what we believe about

Jesus Christ. The preaching of the gospel in our own time must make it clear that to turn to Christ is to turn from our acceptance of nuclear weapons. The fruit of conversion must be visible in an active refusal to follow the leadership of those who are marching the world to nuclear oblivion. Instead converts must become known as peacemakers following the leadership of the one who was willing to bear the cost of making peace in a hostile and violent world. (Wallis 1978)

For Wallis and Sojourners, the antinuclear movement is clearly a Christian mandate for the 1980s, as were the civil rights movement during the 1950s and 1960s and the antiwar movement in the 1960s and early 1970s.

Robertson versus Wallis: An Attempt at Arbitration

Pat Robertson and Jim Wallis share an evangelical acceptance of the Bible as well as the charismatic belief in the power of the Holy Spirit to lead, guide, and direct. Their emphases and scriptural interpretations, however, are worlds apart. Both men are political, but they differ radically on key domestic and international issues. Both Wallis and Robertson brought their political positions with them as they entered the realm of charismatic Christianity. Wallis had already been involved with social activism in the late 1960s. Robertson, raised in a conservative southern milieu, followed the political direction of his father, who once represented Virginia in the United States Senate. Robertson clearly puts evangelism first and his politics seek to create a climate favorable to evangelistic efforts. It is precisely the milieu of free enterprise, capitalistic adventure, and laissez faire that has been hospitable to the rise of CBN. As Robertson views the world, communism, socialism, and big government threaten the very operation that he is using to "save souls."

Wallis, on the other hand, believes the Christian mandate emphasizes caring for the poor and mediating peace. He is sympathetic toward government efforts to relieve poverty and reduce armaments. He emphasizes social justice and believes evangelism can best be accomplished by ministering to material as well as spiritual needs. Many charismatic Christians, particularly the neo-Pentecostals, take a position between these two poles. They may be unaware of the ideological debate between conservative and progressive evangelicals. Viewing social action as part of their own religious traditions, they may be socially concerned but not necessarily politically active.

Charismatic Social Action and Politics: Present and Future

Charismatic Christians claim to have had a personal experience of God that has changed their lives.[8] They believe God is capable of intervening in human affairs, just as He brought about their personal conversions. If God can miraculously heal the sick, control the weather, and speaks directly to believers, the first obligation of charismatics is to understand His leading. For some, the spiritual quest ends with a personal relationship with God that gives little importance to either social action or to political concerns.[9] This particular approach to social issues has been described by Fichter (1975, chap. 5) in his study of Catholic charismatics. Catholic pentecostals may tend to withdraw from social action, but they are not apolitical. Bradfield (1979, pp. 37–42), on the other hand, describes neo-Pentecostals from a Virginia chapter of FGBMFI as being political conservatives who emphasize a need to change hearts rather than to take political action.

Marty's (1975, p. 208) comments on classical Pentecostals probably apply to neo-Pentecostals as well when he asserts that they lack any distinctive political stance. Rather, "their political opinions parallel those of the social classes and majorities in the locales from which they come." Pentecostals and neo-Pentecostals have a religious conception of life that influences their approach to political issues, but they do not have a unified political platform.

Many others, however, recognize the need for political action in movement. Those involved in intentional communities, such as Sojourners and the Church of the Redeemer, attempt to use the spiritual gifts to develop a community that can serve others in need. In some communities the emphasis is on building a relatively insulated social system of mutual support with little outreach; others feel the need for an active social ministry. In either case, those committed to community have moved beyond the purely personal charismatic experience. Some writers (e.g., Christenson 1974) see community as a necessary and vital link between the charismatic experience and social action.

Even those charismatics not involved in intentional communities see a need for social outreach through the church (see Suenens and Camara 1979; Fahey 1977). They view attempts to further social justice and the spiritually oriented charismatic movement as works of the Holy Spirit. These writers are likely to come from religious backgrounds, such as

Roman Catholicism, in which teachings and activities dealing with social issues are traditional. Their message centers on the belief that the gifts of the Holy Spirit, including healing, prophecy, and miracles, are intended for service, both within the church and in the larger society.

Charismatics who attempt to keep alive their personal relationship with God are also likely to believe in the power of prayer and fasting. Those who are also concerned about the problems of humanity are convinced that prayer and fasting can change the world (Prince 1973, 1980). They see prayer and fasting as powerful forces capable of moving men and women to action in accord with the will of God.

Unlike the liberal Christians who accept the power of men and women to alter the course of history through social action, charismatic Christians insist on the need for divine direction. They pray for the Holy Spirit to work through them. By waiting and listening to God, by asking and expecting to receive, they will hear God's instructions.

An example of the kind of divine intervention charismatics expect is the experience of a local minister who came to a charismatic believer to tell him that his ministry was in debt and might be forced to close. The charismatic suggested that he ask God's guidance, including some kind of intervention that would alleviate the financial problem. After their talk, the minister and the charismatic prayed together that God might resolve the financial problems and guide the minister. The minister left the charismatic to return to his office to check his afternoon mail. In the mail was a gift for $10,000, the amount needed to get the ministry out of debt. Accompanying the gift was a note from a woman who had a ''sense'' that God was telling her to send the money to that ministry. The minister was astounded and reported back to the charismatic, ''We are a small operation; we have never in our history received that kind of gift.''

Charismatics maintain that if believers were praying, listening, and responding, the difficulties that plague humankind would not be as great. This is not to suggest that most charismatics claim always to know God's leading or that all they do is a result of His promptings. They aspire to that ideal communication and seek to follow God's direction in areas of social action and politics as well as in other endeavors of life.

Given the range of political views and approaches to solving social problems, charismatics as a group cannot claim a distinct position (Henry 1976). In general, their politics follow rather than resist the trends of American society as a whole.[10] The appeal of Sojourners' call for Christians to identify with the poor is decidedly limited, whereas the plea to repent from sexual immorality in order that God may once again grant prosperity and success is far more amenable to American ears. Charismatics, for the most part, represent a Christ within culture rather than against it.

In the process of maturing, the charismatic movement may heed the call to greater involvement in social issues, but this may not necessarily lead to social action. The efforts of charismatic groups will probably be seen as miniscule by those favoring large-scale political activities. Charismatics are not likely to solve the energy crisis, resolve the issue of the arms race, nor end poverty. Projects providing direct service to those in need, a type of partisan social action, are probably the only kind upon which the divergent group known as "charismatic Christians" can agree.[11]

Charismatic politics, on the other hand, is an ambiguous phenomenon, and it is difficult to predict the direction it will take. It seems to depend more on circumstances, including the social status of adherents, economic interests of spokespersons, and traditional stance of the parent religious denomination, than on spirituality (Remmer 1973, p. 96). Perhaps those who remain apolitical but involved in nonpolitical social action are on the safest ground in terms of Christian theology.

Notes

1. Most conservative Christian believers, including the charismatics, are reluctant to wear the label "fundamentalist," which smacks of past opposition to science, secular education, and social equality. As they became assimilated into the American religious mainstream during this century, the term "evangelical" came to be preferred. There remain hard-core "fundamentalist" believers, of the type represented by Bob Jones and Bob Jones University. Such believers are a minority, but because most social science literature does not attempt to make a distinction between these conservative approaches to religion, use of the hyphenated term here refers to the common heritage and history of self-designated evangelicals and fundamentalists of today.

2. Wallis himself eschews the liberal label in favor of being a radical. In response to a draft of this chapter, he commented: "It is inaccurate to describe Sojourners as having a politically liberal ideology. If there is something Sojourners is not, it is liberal—either theologically or politically. If you must categorize us politically it would be far more truthful to speak of our politics as radical and not liberal."

In consulting with colleagues the author decided to note Wallis's objection but to retain the original label. Sojourners works for reform within the system, and their political position is akin to other groups which the average reader would most probably term "liberal."

3. Jerry Falwell, founder of the Moral Majority and preacher for "The Old-Time Gospel Hour," is a fundamentalist but not a charismatic. Robertson's television program ranks thirteenth in size of audience, as compared to Falwell's sixth position, with a viewing audience of approximately 400,000 as compared with Falwell's 1,500,000 (Hadden and Swann 1981, p. 51–52). Robertson's influence in the charismatic movement goes beyond his own television program; he organizes and speaks at conferences, issues a newsletter, and is president of a major Christian television network. He is the most political of the leaders of the charismatic movement and, like Falwell, has an influence that goes beyond his own television program.

4. For a brief discussion of secular humanism as understood by the religious conservatives, see Woodward and Salholz (1981).

5. Examples of Robertson's propaganda techniques are numerous but one will suffice as an illustration. During the antihumanist film aired on November 28, 1980, viewers were informed that secular humanists favor euthanasia and teach that individuals have a right to commit suicide. After documenting this "fact," Robertson began to present information about the financial distress of the Social Security System and how the condition can only worsen as children of the "baby boom" era reach retirement. He then suggested that their children are learning in the schools that patricide and matricide would be acceptable solutions to social ills, including the problem of how to take care of the aged when the system declares bankruptcy! Similarly specious arguments linked sex education in the schools with Planned Parenthood and teenage pregnancy rates, world crises with the wrath of God, and liberal politics with atheism.

6. An illustration of how Robertson views the Christian responsibility of "feeding the hungry" in light of his opposition to government support of the poor may be seen in the program aired on November 27, 1980. Robertson had just returned from prayer and believed God had spoken to him about ethical righteousness. Our world institutions are going to fail and Christians must learn to be compassionate and sharing with others. He then talked about Operation Blessing, a *700 Club* related local effort that aims to provide food and clothing to those in need. Those who receive material and spiritual aid later come back to serve others. In combining the ministry to physical and spiritual needs, Robertson asserted that Operation Blessing is genuine "Holy Ghost Social Gospel." He then went on to attack liberalism and big government spending, which tries to solve poverty through legislation. Robertson added, "I am a conservative and favor laissez-faire, but we need a Christian alternative between the hard-nosed conservative position and the welfare state. It is important to put a net of Christian love under the welfare state," strongly implying that welfare must be eliminated.

7. While Jim Wallis does not possess the power at Sojourners that Pat Robertson does as president of CBN, Wallis is one of the founders of the Community and is the editor of its publication. As such he can and does serve as a spokesperson for its policies. The operation of Sojourners as a community (described in chapter 7) and as a ministry is quite different in organization and scope from Robertson's multimillion dollar enterprise at CBN. In this sense, Robertson, an undisputed leader who can and does select his own staff, operates very differently from Wallis, who is one member of a community of persons committed to sharing life and resources with one another.

8. Some leaders tend to dress their politics in the cloak of "divine guidance." During the summer prior to the 1980 elections I received a letter from a preacher who reported a prophecy he received: "If you'll begin now to intercede, begin now to paint the picture of a successful, God-oriented, God-chosen man in the presidency of the United States, when the election time comes, I'll tell you who to vote for and you'll back a winner." To my knowledge he did not publicly reveal the name before the election.

9. It is this kind of Christian narcissism that has led some to pray, "Lord, help us to mature" (Buckingham 1980, pp. 21–25), and others to criticize the em-

phasis on self promoted by charismatic experiences (Moltmann 1980; Kaufman 1980).

10. The relationship between the conservative landslide in the 1980 election and the religious right remains an empirical question. The pollster Lou Harris attributed the phenomenon more to a broad repudiation of the Carter policies than to any call to arms by the Christian fundamentalists. This is in accord with a recent Gallup Poll which found no significant differences between the political stance of evangelicals and nonevangelicals (Minney 1980, p. 52).

11. The type of ministry likely to be supported by charismatics and evangelicals is only marginally political, with an emphasis on social action and evangelism. Examples are ex-Watergate figure Charles Colson (1980) and his prison work or David Wilkerson's (1963) work with teenage drug addicts.

CHAPTER 12

One Head, One Body: Summary and Conclusions

There is one body and one Spirit—just as you were called to one hope when you were called—one Lord, one faith, one baptism; one God and Father of all, who is over all and through all and in all. But to each one of us grace has been given as Christ apportioned it. . . . It was he who gave some to be apostles, some to be prophets, and some to be pastors and teachers, to prepare God's people for works of service, so that the body of Christ may be built up until we all reach unity in the faith and in the knowledge of the Son of God and become mature, attaining to the whole measure of the fullness of Christ. (Ephes. 4:4–7, 11–13)

The charismatic movement is but one of numerous social movements that has touched Christendom throughout its 2,000-year history. Its full significance cannot be adequately evaluated at this time, but the movement is potentially as important as the Protestant Reformation that swept through Europe some 450 years ago. The charismatic movement in America is presently at a crossroads.[1]

Social observers of the early twentieth century could not have been aware of the significance of the Azusa Street revival in Los Angeles. Even as Pentecostalism developed into an established sect and began to take its place among the recognized Christian denominations, few people noticed that the charismatic movement initiated by these believers was having a decided impact on contemporary Christianity. Were it not for the development of neo-Pentecostalism during the past twenty-five years, perhaps there would be no need to take special heed of the movement. Pentecostal churches would have served as another illustration of the rise of a new denomination out of attempted reformation of old ones.

The rise of neo-Pentecostalism may be reversing the divisiveness that has marked Christendom since the Reformation. All major denominations have chosen to tolerate, if not endorse, the charismatic movement and, in spite of some conflicts and difficulties, many neo-Pentecostals have been able to remain in mainline churches. At the same time, the belief and experience of the charismatics opposes the rationalistic biases of both the larger culture and established religious denominations, providing charismatics with a common ground on which to unite. Denominational walls begin to crumble as charismatic Catholics seek support from classical Pentecostals, charismatic Lutherans learn from charismatic Episcopalians, and charismatic Baptists share fellowship with charismatic Methodists.

However, many charismatic leaders now recognize that the movement may be in jeopardy, due to the routinization of charisma and internal divisions.

Problems Besetting the New Pentecost

Routinization of Charisma.   The charismatic movement affirms the availability of religious experiences to all believers. Glossolalia, healing, prophecy, revelation, and other gifts of the Spirit accompanying the baptism in the Spirit are not only ideological tenets but also personal experiences promised to the believer. This experiential basis is both the strength and the weakness of the movement, as it has been for many previous religious revival movements. Spontaneous experiences give rise to programs to facilitate them, which in turn produce institutionalization and the routinization of charisma. As religious experience is replaced by socialization within an institution, the importance of the experiential dimension diminishes.

This process of routinization has been described throughout various chapters of this analysis. It may begin subtly, as when charismatic groups in mainline churches begin to delete the term "charismatic" and replace it with the more neutral term "renewal." The focus shifts away from emphasis on Spirit baptism, which may separate charismatics from others in a denomination, toward less controversial teachings that permit greater integration into the structure of the institutional church. The rigidity that has beset many charismatic intentional communities as the development of community size and structure takes precedence over individual experience is another example of routinization. The same ossification occurs in other institutions established by charismatics, including the electronic church and the healing ministry. Religious experience and "waiting on" God to act is the archenemy of efficient and rational bureaucratic organizations. In all but a few cases bureaucracy quickly tends to replace the more tenuous structures that allow charisma to flow freely.

The development of the bureaucratic model based more on General Motors than on the Acts of the Apostles is often viewed as a more mature state by those involved. The success of the community, the television program, or the service ministry depends not on the charismatic gifts in evidence but rather on the size, financial status, and prestige of the organization. Rationalization for the loss of charisma in the development of the structure parallel the dispensationalist argument, which holds that God granted the initial outpouring of charisma only to promote the establishment of the early church.[2]

In addition to this normal unintended routinization, charismatic groups may experience a more deliberate routinization where its ideology and language are employed to further personal or institutional goals. Examples of such "inauthentic routinization" were found in early Pentecostalism, compelling organization of believers as a protection against such exploitation. Although inauthentic routinization does not appear widespread, I have occasionally observed it manifested in parachurch and independent ministries where it is more difficult to check such practices.

I am familiar with a former Akron ministry where the pastor used charismatic ideology and practices for personal gain. The minister, a charismatic personality in the sociological sense, attracted a congregation of approximately 150 persons through his preaching and teaching on the charismatic gifts. Those I knew who once belonged to this church liked the emphasis on the miraculous and the uninhibited worship that characterized the services. When some church elders learned that he had falsified his ministerial credentials and was enjoying sexual relations with some women in the congregation, the minister suddenly moved out of town. The "miracle" of abundant church funds that were a supposed sign of God's approval also disappeared. The church was left in financial shambles, as further evidence was discovered that the man had used church funds for his personal gain.

The minister had adopted the charismatic routine of sponteneity in services and promoted the belief in prophecy, tongues, healings, and miracles, but his ministry was clouded by duplicity and deceit. Despite the disappointment of the congregation in learning their leader had feet of clay, many did not abandon the charismatic movement and still favorably recall their charismatic experiences at this church. Some members did drift away from the movement, but others became involved in established charismatic churches and were more alert to potential abuses of the charismatic gifts by a church leader.

Another use of the charismatic movement that inevitably hastens the routinization process is its being used to support a faltering institution. The use of charismata to further an institutional objective may be described as follows. A small charismatic group develops, having the enthusiasm and generosity often associated with such groups, but lacking strong leadership and organizational features. A leader steps into the vacuum and is able to transform this group into a viable organization to support a valued goal. Additional structures and discipline are rationally incorporated into the group to further institutional goals, but this rational action is clothed in charismatic language.

I was able to observe this process at an unspecified institution that was in danger of closing due to lack of funds and clientele. Once the leader made it clear that this institution would now be part of the charismatic movement, his decision brought both financial advantages (gifts from charismatic believers) and a ready-made clientele for the institution's services. Those who have observed this change in the institution, while not questioning the personal integrity of the leader, have questioned his use of the charismatic movement to "save" the institution. As one man complained, "I am tired of every one of his thoughts being given the status of a prophetic utterance." Others complained that the leader was equating loyalty to the institution with loyalty to Jesus Christ and the movement of the Holy Spirit. These critics, while questioning the authenticity of the charismatic gifts manifested by the leader, do not deny that the leader's action has saved the institution. They continue to believe in possible authentic manifestations of the gifts of the Spirit, but they condemn what they perceive to be the leader's skillfull and rational manipulation of them to further the institution's well being. In the words of one critic, ''——— has prostituted the charismatic movement to save this organization.''

During my contact with charismatic groups, I did not find deliberate inauthenticity, either for personal or institutional gain, to be widespread. On occasion it does occur, and charismatic leaders are sensitive to its dangers. One means of protecting against inauthentic routinization is through organization and regulation of charismatic practices, which is in effect simply another form of routinization.

Routinization of charisma seems inevitable. Max Weber noted that the ''pure'' type of charismatic authority is necessarily a transient and inter- mittent phenomenon. In some segments of the charismatic movement, many believers may still employ the rhetoric of charisma, but much of its original spirit (and Spirit) may be waning. Charisma requires a willing- ness to live with ambiguities and a certain amount of tension.[3] This appears to be too high a price to pay for most, as charisma often gives way to an organizational structure that is bureaucratic, efficient, and more compatible with contemporary rationality.[4] The charismatic movement appears to be following the route of other social movements that replace charisma with a bureaucratic structure attuned to society. Participants, who have a stake in the newly emergent structure, promote the organiza- tion regardless of its ability to attain original goals (Zald and Ash 1964).

Divisions within the Kingdom. A recent evaluation of the charismatic movement in a leading charismatic publication observed: ''There is no doubt that something has happened to the charismatic renewal. It doesn't have the same impetus, vitality, or drive that it had ten or even five years ago'' (Langstaff 1981). The author correctly attributes the problem to fragmentation within the movement. It appears that this fragmentation is denominational (structural), racial and ethnic, and ideological. All are sapping the strength of the movement experienced during the 1970s.

Neodenominationalism. Despite the ecumenical dimensions of the charismatic movement, some charismatics appear to be retreating to the safety of denominational boundaries. There is no single cause for this phenomenon, but the move is apparent as various denominations tackle the task of larger ''church renewal.'' Different problems face different denominations, and in an effort to avoid internal strife, charismatics have placed greater emphasis on denominational cohesion (Whitaker 1981).

The divisions that are more apparent today than a few years ago reflect differences in goals and strategies for the movement. Will the charismatic movement, like the Pentecostal churches, confine itself to charismatic experiences as a means of furthering Christianity, or will it seek integration with the larger denominations in hopes of revitalizing the church? Among neo-Pentecostals, many nondenominational independents appear to be in favor of the former, while mainline denomination leaders recognize the importance of the latter. Charismatics in mainline denominations, a minority within any denomination, face a special dilemma. By isolating themselves they risk further division and ineffectiveness in influencing the policies of the larger denomination, but by accommodating themselves to the denomination they lose some of their integrity as charismatics.

Neodenominationalism, or classical denominationalism practiced by charismatics (Lensch 1981), appears to be on the rise, as evidenced by the splitting of charismatic fellowships into denominational groupings, by the lack of communication that is becoming more evident among leaders, and by the preoccupation with denominational interests. The result is to weaken the effectiveness of the total charismatic movement.[5]

Racial and Ethnic Divisions.   My analysis of the charismatic movement has been limited to one stream of it—white, largely working and middle class Americans. There is much evidence of charismatic belief and practices in other groups less visible in the movement. Hispanic American ghettos are dotted with store-front Pentecostal churches and Catholic churches serving these communities appear to possess a strong charismatic component. Black Americans account for millions of Pentecostal adherents who, like the Hispanics, are not adequately represented in magazines, charismatic conferences, or in the electronic church. Racial and ethnic divisions found in the larger society appear in the microcosm of the charismatic movement.

These divisions have recently been acknowledged by the editor of one leading charismatic magazine. As he assigned a reporter to cover the ministry of a black evangelist, the editor wanted to downplay its racial significance. He confessed, "And I feel awkward now writing about my feelings concerning this article. I'm sensitive to the fact that *Charisma* hasn't covered the black Christian community like it has the white Christian community, and I'm wanting to pretend as if that isn't so by refusing to face up to the racial issue in this article. But it is something that I must face . . ." (Strang, 1981). The editor then called for a tearing down of racial walls as there had been a tearing down of denominational walls, promising to devote more coverage to black and Hispanic charismatics. Whether *Charisma* will prove true to its resolution and other ministries follow its example remains to be determined.

The vast bulk of the charismatic movement's literature, however, does not demonstrate an awareness of the racial and ethnic divisions that are inherent in the movement. Given this lack of awareness, it is not surprising that the black, white, and Hispanic streams of the charismatic movement flow with little evidence of their merging into a powerful river.

Ideology: Heresy Charges and Countercharges. Although most charismatic literature refrains from criticizing different ideological positions, the potential exists for divisiveness due to incompatible ideologies (Maust 1980). In addition to disparate positions on social action and politics there are disagreements about discipleship, the role of women, and positive confession.

Discipleship: Normative Rules versus Personal Guidance. Given the "freedom in the Holy Spirit" and the importance of religious experience, order and discipline can be problematic in charismatic groups. The early Pentecostals experienced a breakdown of order leading to organizational constraints on public expression of religious experience and aberrant behavior. The appropriate balance between personal freedom and institutional control is an issue that continues to be problematic for charismatics. Few would be willing to call for the elimination of normative controls, but many also question the degree of control urged by advocates of discipleship.

Discipleship refers to the practice of making oneself personally responsible and accountable to another believer for all "life decisions." Such decisions may range from figuring a daily time schedule or financial budget to appropriate use of possessions. It assumes that God speaks to individuals through others in positions of authority. Discipleship is usually highly structured. Women become disciples of their husbands and men become disciples of other men in hierarchical relationships. While some degree of discipleship is essential in any organization, the extent of such accountability to another person and the need to follow the rules of extensive discipleship is a definite point of disagreement among charismatic leaders.

The practice of discipleship has been advanced by a number of charismatic leaders (including Mumford 1973; Ortiz 1975). It is practiced in varying degrees in some churches as well as in many intentional communities. Even in the highly structured Roman Catholic Church it has served to divide those Catholics who support the hierarchical church structure from those who assert that the believer must be discipled only to form his/her own conscience and then is accountable directly to God. Supporters and critics of the practice can be found among Protestant as well as Catholic charismatics.[6]

Gender Roles: Traditionalism versus Modernism. Many of the charismatic writings on the family and gender roles are steeped in traditionalism and are critical of changes brought about through the feminist movement (see, for example, Christenson 1970; Christenson and Christenson 1977; Martin 1978). Charismatics charge that gender role changes have caused a breakdown of the contemporary family; they encourage instead that the modern Christian woman return to a housewife role. These ideas agree with those of other conservative evangelical Christians who assert that traditional roles for men and women are God-ordained in the Scriptures.

A highly regarded work on gender roles is charismatic Catholic Stephen Clark's *Man and Woman in Christ* (1980). Clark argues that traditional roles are necessary for the functioning of society and that it is essential for Christians to distinguish between the responsibilities of men and women. He believes that women are "primarily responsible for internal house management and the work which directly serves people's immediate needs," such as cooking and domestic work. Men, on the other hand, are "responsible for the heavy physical work, overall government, and seeing that the family is provided with food, clothing, and a place to live" (Clark 1980, p. 604). The organization of Christian communities and churches should reflect presumed innate differences, with "the elders [heads] of the community chosen from among the men and the husband serving as the head of the family, with women in complementary positions of leadership and subordinate government" (Clark 1980, p. 605).

A minority position in the charismatic movement calls for Christian feminism. A few groups encourage women leaders (Sojourners Community and New Jerusalem Community, for example), and emphasize that "in Christ there is neither male nor female." Those taking this position appear to be less involved in writing about their views and more committed to struggling with yet unresolved issues in providing an alternate model to the traditional one.

Classical Pentecostals, like neo-Pentecostals, are also divided on the issue of gender roles. Some believe in traditional sex roles, which would prevent women from occupying many positions of church leadership. Others recognize that some important figures in the history of Pentecostalism have been women, including the founder of the Foursquare Gospel Church, Aimee Semple McPherson, and the famous healing evangelist, Katherine Kuhlman.[7] Yet few women hold positions of leadership even in those denominations that permit women to assume pastoral roles in the church. The assumptions and teachings about the appropriate role of women in the home and in the church are far more often traditional than modernist.

In one respect the ideological differences regarding gender roles are among the most critical facing the movement. Those groups accepting female leadership are often ostracized by those who in conscience question the legitimacy of such leadership. Few groups follow the nineteenth-century evangelicals who battled for women's rights or some early twentieth-century Pentecostal churches that readily ordained women. Instead, many charismatics are among those evangelicals who oppose the gains made by feminists, particularly gains made in the established churches.

Positive Confession: Health and Wealth for all Believers. Believing and experiencing God's power in daily life has led to an unofficial doctrine repudiated by leaders of most established denominations. Catch-phrases like "name it and claim it" or "confess it and possess it" express the idea that God brings health and wealth to believers for the asking. Failure to receive implies a lack of faith or a failure to employ the correct incantation to move God to action. Critics have denounced extreme teachings of positive confession for making God a kind of divine bellhop, while proponents assert that the doctrine is simply a means of securing the legacy intended for all believers.[8]

Both classical Pentecostals and neo-Pentecostals have cautioned against the emphasis on material blessings and prosperity inherent in this doctrine. Its tenets are perhaps more a reflection of middle-class American affluence than the principles found within the gospels.

Belief in positive confession has less power to fragment the charismatic movement than teachings on discipleship or gender roles, which have both opponents and proponents within denominations as well as among independent charismatics. The teachings on universal health and prosperity may appear in segments of the charismatic media but are unlikely to lead to schism within the larger movement.

Plurality, Unity, and Charismata

No major scholar studying American religions during this century was able to predict the rise of the charismatic movement, particularly the spread of neo-Pentecostalism. Its nonrational, experiential approach to religion defies the rationalistic secular order of our time. At present many signs point to the decline of the movement. It is better organized than it was ten or twenty years ago, but it is also less charismatic. It would thus be easy to write a premature eulogy for the charismatic movement. But just as scholars underestimated the vitality of Pentecostal belief in failing to recognize the potential impact of the charismatic movement, it would be erroneous to read the evidence of plurality as signifying the inevitable breakdown of the movement.

Many leaders are themselves aware of the threats to the charismatic movement, particularly its divisiveness. A renewed emphasis on the distinctive beliefs of charismatic Christians, along with a new call to unity, appear to be revitalizing the movement. Rapport with noncharismatics will continue, but a pluralistic unity may be essential to the movement's survival.

The divergent structures and ideologies of the charismatic movement possess many strengths as well as weaknesses. This is apparent even with regard to the potentially divisive issues of discipleship, gender roles, and positive confession discussed in this chapter. Proponents of discipleship, for example, are critical of the "me and Jesus" individualism of many believers and their refusal to accept authority and responsibility within a corporate structure. Discipleship advocates, on the other hand, may overemphasize the corporate dimension. Both extremes may bring others to a more intermediate ideological position. This moderating effect applies also to the issue of gender role differences. Modernists and traditionalists will find that most Christians take a position somewhere in between the extremes. Even positive confession may serve as a warning against the routinization of charismata.

Some leaders of the movement respond to criticism of their ideology by pointing to the positive contributions of a ministry to the totality of the belief system. Thus television ministries, intentional communities, and healing ministries all further the goals of the charismatic movement. Such a response seeks to promote agreement on core issues rather than controversy over peripheral ones. The core issue for charismatic Christians is their belief and experience of Spirit baptism and the accompanying gifts, along with the role of the gifts in revitalizing and spreading orthodox Christianity. The core issue is, in fact, a struggle against the seemingly inevitable routinization of charisma.[9] Many other issues, including those related to the operation of the gifts and the structure of charismatic organizations, are peripheral to this ideological core.

The movement may actually be strengthened by its pluralism so long as peripheral issues do not become central concerns. If, for example, specific teachings about divine healing overshadow the core belief in the possibility of divine healing today, pluralistic views are divisive and a threat to the movement.[10] The same may be said about other specific teachings on the appropriate structure of Christian communities, the manner in which Spirit baptism is to be experienced, and the frequency of prophecies at gatherings. Emphasis on particular gifts can actually serve to remind believers of the spiritual reality of all the gifts and the contributions of each of the ministries and denominations to the total movement. Interdenominational or intradenominational quarrels over doctrinal emphases fragment and weaken the movement. Distractions from the core belief in Spirit baptism and the gifts, particularly through routinization of charisma, is the greatest threat to the movement. Without charisma the movement remains part of the larger evangelical church but loses its distinguishing identity.

Whether or not the charismatic movement can overcome routinization as a united body remains to be seen. The strength of tradition and denominational beliefs, as well as the quest for doctrinal certainty and precision, may prove too strong for the unity in diversity that has been inherent in the movement from its Azusa Street days. The most recent phase of the charismatic movement is over. The challenge of accepting differences with an open attitude while avoiding routinization will determine the charismatic movement's ability to endure and, in turn, to leave its mark on the larger Christian church. The challenge is a formidable one.

Notes

1. American charismatics have had the resources to take a visible lead in the movement, but reports indicate that the movement is as strong or stronger in other parts of the world. The growth of classical Pentecostalism in North and South America, the Near East, Africa, and the Far East, as well as in Europe has been discussed by Nichol (1966, chaps. 10–11). Evangelical magazines have also featured articles on the growth of the charismatic movement in Britain (*America,* April 29, 1978, and *Christianity Today,* September 8, 1978), Africa (*Christianity Today,* August 26, 1977), South America (*Christianity Today,* November 30, 1977, and *Christianity Today,* December 7, 1979), and India (*Christianity Today,* March 4, 1977). For a discussion of the charismatic movement in both English and French-speaking Canada, see Reimers (1979).

2. This process has been most apparent to the author in the course of observations of "Mana Community" for over six years of its ten-year history. Admission to the community and rules for remaining there have become more bureaucratized. Prophecy, which once flowed spontaneously, is now used as a means of reinforcing teachings. Spontaneous sharings have been excluded from prayer meetings. The "miracles" of God's providing for the community during its early history, when it had few outside resources, have become part of the founding myth, but the day-to-day operations of Mana are highly structured and highly legalistic. The changes experienced during these last few years, however, have also been accompanied by a rapid growth in numbers.

3. The Mary Sisters, a reformed Protestant religious community founded in Darmstadt, Germany, after World War II, provides an illustration of a group that has been able to retain a charismatic dependence on God rather than on bureaucratic organization. Numerous incidents of the Sisters "living by faith" (rather than depending on saved resources, insurance, etc.) are reported by one of the founders (Schlink 1966). She notes that "The laziness and indifference of our human nature does not like to be constantly disturbed by the restlessness of faith. . . . After all the battles connected with the building of our Mother House and chapel, we were frankly tired of believing, tired of praying, tired of hoping" (p. 57). Such living by faith in the power of prayer, as demonstrated by the Mary Sisters, involves a tremendous amount of psychic energy that is difficult to maintain over any period of time.

4. For a brief discussion of the routinization of charisma within Hasidic Judaism and classical Pentecostalism, see Sharot (1980).

5. Some charismatic leaders believe the reason the movement is losing its thrust is its failure to make church unity the prime order of business. The theme of the prophecies given at the Kansas City Charismatic Conference in 1977 was interdenominational unity (see *New Covenant,* October, 1977), yet some leaders assert that the conference was the high point of interdenominational cooperation, which has been on the wane ever since.

6. Charisma (Strang 1980, p. 26) reported that David du Plessis was able to bring together leaders on both sides of the discipleship controversy to share positions with one another. Despite disagreement on the issue, there was a willingness among leaders to come together to discuss these differences. There is also some evidence that those adhering to a rigid discipleship pattern are moderating their position (Mumford 1981).

7. Synan (1971, pp. 188–89) notes that the first woman preacher to become famous in the United States was Mary Woodworth Etter, who led divine healing campaigns during the 1890s. Although she was a forerunner of the charismatic movement, her stress on divine healing was Pentecostal in character. She also was reportedly a thorough feminist who "did much to further the cause of her sex long before the climax of the woman's suffrage movement around 1920."

8. Further discussion on prosperity and wealth may be found in *Charisma* (September, 1980) which provides illustrations of differing positions. Two opposing views are the statements of Anthony Campolo (1980) and Gloria Copeland (1980). Campolo states: "I believe that the Christian lifestyle does deliver success to people but not the kind of success that is understood by society. Jesus never promised wealth, power and prestige to those who would follow Him." Copeland, on the other hand, asserts that "Redemption from the curse of poverty is part of Jesus' substitutionary work at Calvary. He paid the price for my prosperity. I will not scorn any part of His work."

Discussion of positive confession as applied to healing may be found in chapter 5 on "Faith and Healing."

9. This battle against routinization is wrestled with openly by leaders of the Assemblies of God, one of the oldest and largest Pentecostal denominations. They often refer to the AG as a "movement" rather than an "institution." There is limited evidence that such awareness can retard routinization and eventually revive "institutionalized" charisma.

10. One illustration of an awareness of the plurality in the charismatic movement and the manifestation of the desire that it not be divisive may be found in the John 17:21 International Fellowship which held its first meeting in Dallas, Texas, in the Spring of 1980. The meeting was attended by some 450 charismatic pastors and leaders (out of 1,000 who were invited), representing many of the factions within the movement (Maust 1980, p. 44).

Another national organization was formed by the leaders of five denominational charismatic organizations (Episcopal Renewal Ministries, Fellowship of Charismatic Christians in the United Church of Christ, Lutheran Charismatic Renewal Services, Presbyterian Charismatic Communion, and United Methodist Renewal Services Fellowship) in the spring of 1981 (Logos 1981, p. 8). Known as the Parish Renewal Council, it will sponsor regional and national parish renewal conferences, publish position papers, and organize a network of inter-denominational renewal prayer fellowships.

GLOSSARY

AWAKENING (Religious)

A period of religious revitalization that begins in a general crisis of beliefs and values and extends over a period of a generation or so. See also *revival*.

BAPTISM OF THE HOLY SPIRIT

A second encounter with God (the first being conversion) in which the Christian begins to receive the power of the Holy Spirit into his/her life; for most Pentecostals and many neo-Pentecostals, the evidence of having been baptized by the Holy Spirit is glossolalia.

BORN AGAIN

Term applied to evangelical, fundamental, and other Christians based upon the act of repenting from sin and accepting Jesus Christ as one's savior.

CHARISMA (pl. charismata)

A divinely conferred gift or power, specifically the gifts of the Holy Spirit. See also *Gifts of the Holy Spirit*. In sociology, that personal quality giving an individual influence or power over large numbers of people. See also *routinization of charisma*.

CHARISMATICS

Born-again Christians who accept the Bible as an inspired Word of God and who believe they are emphasizing a part of Christian tenet that is often neglected by other Bible believers, namely the power of the Holy Spirit, the Baptism of the Holy Spirit, and the Gifts of the Holy Spirit. While the term is sometimes used to refer to only neo-Pentecostals, it is used throughout this work to include both Pentecostals and neo-Pentecostals.

COGNITIVE DISSONANCE

The process of minimizing discomfort over failures in previous expectations by positively redefining or reinterpreting a situation.

243

CRYPTOMNESIA

A psychological explanation for xenoglossia by which conscious thoughts are believed to be original while in reality they are only memories of something learned earlier.

DANCING IN THE SPIRIT

Spontaneous dance that may occur at some charismatic, particularly neo-Pentecostal, worship services.

DELIVERANCE

A ministry of delivering persons from oppression or possession believed to be demonic in origin.

DISCERNMENT OF SPIRITS

The gift or process of distinguishing the actions of the Holy Spirit from the actions of demonic spirits.

DISPENSATIONALISM

An anticharismatic theological position holding, among other beliefs, that "dispensations" or special blessings were given by God during certain historical epochs; the miracles of the Bible were gifts for that epoch but are not meant for today.

EVANGELICAL

A Christian who accepts the Bible as the Word of God but allows for some flexibility in interpretations. While charismatics tend to be evangelical, not all evangelicals are charismatics. See also *fundamentalism.*

EXHORTATION

A common form of prophecy entailing speech which revives, renews or strengthens the hearer. See also *prophecy.*

FALLING UNDER THE POWER

See *slain in the Spirit.*

FULL GOSPEL BUSINESSMEN'S FELLOWSHIP INTERNATIONAL (FGBMFI)

A worldwide organization began by wealthy California dairyman Demos Shakarian in the 1950s enabling the spread of charismatic beliefs to both former non-Christians and non-Pentecostals.

FULL GOSPEL

A charismatic term referring to emphasizing the baptism of the Holy Spirit and the accompanying gifts as part of orthodox Christian teachings.

FUNDAMENTALISM

Christian belief stemming largely from strict Calvinist theology that insists on a literal interpretation of the Bible. With the erosion of much of its influence during the early twentieth century due to its extreme rigidity, many bible-believing Christians prefer the more moderate label of *evangelical*. Most fundamentalists were opposed to early Pentecostalism and remain opposed to the larger current charismatic movement.

GIFT OF FAITH

A gift of the Holy Spirit enabling the believer to have faith in miracles of the type mentioned by Jesus (Matt. 17:20) of casting a mountain into the sea; "mountain-moving" faith as distinguished from the ability to believe in the teachings of Jesus regarding salvation.

GIFTS OF THE HOLY SPIRIT

Spiritual gifts said to accompany the Baptism of the Holy Spirit including glossolalia, prophecy, revelation, wisdom, faith, healing, miracles, discernment of spirits.

GLOSSOLALIA

"Speaking in tongues"; a form of nondiscursive prayer in an unintelligible language. From a linguistic viewpoint, a meaningless but phenologically structured human utterance believed by the speaker to be a real language but bearing no systematic resemblance to any natural language, living or dead. See also *xenoglossia*.

GOSPEL OF WEALTH or GOSPEL OF PROSPERITY

A teaching espoused, especially by some parachurch ministers, insisting that God wishes health and wealth in this life for all believers.

IDEOLOGY

Any theoretically articulated proposition about social reality expressed by a religious class of persons (i.e., charismatic Christians).

LAYING OF HANDS

A charismatic practice of placing hands on the head, shoulders, arms, etc. of the person being prayed with. In nursing, a practice associated with therapeutic touch practices. See also *therapeutic touch*.

MIRACLE

An extraordinary event manifesting a supernatural work of God.

MODERNISTS

Those forerunners of Christian theology that sought more liberal or de-mythologized interpretations of the Bible who were confronted by the theologically conservative fundamentalists.

NEO-PENTECOSTALS

Christians, largely in mainline denominations and parachurch ministries, who have accepted the Pentecostal doctrine emphasizing the Baptism of the Holy Spirit and the accompanying gifts of the Holy Spirit. See also *charismatic, Baptism of the Holy Spirit, Gifts of the Holy Spirit.*

PENTECOSTALS

Those Christians belonging to "classical" charismatic denominations (Assemblies of God, Apostolic churches, Church of God in Christ, Church of God–Cleveland, etc.) that stemmed from the charismatic revival of the early twentieth century.

PRAYING IN THE SPIRIT

Praying in tongues or glossolalia.

PROPHECY

A gift of the Holy Spirit through which a person speaks in the name of God by giving an exhortation, reporting a vision, providing a revelation, or interpreting a glossolalic utterance.

RAPTURE

The belief that Christians will be removed "in a twinkling of an eye" from the earth to meet the Lord "in the sky" before the earth is destroyed.

REVELATION

A form of prophecy which covers an event or events in a person's life that is not secured through the senses.

REVIVAL

A process entailing a personal conversion, salvation, regeneration or spiritual rebirth in a particular place at a particular time. Contrasts with a period of "extended revival" or *awakening.*

ROUTINIZATION OF CHARISMA

The process of institutionalizing or making normative the operation of the Gifts of the Holy Spirit, often accompanied by retaining a practice or a belief without expectation of personal religious experience said to accompany it; removing the emphasis on the charismatic features of Pentecostal and neo-Pentecostal belief.

SLAIN IN THE SPIRIT

The power of the Holy Spirit so filling a person with a heightened inner awareness that the body's energy fades away and the person collapses to the floor.

SINGING IN THE SPIRIT

Glossolalic song where both melody and "words" are believed to be given by the Holy Spirit; such singing may spontaneously arise in corporate form during charismatic services.

SOCIAL MOVEMENT

A large-scale, widespread, and continuing elementary collective action in pursuit of an objective that affects and shapes the social ordering in some fundamental aspect.

SPEAKING IN TONGUES

See *glossolalia.*

SPIRIT BAPTISM

See *Baptism of the Holy Spirit.*

THERAPEUTIC TOUCH

The act of healing that is akin to the ancient practice of laying-on of hands that is used as an adjunct to orthodox nursing practices.

TONGUES

See *glossolalia.*

UNITARIAN PENTECOSTALS

Those Pentecostal denominations who have rejected the Trinitarian position of Christianity (three Persons in one Godhead), emphasizing instead the unity of God and three *manifestations* (rather than persons) of this Godhead.

WORD OF KNOWLEDGE

See *revelation.*

XENOGLOSSIA

The demonstration of knowledge of a known language not learned in the normal way; contrasts with unintelligible glossolalia.

REFERENCES

Andrews, Sherry

    1978   Evangelists: what are they saying to the body of Christ? *Charisma,* March, pp. 21–28.

    1981   Oral Roberts: expecting a miracle? *Charisma,* March, pp. 22–23.

Angley, Ernest

    1974   *Faith in God heals the sick.* Akron: Winston Press.

    1975   *Miracles are real–I got one.* Akron: Winston Press.

    1979   *Untying God's hands.* Akron: Winston Press.

    n.d.   Let this cup pass. Ernest Angley Cassette Tape, no. 91.

Armstrong, Ben

    1979   *The electric church.* Nashville, Tenn.: Thomas Nelson Publishers.

Assemblies of God

    1980   *The believer and positive confession.* Springfield, Mo.: Gospel Publishing House.

Baker, Dennis

    1981   Parachurch ministries of Pentecost. *Logos,* March–April, pp. 30–34.

Bakker, Jim with Robert Paul Lamb

    1976   *Move that mountain.* Plainfield, N.J.: Logos International.

    1977   *The big three mountain-movers.* Plainfield, N.J.: Logos International.

249

Bartleman, Frank

    1980   *Azusa street.* Plainfield, N.J.: Logos International.

Bartow, Donald W.

    1981   *The adventures of healing.* Canton, Ohio: Life Enrichment Publishers.

Basham, Don

    1971   *A handbook on tongues, interpretation and prophecy.* Springdale, Pa.: Whitaker House.

    1972   *Deliver us from evil.* Lincoln, Va.: Chosen Books.

    1973a   Baptism in the Holy Spirit. In *The Holy Spirit in today's church,* ed. E. Jorstad, pp. 58–65. New York: Abingdon Press.

    1973b   Speaking in tongues. In *The Holy Spirit in today's church,* ed. E. Jorstad, pp. 77–87. New York: Abingdon Press.

Bell, Daniel

    1976   *The cultural contradiction of capitalism.* New York: Basic Books.

Bellah, Robert

    1970   *Beyond belief.* New York: Harper and Row.

Bennett, Dennis J.

    1970   *Nine o' clock in the morning.* Plainfield, N.J.: Logos.

    1975   The gifts of the Holy Spirit. In *The charismatic movement,* ed. Michael P. Hamilton, pp. 15–32. Grand Rapids: William B. Eerdmans Publishing Co.

Berger, Peter, and Luckmann, Thomas

    1966   *The social construction of reality.* Garden City, N.Y.: Doubleday.

Berger, Peter L.

    1967   *The sacred canopy: elements of a sociological theory of religion.* Garden City, N.Y.: Doubleday.

    1969   *A rumor of angels.* Garden City, N.Y.: Doubleday.

    1977   *Facing up to modernity: excursions in society, politics, and religion.* New York: Basic Books.

Berger, Peter L., Berger, Brigitte, and Kellner, Hansfried

    1973   *The homeless mind: modernization and consciousness.* New York: Random House.

Bethell, Tom

    1978   The common man and the electric church. *Harper's* 256 (April): 86–90.

Bibby, Reginald W.

    1978   Why conservative churches *really* are growing: Kelley revisited. *Journal for the Scientific Study of Religion* 17, no. 2, pp. 129–37.

Blau, Peter M.

    1964   *Exchange and power in social life.* New York: John Wiley & Sons.

Bloch-Hoell, Nils

    1964   *The Pentecostal movement.* New York: Humanities Press.

Bloesch, Donald G.

    1974   *Wellsprings of renewal: promise in Christian communal life.* Grand Rapids: William B. Eerdmans Publishing Co.

Boguslawski, Marie

    1979   The use of therapeutic touch in nursing. *Journal of Continuing Education in Nursing* 10, no. 4, pp. 9–15.

Bouvard, Marguerite

    1975   *The intentional community movement.* Port Washington, N.Y.: Kennikat Press.

Bradfield, Cecil David

    1979   *Neo-Pentecostalism: a sociological assessment.* Washington, D.C.: University Press of America.

Bradford, Brick

    1980   Resistance to renewal. *Renewal News,* no. 58, p. 4.

Buckingham, Jamie

    1980   Lord, help us to mature. *Charisma,* January, pp. 21–25.

    1981   End of an era. *Charisma,* December, pp. 48–55.

Bunn, John T.

1973 Glossolalia in historical perspective. In *Speaking in tongues: let's talk about it,* ed. W. E. Mills, pp. 36–47. Waco, Texas: Word Books.

Cada, Lawrence et al.

1979 *Shaping the coming age of religious life.* New York: Seabury Press.

Cameron, William Bruce

1966 *Modern social movements.* New York: Random House.

Campolo, Anthony Jr.

1980 There's more to success and prosperity than money. *Charisma,* September, pp. 42–49.

Casdorph, H. Richard

1976 *The miracles.* Plainfield, N.J.: Logos International.

Castleberry, Jean

1981 Son healed of brain tumor. *Pentecostal Evangel,* August 2, p. 15.

Charisma

1980 Television: is it the answer to evangelism or does it trivialize Christianity? *Charisma,* May, p. 17.

1980a Charismata. *Charisma,* May, p. 19.

1980b Lutheran Leaders. *Charisma,* April, p. 14.

1981 Lutheran renewal: differing views on the gifts. *Charisma,* September, p. 20.

1982 Religious TV viewing up. *Charisma,* May, p. 17.

Christenson, Larry

1970 *The Christian family.* Minneapolis: Bethany Fellowship.

1974 *A charismatic approach to social action.* Minneapolis: Bethany Fellowship.

1976 *The charismatic renewal among Lutherans.* Minneapolis: Lutheran Charismatic Renewal Services.

Christenson, Larry, and Christenson, Nordis

 1977   *The Christian couple.* Minneapolis: Bethany Fellowship.

Christianity Today

 1979   The Christianity Today-Gallup poll: an overview. *Christianity Today* 23, no. 28, pp. 12–19.

Clark, Stephen B.

 1980   *Man and woman in Christ.* Ann Arbor: Servant Books.

Cliffe, Albert E.

 1951   *Let go and let God.* Englewood Cliffs: Prentice-Hall.

Colson, Charles

 1980   Revival is not enough. *Christian Life,* April, pp. 22–24ff.

Conn, Charles W.

 1977   *Like a mighty army.* Cleveland: Pathway Press.

Copeland, Gloria

 1978   *God's will is prosperity.* Tulsa: Harrison House.

 1980   God wants you to prosper, as your soul prospers. *Charisma,* September, pp. 38–41.

Coser, Lewis A.

 1956   *The functions of social conflict.* New York: Free Press.

Coughlin, Peter B.

 1977   Slain in the Spirit. *Catholic Charismatic* 2, no. 4, pp. 22–24.

Culpepper, Robert H.

 1971   *Evaluating the charismatic movement.* Valley Forge: Judson Press.

Damboriena, Prudencio S. J.

 1969   *Tongues as of fire.* Washington, D.C.: Corpus Publications.

Dart, John

 1980   The '80's: setting the scene. *Interpreter,* May, pp. 8–11.

Dayton, Donald W.

1976   *Discovering an evangelical heritage.* New York: Harper and Row.

Demerath, J. N. III

1968   Trends and anti-trends in religious change. In *Indicators of social change,* ed. E. B. Sheldon and W. E. Moore, pp. 349–445. New York: Russell Sage Foundation.

Derstine, Gerald

1980   *Following the fire.* Plainfield, N.J.: Logos International.

Desmond, David, and Maddox, James

1980   Religious programs and careers of chronic heroin users. In *Drug Problems of the 70's: Solutions for the 80's,* ed. R. Faulkinberry, pp. 193–98. Endac Enterprises/Print Media: Lafayette. La.

Dorpat, David

1980   Why doesn't God heal everyone? *New Covenant,* June, pp. 4–6.

Douglas, Jack D., and Johnson, John M., eds.

1977   *Existential sociology.* New York: Cambridge University Press.

Duncan, Hugh Dalziel

1968   *Symbols in society.* New York: Oxford University Press.

du Plessis, David J.

1970   *The spirit bade me go.* Plainfield, N.J.: Logos International.

du Plessis, David (as told to Bob Slosser)

1977   *A man called Mr. Pentecost.* Plainfield, N.J.: Logos International.

Episcopal Charismatic Fellowship

1980a   Reflections on renewal at St. Ambrose. *Acts 29 Newsletter,* April, pp. 1–4.

1980b   Two hills. *Acts 29 Newsletter,* May, pp. 1–4.

Fahey, Sheila Macmanus

1979   *Charismatic social action.* New York: Paulist Press.

Faupel, David W.

1972   *The American Pentecostal movement: a biographical essay.*
            Society for Pentecostal Studies Monograph.

Fee, Gordon D.

1980   The alien 'gospel' of prosperity. *Presbyterian Charismatic
            Communion Renewal News,* July–August, pp. 4–5.

Fenn, Richard E.

1978   *Toward a theory of secularization.* Society for the Scientific
            Study of Religion Monograph Series, no. 1.

Fichter, Joseph H.

1975   *The Catholic cult of the Paraclete.* New York: Sheed and
            Ward.

Flynn, P. A. R.

1980   *Holistic health.* Bowie, Md.: Robert J. Brady Co.

Ford, J. Massyngberde

1976   *Which way for Catholic Pentecostals?* New York: Harper and
            Row.

Fracchia, Charles A.

1979   *Living together alone: the new american monasticism.* New
            York: Harper and Row.

Friedrichs, Robert W.

1970   *A sociology of sociology.* New York: Free Press.

Frodsham, Stanley Howard

1946   *With signs following.* Springfield, Mo.: Gospel Publishing
            House.

Full Gospel Business Men's Fellowship International

1976   *A sure cure: the acts of the Holy Spirit within the medical
            profession today.* Costa Mesa, Calif.

Gee, Donald

  1963   *Spiritual gifts in the ministry today.* Springfield, Mo.: Gospel
              Publishing House.

Geertz, Clifford

  1973   *The interpretation of cultures.* New York: Basic Books.

Gelpi, Donald L.

  1971   *Pentecostalism: a theological viewpoint.* New York: Paulist
              Press.

Gerlach, Luther P., and Hine, Virginia H.

  1970   *People, power, change movements of social transformation.*
              New York: Bobbs-Merrill.

Gerlach, Luther P.

  1974   Pentecostalism: Revolution or counter-revolution? In *Reli-*
              gious movements in contemporary America, ed. I. Zaretsky
              and M. Leone, pp. 669–99. Princeton: Princeton University
              Press.

Ghezzi, Bert

  1980   From the editor. *New Covenant* 10 (August): inside front
              cover.

Gibbons, Don, and DeJarnette, James

  1972   Hypnotic susceptibility and religious experience. *Journal for*
              the Scientific Study of Religion 11 (June): 152–56.

Giordano, Daniel, and O'Brien, Sheila

  1978   Entering into life together. *Catholic Charismatic* 2
              (February–March): 22–24.

Glock, Charles, and Stark, Rodney

  1965   *Religion and society in tension.* Chicago: Rand McNally.

Glock, Charles, and Bellah, Robert

  1976   *The new religious consciousness.* Berkeley: University of
              California Press.

Goodykoontz, Lynn

1977   Touch: attitudes and practice. *Nursing Forum* 18, no. 1, pp. 4–17.

Gordon, Ernest

1980   *Me, myself and who? (humanism: society's false premise).* Plainfield, N.J.: Logos International.

Gouldner, Alvin W.

1970   *The coming crisis of Western sociology.* New York: Basic Books.

1976   *The dialectic of ideology and technology.* New York: Seabury Press.

Grad, Bernard

1979   Healing by the laying on of hands: a review of experiments. In *Ways of health,* ed. D. S. Sobel, pp. 267–87. New York: Harcourt, Brace, Jovanovich.

Greeley, Andrew M.

1972   *The denominational society.* Glenville, Ill.: Scott, Foresman, and Co.

Gruner, LeRoy

1979a   Heroin, hashish, and hallelujah: the search for meaning. Paper presented at the annual meeting of the Southern Sociological Society.

1979b   Comparative analysis of therapeutic models using the Teen Challenge paradigm. *Cornell Journal of Social Relations* 14 (Winter): 191–211.

Hadden, Jeffrey K.

1970   *The gathering storm in the churches.* New York: Doubleday.

1971   *Religion in radical transition.* New York: Aldine Publishing Co.

1980a   Soul-saving via video. *Christian Century,* May 28, pp. 609–13.

1980b   Born again politics. *Presbyterian Outlook,* October 20, pp. 5–6.

1980c   Soul-saving via media. *Christian Century,* May 28, pp. 619–13.

Hadden, Jeffrey K., and Swann, Charles E.

    1981   *Prime time preachers.* Reading, Mass.: Addison-Wesley.

Hagin, Kenneth E.

    1979   *Seven things you should know about divine healing.* Tulsa: Kenneth Hagin Ministries.

Hale, C. Benjamin

    1974   Radio church: is anyone listening? *Christianity Today* 18 (January 18): 5–6.

Hardon, John A.

    1969   *The Protestant churches of America.* New York: Image Books.

Harper, Michael

    1973   *A new way of living.* Plainfield, N.J.: Logos International.

Harris, Ralph W.

    1973   *Spoken by the spirit.* Springfield, Mo.: Gospel Publishing House.

Harrison, Michael Isaac

    1972   The organization of commitment in the Catholic Pentecostal movement. Ph.D. dissertation, University of Michigan.

Harrison, Michael

    1974   Preparation for the life in the spirit seminar. *Urban Life and Culture* 2 (January): 387–414.

Harthern, Roy

    1979   Building the body through fellowship groups. *Charisma,* July–August, pp. 36–40.

Hawn, Robert

    1979   How a Christian community changed my life. *Charisma,* July–August, pp. 48–53.

Hay, David, and Morisy, Ann

    1978   Reports of ecstatic, paranormal, or religious experience in Great Britain and the United States—a comparison of trends. *Journal for the Scientific Study of Religion* 17, no. 3, pp. 255–68.

Hay, David

    1979   Religious experience amongst a group of post-graduate students—a qualitative study. *Journal for the Scientific Study of Religion* 18, no. 2, pp. 164–82.

Heberle, Rudolf

    1951   *Social movements.* New York: Appleton-Century-Crofts.

Heidi, S.

    1980   The religious life. Life Together. Orleans, Mass.: Community of Jesus.

Henry, C. F. H.

    1976   Strife over social concerns. *Christianity Today* 20 (June 4): 32–33.

Hess, Catherine B.

    1975   An evaluation of the Teen Challenge treatment program. Washington, D.C.: U.S. Dept. of Health, Education, and Welfare, Public Health Service.

Hine, Virginia H.

    1969   Pentecostal glossolalia: toward a functional interpretation. *Journal for the Scientific Study of Religion* 8 (Fall): 211–26.

Hinson, Glenn E.

    1973   The significance of glossolalia in the history of Christianity. In *Speaking in tongues,* ed. W. E. Mills, pp. 61–80. Waco, Texas: Word Books.

Hocken, Peter

    1979   Charismatic renewal and Christian unity. *America,* December, pp. 340–42.

Hoge, Dean R., and Roozen, David A., eds.

    1979   *Understanding church growth and decline.* New York: Pilgrim Press.

Hollenweger, W. J.

    1972   *The Pentecostals: The charismatic movement in the churches.* Minneapolis: Augsberg Publishing House.

    1972   *The Pentecostals.* Minneapolis, Minn.: Augsberg Publishing House.

Hood, Ralph W.

  1980   Social legitimacy, dogmatism, and the evaluation of intense
              experiences. *Review of Religious Research* 21 (Spring):
              184–93.

Humbard, Rex

  1975   *To tell the world.* Englewood Cliffs, N.J.: Prentice-Hall.

Hummell, Charles C.

  1978   *Fire in the fireplace: contemporary charismatic renewals.*
              Downers Grove, Ill.: Inter Varsity Press.

Hunter, Harold

  1980   Tongues-speech: a patristic analysis. *Journal of the Evangel-
              ical Theological Society* 23 (June): 125–38.

Inch, Morris A.

  1978   *The evangelical challenge.* Philadelphia: Westminster Press.

Jacquet, Constant H., ed.

  1980   *Yearbook of American and Canadian churches.* Nashville,
              Tenn.: Abingdon Press.

Jadot, Jean

  1978   An assessment of the Catholic charismatic renewal. *New
              Covenant,* November, pp. 16–18.

James, William

  1961   *The varieties of religious experience.* New York: Mentor
              Books.

John Paul II

  1981   The church has seen the fruits of your devotion. *New Coven-
              ant,* August, pp. 7–9.

Johnstone, Ronald L.

  1971   Who listens to religious radio broadcasts anymore? *Journal
              of Broadcasting* 16 (Winter): 91–102.

Jorstad, Erling

    1972   *That new-time religion: the Jesus revival in America.* Minneapolis: Augsberg Publishing House.

    1973   *The Holy Spirit in today's church.* New York: Abingdon Press.

Jungkuntz, Theodore R.

    1977   Occasional Paper: II. The Cresset. Valparaiso University Press.

Kanter, Rosabeth Moss

    1973   *Communes: creating and managing the collective life.* New York: Harper and Row.

Kaufman, Jonathan

    1980   Old-time religion. *Wall Street Journal,* July 11, p. 1.

Kehl, D. G.

    1980   Peddling the power and the promises. *Christianity Today* 24 (March 21): 16–19.

Kelley, Dean M.

    1972   *Why conservative churches are growing.* New York: Harper and Row.

Kellsey, Morton

    1978   *Discernment: a study in ecstasy and evil.* New York: Paulist Press.

Kelly, Otha M.

    1976   *Profile of a churchman.* Jamaica, N.Y.: K. & C. Publishers.

Kelsey, Morton T.

    1968   *Tongue speaking: an experiment in spiritual experience.* New York: Doubleday.

    1972   *Encounter with God.* Minneapolis, Minn.: Bethany Fellowship.

1973		*Healing and Christianity.* New York: Harper and Row.

1979		Faith: its function in the holistic healing process. In *Dimensions in holistic healing,* ed. H. Otto and J. Knight, pp. 213–25. Chicago: Nelson-Hall.

Kildahl, John P.

1972		*The psychology of speaking in tongues.* New York: Harper and Row.

1975		Psychological observations. In *The charismatic movement,* ed. M. P. Hamilton, pp. 124–42. Grand Rapids: William B. Eerdmans Publishing Company.

Kotarba, Joseph A.

1977		The chronic pain experience. In *Existential sociology,* ed. Jack D. Douglas and John M. Johnson. New York: Cambridge University Press.

1979		Existential sociology. In *Theoretical perspectives in sociology,* ed. Scott G. McNall, pp. 348–68. New York: St. Martin's Press.

Krieger, Dolores

1973		The relationship of touch, with intent to help or heal to subjects' in-vivo hemoglobin values: a study in personalized interaction. *American Nurses' Association Ninth Nursing Research Conference,* pp. 39–65. San Antonio, Texas.

1975		Therapeutic touch: the imprimatur of nursing. *American Journal of Nursing* 75, no. 5, pp. 784–87.

1979		Therapeutic touch and contemporary applications. In *Dimensions of holistic healing,* ed. Otto and Knight, pp. 297–305. Chicago: Nelson-Hall.

Krieger, Dolores, Peper, Erik, and Ancoli, Sonia

1979		Therapeutic touch: searching for evidence of physiological change. *American Journal of Nursing* 79, no. 4, pp. 660–65.

Kuhlman, Kathryn

1962		*I believe in miracles.* Englewood Cliffs, N.J.: Prentice-Hall.

Labonte, Arthur

1974		*Exploring the gift of prophecy.* Pecos, N.M.: Dove Publications.

Lamott, Kenneth

1975 *Escape from stress.* New York: G. P. Putnam's Sons.

Lang, Kurt, and Lang, Gladys Engel

1961 *Collective dynamics.* New York: Thomas Y. Crowell Company.

Langrod, John, Joseph, Herman, and Valdes, Katherine

1972 The role of religion in the treatment of opiate addiction. In *Major modalities in the treatment of drug-abuse behavioral publications,* ed. Leon Brill and Louis Lieberman. New York: Behavioral Publications.

Langrod, John, Alksne, Lois, and Gomez, Efrain

1981 A religious approach to the rehabilitation of addicts. In *Substance abuse: clinical problems and perspectives,* ed. J. H. Lowinson and P. Ruiz. Baltimore: Williams and Wilkins Co.

Langstaff, Alan

1981 Leadership: A new breed of leaders. *Logos Journal,* January–February, pp. 14–17.

Larrain, Jorge

1979 *The concept of ideology.* Athens, Ga.: University of Georgia Press.

Lawson, Jo

1977 Healed of cancer. Plainfield, N.J.: Logos International.

Leggatt, Dick

1978 A personal interview with Kevin Ranaghan. *New Wine,* July–August, pp. 23–30.

Lehmann, Danny

1979 Rich religion: the hundredfold heresy. *Last Days Newsletter* 2 (September–October): 5, 8, 10.

Lensch, Rodney G.

1981 Opinion: The charismatic army has been fragmented. *Logos Journal,* January–February, pp. 28–30.

Lindsey, Hal

1970 *The late great planet earth.* Grand Rapids: Zondervan Publishing House.

Logan, James C.

1975 Controversial Aspects of the Movement. In *The charismatic movement,* ed. Michael Hamilton, pp. 33–48. Grand Rapids: William B. Eerdmans Publishing Co.

MacArthur, John F. Jr.

1978 *The charismatics.* Grand Rapids: Zondervan Publishing House.

1979 The charismatics. *Moody Monthly* 80 (December): 82–85.

McCartney, Chris

1978 The experience of healing. *Catholic Charismatic* 3, no. 3, pp. 20–23.

McClory, Robert

1980 People of praise. *National Catholic Reporter* 16 (October 3): 1, 4–5.

McCready, William C., and Greeley, Andrew

1976 *The ultimate values of the American population.* Beverly Hills: Sage Publications.

McDonnell, Killian

1978 Prayer groups and communities. *New Covenant* 8 (July): 23–27.

McDonnell, Killian, ed.

1981 *Presence, power and praise.* 3 vols. Collegeville, Minn.: Liturgical Press.

McGaw, Douglas B.

1979 Commitment and religious community: a comparison of a charismatic and a mainline congregation. *Journal for the Scientific Study of Religion* 18 (June): 146–63.

1980 Meaning and belonging in a charismatic congregation: an investigation into sources of neo-Pentecostal success. *Review of Religious Research* 21 (Summer): 284–301.

McGuire, Meredith

    1977   Testimony as commitment mechanism in Catholic Pentecostal prayer groups. *Journal for the Scientific Study of Religion* 16: 165–68.

McLoughlin, William G.

    1978   *Revivals, awakenings, and reform.* Chicago: University of Chicago Press.

MacNutt, Francis

    1974   *Healing.* Notre Dame, Ind.: Ave Maria Press.

    1977   *The power to heal.* Notre Dame, Ind.: Ave Maria Press.

    1977   Resting in the Spirit. *Catholic Charismatic* 2, no. 4, pp. 18–23.

McWilliams, Carey

    1979   Second thoughts: TV evangelists. *Nation* 229 (December 1): 552.

Mainse, David with David Manuel

    1979   *100 Huntley Street.* Plainfield, N.J.: Logos International.

Maloney, George A.

    1977   Understanding and evaluating "slaying in the Spirit." *Catholic Charismatic* 2, no. 4, pp. 27–30.

Maloney, H. Newton and Adams Lovekin

    In Press   *Glossolalia: social and psychological perspectives.* New York: Oxford University Press.

Manney, James, and Bourassa, Louise, eds.

    1976   *Come and see.* Ann Arbor: Work of Life.

    1980   Critics, electronic church try two-way communication. *Christianity Today,* March 7, p. 66.

Manuel, David

    1977   *Like a mighty river.* Orleans, Mass.: Rock Harbor Press.

    1981   But who is John Gimenez? *Charisma,* July–August, pp. 22–27.

Mardsden, George M.

1975   From fundamentalism to evangelism: a historical analysis. In *The evangelicals,* ed. D. F. Wells and J. D. Woodbridge, pp. 122–42. New York: Abingdon Press.

Mariani, John

1979   Television evangelism: milking the flock. *Saturday Review* 6 (February 3): 22–25.

Marshall, Catherine

1978   *The helper.* Waco, Texas: Chosen Books.

Martin, Ralph

1978   *Husbands, wives, parents, children.* Ann Arbor: Servant Books.

1980   Catholic assesses charismatic renewal in his church. *Christianity Today* 24 (March): 18–19.

Martin, William

1981   The birth of a media myth. *Atlantic,* June, pp. 7–16.

Marty, Martin

1975   Pentecostalism in the context of American piety and practice. In *Aspects of Pentecostal-charismatic origins,* ed. Vinson Synan, pp. 193–233. Plainfield, N.J.: Logos International.

1979   Almost persuaded. *Christian Century* 96 (December): 991.

Maslow, Abraham H.

1970   *Religions, values, and peak-experiences.* New York: Viking Press.

Matzat, Don

1977   A renewal at faith. *Bread of Life,* July–August, pp. 2–9.

Maust, John

1980   Charismatic leaders seeking faith for their own healing. *Christianity Today,* April 4, pp. 44–46.

1980   Critics, electronic church try two-way communication. *Christianity Today,* March 7, pp. 66.

References   267

Menzies, William W.

1971   *Anointed to serve: the story of the Assemblies of God.* Spring-
              field, Mo.: Gospel Publishing House.

1975   The non-Wesleyan origins of the Pentecostal movement. In
              Aspects of Pentecostal-charismatic origins, ed. A. Synan,
              pp. 81–97. Plainfield, N.J.: Logos International.

Messerano, Frank C.

1965   A study of worship forms in the Assemblies of God. M.Th.
              thesis, Princeton Theological Seminary. Abstracted in *The
              American Pentecostal movement: a bibliographical essay,* by
              David W. Faupel, p. 15. Wilmore, Ky.: Asbury Theological
              Seminary.

Miller, Holly G.

1979   Science and prayer: keys to the City of Faith. *Saturday
              Evening Post* 251 (July): 22–26.

Miller, Lynn Agoglia

1979   An explanation of therapeutic touch. *Nursing Forum* 18, no.
              3, pp. 278–87.

Mills, Watson E., ed.

1973   *Speaking in tongues: let's talk about it.* Waco, Texas: Word
              Books.

Minnery, Tom

1980   The religious right: how much credit can it take for electoral
              landslide. *Christianity Today,* December 12, pp. 52–53.

Moberg, David O., ed.

1979   *Spiritual well-being: sociological perspectives.* Washington,
              D.C.: University Press of America.

Moltmann, Jurgen

1980   How my mind has changed: challenge of religion in the 80's.
              Christian Century 97 (April 23): 465–68.

Montague, George T.

1977   Slain in the Spirit—a biblical assessment. *Catholic Charis-
              matic* 2, no. 4, p. 32.

Moore, Dan

    1980   Of catered meals, clothing exchanges, and child swapping. *Lord Jesus Body News* 5 (March–April): 7.

Mumford, Bob

    1973   *The problem of doing your own thing.* Ft. Lauderdale, Fla.

Munk, Gerald W.

    1978   The charismatic experience in Orthodox tradition. *Theosis* 1, no. 7 (November): 1–3.

Neal, Emily Gardiner

    1958   *God can heal you now.* Carmel, N.Y.: Guideposts.

Neitz, Mary Jo

    1981   Slain in the Spirit: creating and maintaining a religious social reality. Ph.D. dissertation, University of Chicago.

New Covenant

    1977   Prophecies from the general sessions. *New Covenant* 7 (October): 10.

    1978   International Update: Belgium. *New Covenant* (January): 11–13.

Newsweek

    1980   Sister Ruth: Living the whole life. *Newsweek,* March 24, pp. 17–18.

    1981   When God talks, Oral listens. *Newsweek,* November 16, p. 64.

Nichol, John Thomas

    1966   *Pentecostalism.* New York: Harper and Row.

Niebuhr, H. Richard

    1929   *The social sources of denominationalism.* Cleveland: World Publishing Co.

Niebuhr, Reinhold

    1960   *Reinhold Niebuhr on politics,* ed. H. R. Davis and R. C. Good. New York: Charles Scribner's Sons.

O'Connor, Edward

  1971   *The Pentecostal movement in the Catholic Church.* Notre
          Dame, Ind.: Ave Maria Press.

Oliver, John

  1975   A failure of evangelical conscience. *Post-American,* May,
          pp. 26–30.

Oritz, Juan Carlos with Jamie Buckingham

  1975   *Call to discipleship.* Plainfield, N.J.: Logos International.

Otto, Herbert A., and Knight, James W.

  1979   The basis of holistic healing. In *Dimensions in holistic heal-
          ing,* ed. Otto and Knight, pp. 1–27. Chicago: Nelson-Hall.

Park, Robert E.

  1950   *Race and culture.* Glencoe, Il.: Free Press.

Pattison, E. Mansell

  1974   Ideological support for the marginal middle class: faith heal-
          ing and glossolalia. In *Religious movements in contemporary
          America,* ed. Irving I. Zaretsky and Mark P. Leone, pp.
          418–55. Princeton: Princeton University Press.

Pelletier, Joseph A.

  1977   A mysterious but mighty ministry—resting in the Spirit.
          Catholic Charismatic 2, no. 4, pp. 33–36.

Pelletier, Kenneth R.

  1977   *Mind as healer, mind as slayer.* New York: Dell Publishing
          Co.

Pinnock, Clark

  1975   Charismatic renewal and the radical church. Washington,
          D.C.: Sojourners Reprints.

  1981   Opening the church to the charismatic dimension. *Chris-
          tianity Today,* June 12, p. 16.

Plowman, Edward E.

  1975   The threat to broadcasting: is it real? *Christianity Today* 19
          (February 28): 44–45.

Poloma, Margaret M.

    1980   Christian covenant communities: an adaptation of the inten-
                    tional community for urban life. In *A reader in sociology: a
                    Christian perspective,* ed. Charles DeSanto et al., pp. 609–
                    30. Scottsdale, Pa.: Herald Press.

Prince, Derek

    1973   *Shaping history through prayer and fasting.* Tappan, N.J.:
                    Fleming H. Revell Company.

    1980   Standing in the gap. *New Wine,* February, pp. 9–13.

Pritchard, Linda K.

    1976   Religious change in nineteenth-century America. In *The new
                    religious consciousness,* ed. Charles Y. Glock and Robert N.
                    Bellah, pp. 297–330. Berkeley: University of California
                    Press.

Pulkingham, W. Graham

    1972   *Gathered for power.* New York: Morehouse-Barlow Co.

    1976   Interview: advice to new communities. *Sojourners,* May–
                    June.

Quebedeaux, Richard

    1978   *The worldly evangelicals.* New York: Harper and Row.

Ranaghan, Kevin, and Ranaghan, Dorothy

    1969   *Catholic Pentecostals.* New York: Paulist Press.

    1971   *As the spirit leads us.* Paramus, N.J.: Paulist Press.

Ranaghan, Kevin

    1980   Has the charismatic renewal peaked? *New Covenant,* April,
                    pp. 18–19.

    1981   The Catholic charismatic renewal. *Logos* March–April, pp.
                    25–29.

Randall, John

    1973   *In God's providence: the birth of a Catholic charismatic
                    parish.* Locust Valley, N.Y.: Living Fame Press.

Reid, Thomas F. with Doug Brendel

    1979   *The exploding church.* Plainfield, N.J.: Logos International.

Reimers, Al

    1979   *God's country.* Toronto: G. R. Welch Co.

Remmert, Gunther

    1973   Spiritual movements and political praxis. In *Spiritual revivals,* ed. C. Duquoc and C. Floristan, pp. 85–97. New York: Herder and Herder.

Richardson, James C.

    1980   *With water and spirit.* Washington, D.C.: Spirit Press.

Richardson, James T.

    1973   Psychological interpretations of glossolalia: a reexamination of research. *Journal for the Scientific Study of Religion* 12 (June): 199–207.

Rice, John R.

    1976   *The charismatic movement.* Murfreesboro, Tenn.: Sword of the Lord Publishers.

Rifkin, Jeremy with Ted Howard

    1979   *The emerging order: God in the age of scarcity.* New York: G. P. Putnam's Sons.

Rigney, Daniel, Machalek, Richard, and Goodman, Jerry

    1978   Is secularization a discontinuous process? *Journal for the Scientific Study of Religion* 17 (December): 381–87.

Roberts, Dennis

    1980   Time didn't stop at nine o'clock in the morning. *Charisma,* May, pp. 23–27, 60.

Roberts, Oral

    1971   *The call.* New York: Avon Books.

Robertson, Pat

    1972   *Shout it from the housetops.* Plainfield, N.J.: Logos International.

    1980   Pat Robertson's perspective. Monthly Newsletter. August. Virginia Beach, Va.: Christian Broadcasting Network.

Roof, Clark Wade

1978   *Community and commitment: religious plausibility in a liberal Protestant church.* New York: Elsevier.

Roszak, Theodore

1975   *Unfinished animal.* New York: Harper and Row.

Sabeth, Bob

1980   A community of communities. *Sojourners,* January, pp. 17–19.

Samarin, William J.

1968   The linguisticality of glossolalia. *Hartford Quarterly* 8, no. 4, pp. 49–75.

1973   Glossolalia as a vocal phenomenon. In *Speaking in tongues,* ed. W. E. Mills, pp. 128–42. Waco, Texas: Word Books Publishers.

Sandidge, Jerry

1976   The origin and developments of the Catholic charismatic movement in Belgium. M.A. thesis, Louvain: Catholic University.

Sandroff, Ronni

1980   A skeptic's guide to therapeutic touch. *RN,* January, pp. 25–30.

Sanford, Agnes

1947   *The healing light.* Plainfield, N.J.: Logos International.

Scanlan, Michael

1974   *Inner healing.* New York: Paulist Press.

1979   *A portion of my spirit.* St. Paul, Minn.: Carillon Books.

1980   The College of Steubenville. *Catholic Charismatic,* December–January, pp. 39, 51.

Scanlan, Michael, and Cirner, Randall J.

1980   *Deliverance from evil spirits.* Ann Arbor: Servant Books.

Schiffmayer, Jeffrey

    1979   Church of the Redeemer: a new look. *Acts 29 Newsletter,* pp. 1, 3, 7.

Schlink, M. Basilia

    1966   *Realities: the miracles of God experienced today.* Grand Rapids: Zondervan Publishing House.

Schwab, A. Wayne

    1980   Implications for evangelism and renewal in Episcopalians–Profile 1979. *Evangelism News.*

Schwartz, Gary

    1970   *Sect ideologies and social status.* Chicago: University of Chicago Press.

Seyle, Hans

    1978   *The stress of life.* New York: McGraw-Hill.

Shakarian, Demas

    1975   *The happiest people on earth.* Old Tappan, N.J.: Fleming H. Revell Co.

Sharot, Stephen

    1980   Hasidism and the routinization of charisma. *Journal for the Scientific Study of Religion* 19 (December): 325–36.

Shenk, Phil M.

    1980   Washington for Jesus. *Sojourners,* June, pp. 10–11.

Sherrill, John L.

    1964   *They speak with other tongues.* Old Tappan, N.J.: Fleming H. Revell Co.

Slater, Philip

    1970   *The pursuit of loneliness.* Boston: Beacon Press.

Sloan, Allan

    1980   The electronic pulpit. *Forbes,* July 7, pp. 116–24.

Slosser, Bob

1979   *Miracle in Darien.* Plainfield, N.J.: Logos International.

Smark, Peter

1978   Mass marketing God: Australian notes on an American phenomenon. *Atlas* 25 (July): 30.

Smith, Timothy L.

1957   *Revivalism and social reform: American Protestantism on the eve of the Civil War.* New York: Harper and Row.

Sojourners

1977   Crucible of community. *Sojourners,* January, pp. 14–21.

Spring, Beth

1982   Pat Robertson's network breaks out of the Christian ghetto. *Christianity Today,* January 1, pp. 36–37.

Stapleton, Ruth Carter

1976   *The gift of inner healing.* Waco, Texas: Word Books.

1977   *The experience of inner healing.* Waco, Texas: Word Books.

Stark, Rodney

1965   A taxonomy of religious experience. *Journal for the Scientific Study of Religion* 5 (October): 97–116.

Stark, Rodney, and Gock, Charles W.

1968a   *American Piety.* Berkeley: University of California Press.

1968b   Will ethics be the death of Christianity? *Transaction,* June.

Stark, Rodney, and Bainbridge, William Sims

1979   Of churches, sects and cults: preliminary concepts for a theory of religious movements. *Journal for the Scientific Study of Religion,* June, pp. 117–31.

Strang, Stephen

1980   Five years of renewal. *Charisma,* September, p. 26.

Strang, Stephen

1981   Bring body together. *Charisma,* May, p. 9.

Strout, Cushing

    1974   *The new heavens and new earth.* New York: Harper Torchbooks.

Suenens, Cardinal

    1978   *Ecumenism and charismatic renewal: theological and pastoral orientation.* South Bend, Ind.: Servant Books.

Suenens, Cardinal, and Camara, Dom Helder

    1979   *Charismatic renewal and social action.* Ann Arbor: Servant Books.

Suenens, Leon Joseph

    1975   *A new Pentecost?* New York: Seabury Press.

Sumrall, Ken

    1973   Miracles and healing. In *The Holy Spirit in today's church,* ed. E. Jorstad, pp. 105–8. New York: Abingdon Press.

Synan, Vinson

    1971   *The Holiness-Pentecostal movement in the United States.* Grand Rapids: William B. Eerdmans Publishing Co.

    1974   *Charismatic bridges.* Ann Arbor: Word of Life.

    1975   *Aspects of Pentecostal-charismatic origins.* Plainfield, N.J.: Logos International.

    1979   From a classical Pentecostal. *Catholic Charismatic,* June–July, pp. 11–13.

Thomas, W. I.

    1928   *The child in America.* Cited in *On social organization and social personality,* ed. Morris Janowitz, p. xl. Chicago: University of Chicago Press.

Thorner, Isidor

    1965   Prophetic and mystic experience: comparison and consequences. *Journal for the Scientific Study of Religion,* October, pp. 82–96.

Time

    1980   Stars of the cathode church. *Time.* 115 (February 4): 64–66.

Tinney, James S.

    1975   Black Pentecostals: setting up the kingdom. *Christianity Today,* December 5, pp. 42–43.

    1978   Editorial. *Spirit* 1, no. 2, pp. 9–10.

    1979   Exclusivist tendencies in Pentecostal self-definition: A critique from black theology. *Journal of Religious Thought* 36 (Spring–Summer): 32–48.

    1980a   Black Pentecostals: the difference is more than color. *Logos,* May–June, pp. 16–19.

    1980b   Personal correspondence with author. October 1.

    1981   Personal correspondence with author. February 10.

Tinney, James S., and Short, Stephen N., eds.

    1978   *In the tradition of William J. Seymour.* Washington, D.C.: Spirit Press.

Tocqueville, Alexis de

    1945   *Democracy in America.* Vol. 1. New York:. A. A. Knopf.

    1974   Principal causes which tend to maintain the democratic republic in the United States. In *American society in Tocqueville's time and today,* ed. R. Taub and D. Taub, pp. 371–84. Chicago: Rand McNally.

Tutle, Robert G. Jr.

    1978   *Wind and flame: a study of the Holy Spirit.* Nashville: Graded Press.

Ujhely, Gertrud B.

    1979   Touch: reflections and perceptions. *Nursing Forum* 18, no. 1, pp. 18–32.

Vaagenes, Morris G. C.

    1980   Renewal—for the whole church or just a remnant? *Lutheran Renewal International.* 1, no. 2, pp. 6–9.

Vogt, Virgil

    1976   Advice to new communities. *Sojourners,* May–June, pp. 28–29.

Wall, James M.

    1980   God's piece of cheese. *Christian Century* 97 (February 27): 219–20.

Wallis, Jim

    1976   *Agenda for biblical people.* New York: Harper and Row.

    1978   A matter of faith. Reprinted from *Sojourners,* November, 1977, March, 1978, and August, 1978. Washington, D.C.: Sojourners Reprints.

    1979   Idols closer to home. Washington, D.C.: Sojourners Reprints.

    1980   Rebuilding the church. *Sojourners,* January, pp. 10–15.

    1981   Over the long haul. *Sojourners,* January, pp. 26–27.

Ward, Horace S.

    1975   The anti-Pentecostal argument. In *Aspects of Pentecostal-Charismatic Origins,* ed. V. Synan, pp. 99–122. Plainfield, N.J.: Logos International.

Wardell, Mark R. and Benson, J. Kenneth

    1979   A dialectical view: Foundation for an alternative sociological method. In *Theoretical perspectives in sociology,* ed. Scott G. McNall, pp. 232–40. New York: St. Martin's Press.

Wardwell, Walter I.

    1972   Limited, marginal, and quasi-practioners. In *Handbook of Medical Sociology,* ed. Howard E. Freeman, Sol Levine, and Leo G. Reeder, pp. 250–73. Englewood Cliffs, N.J.: Prentice-Hall.

Weber, Max

    1968   *Economy and society.* New York: Bedminister Press.

    1978   The nature of charismatic domination. In *Weber: selections in translation,* ed. W. G. Runciman, pp. 226–50. England: Cambridge University Press.

Wehmeyer, Peggy

    1981   Oral Roberts opens his Tulsa hospital. *Christianity Today,* December 11, pp. 41–42.

Weiss, Sandra J.

1979   The language of touch. *Nursing Forum* 18, no. 3, pp. 76–79.

Wells, David F., and Woodbridge, John D.

1975   *The Evangelicals: what they believe, who they are, where they are changing.* New York: Abingdon Press.

Whitaker, Robert C.

1981   Leadership: pastors are the key to denominational renewal. *Logos Journal,* January–February, pp. 20–23.

Wills, Gary

1978   What religious revival? *Psychology Today,* April, pp. 74–81.

1980   *The Pecos Benedictine: Newsletter of the Benedictine Abbey* (Pecos, New Mexico), September.

Wilkerson, David

1963   *The cross and the switchblade.* Old Tappan, N.J.: Fleming H. Revell Co.

1974   *The vision.* Old Tappan, N.J.: Fleming H. Revell Co.

1976   *Racing toward judgment.* Old Tappan, N.J.: Fleming H. Revell Co.

Wilkinson, Paul

1971   *Social movement.* New York: Praeger.

Williams, George H., and Waldvogel, Edith

1975   A history of speaking in tongues and related gifts. In *The charismatic movement,* ed. M. P. Hamilton, pp. 61–113. Grand Rapids: William B. Eerdmans Publishing Co.

Williams, J. Rodman

1978   Why speak in tongues? *New Covenant* 7 (January): 14–16.

Williams, Russ

1979   Heavenly message, earthly designs. *Sojourners,* September, pp. 17–20.

Wilson, Bryan

1966   *Religion in a secular society.* Baltimore: Penguin.

1979   The return of the sacred? *Journal for the Scientific Study of Religion* 18 (September): 269–80.

1970   *Religious sects.* London: World University Press.

Womack, David A.

1968   *The wellsprings of the Pentecostal movement.* Springfield, Mo.: Gospel Publishing House.

Wood, William W.

1965   *Culture and personality aspects of the Pentecostal Holiness religion.* The Hague: Mouton & Co.

Woodbridge, John D., Noll, Mark A., and Hatch, Nathan O.

1979   *The Gospel in America.* Grand Rapids: Zondervan Publishing House.

Woodward, Kenneth L.

1978   Sister Ruth. *Newsweek,* July 17, pp. 58–66.

Woodward, Kenneth L., and Salholz, Eloise

1981   The right's new bogyman. *Newsweek,* July 6, pp. 48–50.

Wuthnow, Robert

1976   Recent patterns of secularization: a problem of generalizations. *American Sociological Review* 41 (October): 850–67.

Yancey, Philip

1979   Ironies and impact of PTL. *Christianity Today* 23 (September 21): 28–33.

Yocum, Bruce

1976   *Prophecy.* Ann Arbor: Word of Life.

Zablocki, Benjamin

1980   *Alienation and charisma: a study of contemporary American communes.* New York: Free Press.

Zald, Mayer N., and Ash, Roberta

1964   Social movement growth, decay and change. *Social Forces* 44: 327–41.

Zaretsky, Irving, and Leone, Mark, eds.

1974   *Religious movements in contemporary America.* Princeton: Princeton University Press.

1970   *Report of the special committee on the work of the Holy Spirit (to the 182nd General Assembly of the United Presbyterian Church).* New York: Office of the General Assembly.

1977   *The Lutheran Church and the charismatic movement.* A Report of the Commission on Theology and Church Relations of the Lutheran Church–Missouri Synod.

1979   *International directory: charismatic prayer groups.* Ann Arbor: Servant Publications.

1979   *Minutes of the thirty-eighth session of the assemblies of God.* Springfield, Mo.

1980   *The Pecos Benedictine: Newsletter of the Benedictine Abbey* (Pecos, New Mexico), September.

INDEX